CW00799178

My Funny Africa

A compendium of short stories

Greer Noble

Cover photographs...

Cecil the famous Zimbabwean lion with one of his cubs... there are many pictures taken by Cecil's admirers, proudly watching over his pride and depicting his humorous and remarkably tolerant nature...

The warthog family that grew up around the author... their comical antics causing much hilarity especially when all four piglets, accustomed to the parasitical practice of sleeping on top of their spinster aunt, now twice their size, persisted with this ridiculous obsession...

The author doing what she enjoys best... soaking up the night sounds of the African bush - a lion calling, hyena with their obscenely funny giggles, the haunting hoot of an owl, the secret cough of a leopard...

Amazon Customer Reviews...

Kim Lepper ~ UK ★ ★ ★ ★ ★
A laudable aim and a laugh-out-loud result. Stories to amuse, elucidate and to share some of the magic of life in Africa. The stories being short, even someone with the attention of a well-rounded Jack Russell terrier can find something brief enough to hold them rapt for a few minutes... or a few days.

Colin Brown ~ UK ★ ★ ★ ★ ★
I stole my copy of My Funny Africa – it cost me a lunch, the best investment I have made this year... its superb collection of African Short Stories, sketches and anecdotes, by a truly wonderful selection of some of Africa's favourite writers. How on earth does Ms Noble manage to get them together... and keep them sober enough to produce such magic? An absolute *must read* for anyone who is already under Africa's Spell, or who might fall there.
I shall be VERY surprised if anyone who reviews this book gives it anything LESS than the full five stars.

My Funny Africa

by Greer and friends

Greer Noble

Published by Noble House International   April 2018 Expanded Edition

Cover design © Greer Noble
Illustrations: Friends of Greer Noble
Editor: Michael Ballantine
Editor's Note: To preserve the individuality of each and every writer, the editing of these stories has been kept to a minimum where possible so that the different styles, grammar and idiosyncrasies afford the reader a continual, refreshing feel of the varied experiences.

ISBN 978-0-9956331-9-3

www.greernoble.com

About the Author

Wild about Africa, Greer Noble has experienced the bush in ways few have - she's skied with hippos, bathed with crocs, had a sundowner with a wild, obstreperous young elephant, dodged sly hyenas over dinner, been attacked by a lemur and gone to bed with an Egyptian cobra, to mention a few.

Educated in the then Rhodesias, she wrote her first book, Veiled Madness by hand, while on a sabbatical in Matusadona National Park on Lake Kariba, her home in earlier years. She's lived in the Seychelles, South Africa, Kenya and Britain and spent months at a time in Moçambique, Mauritius and Thailand. Her travels include the Middle and Far East, Australia, Europe, the Mediterranean and Indian Ocean Islands and most Central, Southern, East and North African countries.

Her life spans careers as diverse as photographic modelling, game ranching (her teenage years were spent on their 60 thousand hectare game ranch), designing-building-running holiday resorts and real estate companies to many explorations across Africa. Running their family hotel on Lake Kariba as well as being privy to secrets as a reservist there during the bush war provided material for many of the incidents and characters in her books.

Presently living between Africa and Europe, she's blessed with a husband of similar sentiments, two adorable children and two equally adorable grandsons and considers it most fortunate to have been brought up in the splendid, balmy, blissful, carefree Africa of old.

Twenty years from now you will be more disappointed by the things that you didn't do than by the ones you did do. So throw off the bowlines. Sail away from the safe harbour. Catch the trade winds in your sails. Explore. Dream. Discover. – **Mark Twain**

*The greatness of a nation and its moral progress
can be judged by the way it treats its animals*
Mahatma Ghandi

In Dedication...

To my courageous hunter-turned-conservationist father, his huge, generous nature, boundless energy, unlimited imagination and innovative ideas '*are before your time*,' my mother would say. A difficult man but an inspiration to all who really knew him. An honorary game warden for life, a far cry from when he was chairman of the Hunter's Association of Rhodesia. A true patriot, he raised money for museums and other worthy causes. I loved him for his selflessness; for establishing a game sanctuary in our home town, transforming a derelict area into a new habitat for animals he helped rescue from the rising waters of Lake Kariba during the famous Operation Noah, just another example. But above all, I loved him for the way he treated my mother – he adored her, he was so very proud of her.

To my unusual ex-soldier, volunteer-nurse, classical-pianist, gourmet-cook, landscape-gardener, ballroom-dancer, exquisitely beautiful, extraordinarily talented mother who excelled in everything she did. Her piano recitals would move the hardest heart, her many pupils passed with nothing less than honours or distinctions, her innovative cooking in the bush astounded everyone. She danced the tango like a goddess, transformed virgin bush into a tropical paradise and when you were ill, blessed with the gift of healing, she was the proverbial Mother Theresa. The warmth that radiated through those dark, knowing eyes and her quick easy smile endeared her to everyone – be it a statesman, a student, a philanthropist or a tramp, she was always the same and they all loved her.

With many fond memories, their invaluable life skills I've tried to live by but more especially their love and appreciation for the African bush and all its creatures, I dedicate this work.

Also by Greer Noble

The Colonial Hunters Daughter (Revision – previously Veiled Madness)
A wild and compelling classic immortalising 20th century Africa – intrigue, violence, decadence and seduction – expect the unexpected – not your usual murder mystery.

The Stone Conspiracy (Revision – previously Checkmate Conspiracy)
A racy, sleep-disturbing thriller, its intermittent injection of mischievous humour and unpredictable twists – riveting.

An Idea is Born

While revelling with a group of fellow bushwhackers, captivated by the array of campfire stories, a shooting star clinched the idea of capturing them – the stories not the revellers!

As enthused as I was about the idea, uppermost in my mind was how best to make it *really* meaningful when just then, as if another sign, a lion called. Of course! Born Free! The Adamsons! It was in the sixties when we met Joy and George Adamson of Born Free fame at our family hotel on the shores of Lake Kariba. I would pledge a percentage of the royalties from sales of the book to Born Free!

And about the name? Well, during that particular safari, so many funny things happened (as they often do in the African bush) that the most fitting and appropriate name I could think of was '**My Funny Africa**'... funny, of course, not always meaning funny haha but also funny peculiar, odd, silly, serious (as in scary), strange, bizarre, weird, perplexing and a host of other meanings... but mostly because Africa has always given me so much happiness.

I hope you enjoy **My Funny Africa** as much as I did putting it together. Not only are these authentic anecdotes entertaining but many are enlightening and even a little educational in bush lore– **GN**

'No one who met George could fail to have been inspired and touched by this remarkable man.' **Virginia McKenna** (Star of the movie Born Free)

Look deep into nature, and then you will understand everything better
Albert Einstein

My Funny Africa

Contents

The only man I envy is the man who has not yet been to Africa –
for he has so much to look forward to
Richard Mullins

Acknowledgements

I would like to thank Virginia McKenna OBE, legendary star in the film Born Free and her son, Will Travers OBE, President and co-founders of the Born Free Foundation, for agreeing to let me use the Born Free logo on the cover of **My Funny Africa** and Will himself for finding the time to submit his own wildlife story; Dr Jane Goodall PhD, DBE, founder of the Jane Goodall Institute and UN Messenger of Peace, who found time in her busy schedule to write a special story too; Wilbur Smith and Professor Bob Shacochis, best seller authors for their stories; Brian Jackman, award-winning journalist, best known as Britain's foremost African wildlife safari writer; legendary game guides, among the best in Africa; Rob Fynn, Lloyd Wilmot and Rory Young, whose very special lives in the wilds must surely be the envy of most men and certainly have my utmost respect and admiration, thank you for your extremely generous contributions to **My Funny Africa**; thank you to Mike Ballantine, my lifelong friend, mentor and partner, for so arduously and tirelessly helping me edit and authenticate every story (including my own), for your endless encouragement and for also finding time to submit a few of your own; a huge, huge thank you to all my bushwhacker friends, old and new, who so gallantly put pen to paper and contributed their stories too, in true African spirit, making this book a reality (*you'll find snippets about all fifty one of us at the back of the book*); and especially to our seven very talented award-winning artists in bringing these stories to life… to my college friend Sue Maas in particular, for going the extra mile and to this end, I would also like to include another fellow countryman, Russell Barnett for his equally brilliant sketches (remarkably, all the artists are either from or have frequented the areas where most of these stories took place). **My Funny Africa** is truly privileged to have your personal contributions and support– **GN**

'Who will now care for the animals, for they cannot look after themselves?
Are there young men and women who are willing to take on this charge?
Who will raise their voices when mine is carried away on the wind,
to plead their case?'
George Adamson

Bushwhackers' Idyll

Have you ever come to notice
In your travels overland
Folk who like to venture
Gladly give a hand

Addicted to their freedom
Uncluttered minds a must
No anchor to society
And hearts of gold and trust

Children of adventure
Responsibilities are few
Values not material
And humour through and through

Roaming and exploring
Second nature to them now
A better friend is hard to find
To share life's path with all its kind

Laughter comes more easily
These special folk you'll meet
Share stories with and celebrate
Life's wilderness retreat

Have you ever come to notice
In your travels overland
Folk who like to venture
Are the kindest in the land

GN

Everything in Africa bites…. but the safari bug is worst of all
Brian Jackman

Moving Tembo

Will Travers

Sue Maas

In the heart of a dense thorn thicket, a massive bull elephant lay on his side, fully alert but immobilised. The Kenya Wildlife Service (KWS) and Born Free team scurried around preparing to haul him, side on, onto the transport crate. A towel covered his eyes and a technician with a backpack sprayer doused him with water to keep him cool, particularly his ears. Someone had thoughtfully put a small peg into the end of his trunk to keep it open and to avoid the risk of suffocation. Vets were taking blood samples.

The specially designed crate was placed a few feet away by a huge Volvo truck called Hannibal and sometimes East 17 after the English pop boy band that co-sponsored it. It was adapted from a refuse skip which could lift the crate complete with a massive 12 ton elephant on to its flat-bed in a single move and had been donated by Born Free to KWS as part of its fledgling elephant translocation programme. But first we had to get Tembo (Swahili for elephant) into the crate and quickly!

Tying ropes to his massive legs, 30 of us strained to flip him over onto the pallet. It looked bizarre. It looked far from dignified. But it was effective. The pallet, a sheet of reinforced steel, designed to fit snuggly into the crate, was attached to Hannibal's winch. Slowly and carefully it slid into the box, complete with elephant.

Four of us went inside the open crate with Tembo to take final measurements – tusks, feet, etc. Despite the fact that this was our very first elephant relocation and we were all learning fast, things had gone relatively smoothly. Our objective was to administer the reversing agent for the anaesthetic as soon as we could and to keep Tembo under for the shortest time possible.

Then something unexpected happened. Our colleagues outside the box decided to shut the main door!

I suppose, at the time, we did not fully register the implications of this as we were so busy - the four of us - finishing our data gathering. But perhaps, in the back of my mind, I understood that something had potentially gone very wrong. My colleagues, Patrick Omondi, then head of the KWS elephant programme, Clem Coetzee, an extremely experienced technician from Zimbabwe and wildlife biologist Catherine Muir, seemed somewhat oblivious of what could well prove to be impending disaster.

It was almost as if Tembo read my thoughts. His huge body convulsed and moved and the space around us seemed suddenly even smaller. I realised we were trapped in a 'steel coffin' with a wild elephant that was just about to come round. There was probably no more than a metre's space in any direction.

Clem was clear and decisive '*Move*' he shouted. The only way out was through a tiny escape hatch built into the top of the crate, about 2 feet square. Catherine, young and slim, was out first followed by Clem – wiry and lean. Patrick pushed me forward and I was out too. Now it was Patrick's turn. We spun around to witness his head and shoulders appear through the hole but the rest of his ample frame was wedged! Inside, the sound of Tembo regaining consciousness became startlingly clear. The thought of Patrick being crushed filled us and our watching colleagues with horror.

Fortunately, Patrick had attempted to exit the crate by putting his arms in front of him. Clem and I rushed forward and grabbed an arm each and with a mighty heave, accompanied by what sounded like a champagne cork flying out of a bottle, Patrick was free and the hatch slammed shut.

There was a long moment of almost surreal silence. Time seemed to be suspended. I think we were all in shock, realising how close we had come to losing a colleague. I went up to Patrick and put my hand on his shoulder and asked if he was ok. It is hard to describe but as a black African man, the colour had drained from his cheeks. He was, in some respects, grey. He put out his hands and so did I and we both noticed how much they were shaking. *'Fine'* he said with a smile. But I know he meant *'only just'*. After that the rest of the process almost went according to plan!

The crate, now containing a fully alert, awake and somewhat annoyed Tembo was loaded on to the back of Hannibal in a single huge swoop and to the applause (and I have to say tears) of the assembled rescue team – hard-bitten wildlife professionals are emotional too.

Then an eight-hour drive, in convoy, to the release site on the northern banks of the Tana river in Kenya's Tsavo East National Park, one of the world's last great protected wilderness areas.

Naturally, this first elephant translocation had attracted a lot of interest and there were senior officials from KWS, media representatives, including the presenter from the BBC's Blue Peter programme who had followed the story from start to finish and helped raise funds to buy Hannibal in the first place, together with members of other wildlife organisations. Everyone was keen to see how well Tembo had made the journey and to witness the elephant translocation process first-hand.

It was decided that once the crate had been placed on the ground and Hannibal had been driven off to a safe distance, Clem, myself and Stuart Miles, the Blue Peter presenter, would install ourselves on top of the crate and open the door. We anticipated, and hoped, that Tembo would come out and just wander off. All the dignitaries were parked-up about 200 yards away, at what we thought was a safe and reasonable distance.

Clem gave the signal. The enormous steel door swung open and it did not take more than a moment for Tembo to make his exit. Looking around he had two options. Turn right towards open expanses of bush and the river. Turn left, uphill, to where the spectators were assembled. He made his decision! Turning left and with a shake of his massive head and a bellow of frustration and anger, he charged up the hill. Never have I seen people move so fast. If they were outside their cars they got in or under or behind. If they were sitting on the roof, they dropped through the roof-hatches like parachutists leaping from a plane. Cameras and tripods were abandoned as Tembo rapidly approached.

In a cloud of dust, ears spread, trunk up, he screeched to a halt perhaps 10 yards short of the first vehicle. For a moment he contemplated the scene in front of him and then, I think, having decided that he had made his point and that he had let us know, in no uncertain terms, how disapproving he was of the indignities he had suffered over the previous day or so, he turned back downhill and disappeared.

I was moving an elephant. In fact, I had moved an elephant and it was the start of KWSs ongoing programme of relocating elephants from areas of high vulnerability to areas of relative safety. Since Tembo, with support from Born Free, they have moved hundreds of elephants at considerable risk to themselves but always with the best of intentions. They still use Hannibal but they have bought new equipment and have refined the translocation process to such an extent that they can move six elephants in a day. It is a world-class operation. But it all started under the baking sun, in a small reserve called Mwea*, with a truck called Hannibal and an elephant called Tembo.

*Mwea – 42 sq km in size, about 200km north-east of Nairobi, Kenya

The only good cage is an empty cage – **Lawrence Anthony**

Gentle Jomeo

Jane Goodall

Dame Jane Morris Goodall, DBE, formerly Baroness Jane van Lawick-Goodall, is a world famous primatologist, ethologist and anthropologist.

Sue Maas

The late Jomeo was a very large and somewhat uncoordinated chimpanzee. When I first knew him he was a young adolescent, very self-confident, beginning to challenge the lowest ranking adult males. But one day, after we had not seen him for a week or so, I encountered him with a wounded foot. He had lost one of his toes. I shall never know what happened, but presumably he was soundly beaten up. Whatever it was, he lost all his self-confidence, and for the rest of his life seemed content to remain a low ranking male.

Things never went quite right for Jomeo. There was the botched charging display. This display is normally a magnificent performance: a male charges across the ground, hair bristling, mouth bunched in a furious scowl, slapping with his hands, stamping with his feet. And, to make the display really spectacular, he may throw rocks or drag a branch or palm frond, flailing it wildly. All of this enables him to make a 'grand entrance' as he arrives to join a

25

group. On this occasion Jomeo was in full display mode, charging down towards a group of peacefully grooming females. He seized a large branch to enhance his performance, only to find it firmly attached to its tree. Any other male would simply have carried on without it. Not Jomeo – he stopped, seized the branch with both hands, and tugged and tugged. Lost momentum, lost the chance of scattering the females and enjoying his moment. And as for the females, no doubt they were as amused as I was.

Then there was the failed hunt. Chimpanzees sometimes hunt monkeys. On this occasion Jomeo was chasing a blue monkey through the branches. The monkey, running for his/her life, made a spectacular leap from one tree to the next. Jomeo, hot in pursuit, made the same leap. At least, he intended to. But as he took off, the branch bent down under his weight and half way across the gap he ran out of jump and landed, ignominiously, on the ground. If he had been hurt it would have been tragic but instead it was just terribly funny. Well for me and possibly the monkey though Jomeo was certainly not amused.

And then there was the slippery tree trunk. It had been raining all night and everything in the forest was wet. Only Jomeo would have attempted to climb this tall tree, with its very straight trunk. He proceeded cautiously, determined to feast on the delicious leaf buds at the top. Every so often a foot or hand slipped, but he still continued. Until suddenly, when he had almost reached the lowest branch, he lost it – and landed back on the ground with a bump. He sat for a moment, glanced up at his unreachable breakfast, and vanished into the undergrowth.

The last vignette – the unsuccessful consortship - is comic and tragic at the same time. A male chimpanzee sometimes tries to persuade a female to follow him, away from all other males, to a faraway place. If he is successful they will stay there together for a few days during which she may become pregnant. We call it a consortship. Low ranking males like Jomeo often attempt to go off with a female who is not at her most sexually alluring – because at that stage of her cycle the dominant males are not interested in her. So it was on this occasion. Jomeo's chosen female, Melissa, had just got back from a consortship with another male. She had an open wound and she had terrible diarrhoea. She was, most definitely, not in the mood to go off with Jomeo. And as for Jomeo, he had a terrible abscess and his face was hugely swollen on one side. A less likely pair for a romance in the jungle would be hard to imagine. Nevertheless, Jomeo did his best to play macho suitor, moving ahead of her, shaking branches with bristled hair – and, if she refused to follow, swaying vegetation over her with both hands, effectively beating her on the back. In this way he managed to get her to follow for a few minutes every half hour or so. And then both would collapse, exhausted, she to wipe her wound and he to nurse his grotesque looking face. In the end she simply climbed a tree and made a nest – even though it was only 3 o'clock. Jomeo sat below, vaguely waved a few plants at her – which she ignored - then lay at the foot of the tree and went to sleep! And that was that. Eventually he wandered off to make his own bed, and in the morning they went their separate ways. Another failure for Jomeo.

I need hardly add that he was one of my very favourite Gombe chimpanzees. And because he was so laid back he was beloved by successions of young males when they first travelled away from their mothers. Sometimes Jomeo would be followed by as many as six as he wandered from one food source to another, then lay to rest with one or more of his followers grooming him. The gentle giant.

Most Africans don't get to see these wild animals at all. Once they see and learn about them, they are much more likely to become involved in protecting the environment – **JG**

The Adamsons of Africa

Brian Jackman

I will never forget the day I met George Adamson, the grand old Lion Man of East Africa. It was in January 1980 and I had flown to Nairobi to report on the death of his wife, Joy Adamson, the author of *Born Free* fame.

Only two months earlier I had been talking to her at her camp in Kenya's Shaba game reserve. Now she was dead, murdered by one of her camp staff, and although the couple had long since separated, George had come to Nairobi for her funeral.

Afterwards I spoke to George and to my great surprise he invited me to fly back with him to meet his lions at *Campi ya Simba*, his remote bush camp in the wilds of Kora.

When we landed on Kora's dusty airstrip the first thing George did was to load his decrepit old Land Rover with camel meat and drive down to the Tana River in search of his lions.

We parked close to the river and George stepped out, cupped his hands to his face and began to call. '*Arusha old girl,*' he cried. '*Arusha, where are you?*' And at the sound of his voice a fully-grown lioness emerged from the bushes where she had been lying on the carcass of a waterbuck.

What happened next I can still hardly believe although the image is still printed on my mind. As soon as she saw George she ran at him, then rose on her hind legs and draped her huge paws over the old man's shoulders, grunting with pleasure while he hugged her tawny body and made little moaning lion noises of his own in reply.

I was sitting where George had left me, in the front passenger seat of the Land Rover whose window, if indeed it existed at all, was impossible to close. "I shouldn't get out if I were you, old boy," he said casually. I had no intention of doing so, especially as Arusha had wandered over to inspect me. Her muzzle was still wet with blood and I could smell her warm breath as she panted through the open window only inches from my face before padding back to George and rubbing herself sinuously against his bare legs.

So began a friendship that continued until at the age of 84, George was gunned down in August 1989 by Somali bandits. The world mourned his passing and so did I. Some scientists had belittled his work at Kora, claiming all he had done was to rescue a handful of lions and return them to the wild. But that was to miss the point. It was he who alerted the world to the fact that the king of beasts was in trouble. His critics failed to see that what he discovered through living with them told us more about ourselves. Deep down, he believed in the unassailable dignity of lions, and helped us to believe it, too.

George Alexander Graham Adamson was born in Etawah, India.. His mother was English and his father, who helped train an army for the Rajah of Dholpur, was Irish. **Information.html**

A Baboon's Tale

Gareth Patterson

S ome of you might know that after the tragic death of my friend George Adamson of Born Free fame, I rescued George's last lion cub orphans, and rehabilitated them back into the wilds in the Tuli bushlands, Botswana. It was an intense learning period for the three young lions, Batian the male and Rafiki and Furaha, his two sisters. It was an intense learning period for me too, as I lived as a human member of a lion's pride, seeing life through their eyes as we patrolled, hunted, and rested together for months on end. On one occasion the lions even saved my life from an injured leopard. But that is a tale for another day... There were also many humorous times in the life I shared with the lions.

In the Tuli, baboons, whenever confronted by lions, generally shout warnings, and scamper to the nearest tall trees, where when aloft, hurl down insults (and at times, hurl down insults of a different form) at the golden big cats below them.

My lions, being east African lions, were more adapt to tree climbing, than their southern African cousins, like those in the Tuli, and this created consternation and terror for the local baboons. Whenever we encountered baboons, the baboons would shriek and race to the nearest trees, but to their utter surprise would discover with backward glances, my lions pursuing them up along the branches.

On one occasion a young male baboon found himself trapped in a solitary tree, with Batian and Furaha climbing rapidly up towards him. With no other nearby trees to leap across into, the baboon flung himself blindly out of the tree. At this time, Rafiki was below, walking away. Whenever I visualize the scene today, it seems that what occurred next, took place in slow motion. The baboon plummeted earthwards, and landed directly on Rafiki's back. For a split second he looked like an oversized jockey on a small mount. Rafiki grunted loudly in surprise, and no doubt, some pain.

Eye's wide, the baboon screamed, and fled away, pursued by Batian and Furaha. He made good his escape though, now for the second time.

Whenever I tell this story at lectures or presentations, I deliberately humanize the ending, telling that today there is a very grizzled and grey baboon, who with his troop in the evening, aloft in trees, preparing for the night, bores his family to distraction by telling the story, '*You'll never guess what happened to me one day many years ago...*'

Footnote: It's remarkable how George and Joy Adamson touched so many of our lives personally and how that has brought us together, here, in **My Funny Africa – GN**

Conservationists – by Default!

Tom Lang

Five of us during the Rhodesian bush war were on patrol in the Zambezi valley below the Kariba dam wall when we came upon a rhino on its side, legs stiff, sticking straight out. After deciding that it was dead we walked up to it. I was just about to touch it when an eye opened.

Before I could shout, it was up on its feet. Luckily it was facing away from us when it took off – like a bullet. We took off the other way. What probably saved us was the rhino's really bad eyesight for which they are known to be afflicted.

I think the brass would have been impressed on how quickly a section could retreat even though we had five FN rifles to repel an attack if necessary. So we're conservationists – by accident, not design!

Do not speak of a rhinoceros if there is no tree nearby – **African Proverb**

The Last Straw

Greer Noble

Some of the many hunting concessions in Zimbabwe are along the banks of the Zambezi River below the Kariba dam wall, demarcated as A, B & C camps. It was at one of these camps that my parents were based with two VIP guests of the then Rhodesian government and their cameraman. My father was often sequestered by Ian Smith the then Prime Minister, to take such guests big game hunting. On this particular occasion they were after elephant – the biggest tusker they could find.

It was pleasantly cool in the Zambezi valley at first light. The whiff of coffee from the old pot that perched precariously on the newly fanned embers of the previous night's fire mingled with wisps of smoke seeping from the burning log. Somewhere along the river a fish eagle's soulful call was immediately echoed by its mate from the far bank on the Zambian side. Five wazungu * sat around the fire-pit quietly sipping coffee, wondering what the new day would bring. Their thoughts were cut short, however, with the sudden appearance of Phineas, my father's gun-bearer and tracker. Wide-eyed he whispered hurriedly to my father in his native tongue. The rest of the party hardly needed a translation to pick up on the excitement and the urgency it implied. It was their third and last day... was their luck about to change?

'Come,' my father directed. 'Small herd – big tusker – on the island!' he said over his shoulder as he grabbed his gun, already on his way down the slope cut into the embankment where the boat was beached. 'I'll see you at the boat.'

A mad scramble ensued with hats, binoculars, camera equipment and guns grabbed. The long boat loaded with Phineas and four mzungu started up, my father at the helm. They were just about to head off across the channel to the island beyond when my mother, caught up in the excitement, came running down the slope towards them, waving. 'Wait... wait for me.'

My father was not happy. 'You're not properly dressed, you're in slops* and you don't have a hat,' he castigated fatherly.

33

With a mischievous smile she shrugged her indifference and climbed in. No time to waste, engine at full throttle, they sped over to the island and beached the boat. Keeping a sharp lookout for crocs they hurriedly clambered out into the shallows while Phineas tethered it against the current to a protruding root. Soon they were filing after Phineas and my father.

The day was already hot, the sun unforgiving and the midges* sent to try them, lusting after any moisture, especially the eyes. Soon the visitors started to lag behind. My mother, even further back, struggled to keep up, hampered by her slops. Sinking into the thick sand they became wedged, making it necessary to plough through the sand with each step. In their anxiety to keep up, the guests offloaded their binoculars, water bottles and cameras onto her, as if she was some mobile hat-rack. Now laden, she dropped back still further until soon the others were out of sight.

It was then that she heard the rumbling. She automatically looked up, expecting to see dark cloud typical of a pending storm. She frowned, wondering how there could be thunder without cloud. Turning, she froze. Amidst a huge cloud of dust looming towards her was a herd of stampeding buffalo. Flashing through her mind, she contemplated dumping her trammels, kicking off her slops and running for the river as there were no trees within easy reach. But then, if she even made it in time, there were the crocodiles and hippos. *Oh God, what to do?* She felt trapped, as if in a dream, the kind where you want to move but can't. Too late, they were almost upon her – all she could do was crouch down on her haunches next to a clump of vegetable ivory and hold her breath.

Her heart thumped wildly. She watched in terror as they tore past on either side of her. Their nostrils flared and the whites of their eyes crazed in panic as if pursued by some demonic monster, their smell so pungent it was almost suffocating. Precariously balanced on her haunches like a living-statue mime artist, unevenly weighted, she strained with all her might to keep from toppling over – one faltering move and she knew she would be trampled to death... which could happen anyway if one happened to collide into another.

It seemed like an eternity when just as suddenly she realised all was quiet. She stood slowly, trembling, and looked around as the

34

dust settled. Miraculously she had survived and without a scratch... or even time for a prayer. What had scared them no one will ever know, only that they are very easily spooked. Now she feared for the men but the stampeding herd had mercifully veered off in another direction!

Meanwhile Phineas, renowned for his tracking skills, found it easy following the small herd despite numerous other big, round veined imprints in the fine soft dry sand and erratic mounds of elephant dung, calling-cards from a previous herd possibly during the night, scattered like manure in a corral. The island wasn't that long and soon the tracks of the herd branched off back down towards the river. My father cursed for that's exactly what he didn't want. Suddenly the herd came into view. Phineas' estimation of four elephants was accurate but it was the size of the leader that took their breath away. He was by far the biggest tusker my father and Phineas had ever seen. They watched with sinking hearts as the herd waded through the flowing water, much deeper at that point, back towards the far bank, probably no more than a couple of kilometres downstream from their camp.

'Quick, set up your tripod,' he prompted his guest's cameraman. He then indicated to the guest after the tusker, to stand beside him. *'Wait until the old man is on terra firma before you shoot.'* Not that anyone, except for Phineas, was any the wiser that my father, with

his no-tolerance attitude towards wounding an animal, would always shoot almost simultaneously when the skills of the shooter were unfamiliar to him. *'Get ready and wait for my signal,'* he instructed.

The island was not far from the mainland. The elephants waded across in single file, the gentle giants they were, and the big tusker, reaching the bank first, began his awkward amble up the steep incline. Suddenly a shot rang out. My father swung around to see the guest shaking like a gecko's tail, wide-eyed and grinning – the proverbial Cheshire, smoke still curling from the barrel of his rifle.

Then all hell broke loose. The huge tusker toppled and fell back into the river. My father cursed and Phineas shook his head. The other three elephant rallied around him, trying to lift their leader's head out of the water to save him but his tusks were too heavy. They kept trying but after several attempts they gave up and slowly clambered up to where the ground levelled out. Time stood still for a long while before they stood in a circle; trunks touching high in the air and trumpeted, then, the biggest of the three led the way. They'd selected a new leader!

From that day forward my father never shot another thing, not even a pheasant for the pot. He couldn't. To bear witness to what had happened had broken his heart. It was the last straw... the turning point in his life. He resigned from the Hunter's Association and sold all his guns. He'd long since donated his prize tusks to the *Umtali* (Mutare) Museum, the renovations in which he'd had a big hand. Some years later he was awarded the title of Honorary Warden for Life by the Department of National Parks and Wildlife. He remained a devout conservationist for the rest of his days.

*wazungu –white persons *slops – thong sandals   *midges – mopane bees

Elephants are living treasures. Nature's gardeners. Nature's great teachers. Tragically some people don't give a damn. They prefer the dead treasure to the living one. The ivory. We must challenge this so-called 'trade' with all our might and shame on those who would condone it. **Virginia McKenna**

Desperation Slash

Nick Bornman

O nce on a safari with a German group in Botswana's Moremi Game Reserve lion were close to our camp and grunted, growled and roared all night. Next morning one of the German tourists asked me how much my safari tents cost. I asked him if he wanted to buy one of my tents. He'd defaced his, he confessed.

During the night he desperately needed to relieve himself but was scared of venturing out with all the lion activity, so decided to cut a neat, typically German, cross in the side of the tent with his Swiss army knife then proceeded to pee through the tiny opening by putting his *thingy* through it. I told him he was lucky that no hyena had come by his tent at that moment or he would have been *thingyless!*

You either get the point of Africa or you don't. What draws me back year after year is that it's like seeing the world with the lid off – **A.A. Gill**

Black Rhino Chuckle

Wilbur Smith

Best-seller author of over 40 books and more than 122 million copies sold, at least five of which have been made into films. Six of his latest titles were the result of a £15m deal with Harper Collins.

The plight of the black rhinoceros is, of course, due mostly to the value of its horn and the ferocious poaching that this engenders. However, a contributory factor to the declining rhino population is the animal's disorganized mating habits. It seems that the female rhino only becomes receptive to the male's attentions every three years or so, while the male only becomes interested in her at the same intervals; a condition known quite appropriately as 'Must'. The problem is one of synchronization, for their amorous inclinations do not always coincide.

In the early Sixties, I was invited, along with a host of journalists and other luminaries, to be present at an attempt by the Rhodesian Game and Tsetse Department to solve this problem of poor timing. The idea was to capture a male rhino and induce him to deliver up that which could be stored until that day in the distant future when his mate's fancy turned lightly to thoughts of love.

We departed from the Zambezi Valley in an impressive convoy of trucks and Land Rovers, counting in our midst none other than the director of the game department in person, together with his minions, a veterinary surgeon, an electrician and sundry other technicians, all deemed necessary to make the harvest.

The local game scouts had been sent out to scout the bush for the largest, most virile rhino they could find. They had done their job to perfection and led us to a beast at least the size of a small granite koppie with a horn on his nose considerably longer than my arm. The trick was to get this monster into a robust mobile pen, which had been constructed to accommodate him.

With the director of the game department shouting frantic orders from the safety of the largest truck, the pursuit was on. The tumult and the shouting were apocalyptic. Clouds of dust flew in all directions, trees, and vegetation were destroyed, game scouts scattered like chaff, but finally the rhino had about a litre of narcotics shot into his rump and his mood became dreamy and benign. With forty black game guards heaving and shoving, and the director still shouting orders from the truck, the rhino was wedged into his cage, and stood there with a happy grin on his face.

At this stage, the director deemed it safe to emerge from the cab of his truck and he came amongst us resplendent in starched and immaculately ironed bush jacket with a colourful silk scarf at this throat. With an imperial gesture, he ordered the portable electric generator to be brought forward and positioned behind the captured animal. This was a machine, which was capable of lighting up a small city, and it was equipped with two wheels that made it resemble a roman chariot.

The director climbed up on the generator to better address us. We gathered around attentively while he explained what was to happen next. It seemed that the only way to get what we had come for was to introduce an electrode into the rhino's rear end, and to deliver a mild electric shock, no more than a few volts, which would be enough to pull his trigger for him.

The director gave another order and the veterinary surgeon greased something that looked like an acoustic torpedo and which was attached to the generator with sturdy insulated wires. He then went up behind the somnolent beast and thrust it up him to a full arm's length, at which the rhino opened his eyes very wide indeed.

The veterinarian and his two black assistants now moved into position with a large bucket and assumed expectant expressions. We, the audience, crowded closer so as not to miss a single detail of the drama.

The director still mounted on the generator trailer, nodded to the electrician who threw the switch and chaos reigned. In the subsequent departmental enquiry the blame was placed squarely on the shoulders of the electrician. It seems that in the heat of the moment his wits had deserted him and instead of connecting up his apparatus to deliver a gentle 5 volts, he had crossed his wires and the rhino received a full 500 volts up his rear end.

His reaction was spectacular. Four tons of rhinoceros shot six feet straight up in the air. The cage, made of great timber baulks, exploded into its separate pieces and the rhinoceros now very much awake, took off at a gallop.

We, the audience, were no less spritely. We took to the trees with alacrity. This was the only occasion on which I have ever been passed by two journalists half way up a mopane tree.

From the top branches we beheld an amazing sight, for the chariot was still connected to the rhinoceros per rectum, and the director of the game department was still mounted upon it, very much like Ben Hur, the charioteer.

As they disappeared from view, the rhinoceros was snorting and blowing like a steam locomotive and the director was clinging to the front rail of his chariot and howling like the north wind, which only encouraged the beast to greater speed.

The story has a happy ending for the following day after the director had returned hurriedly to his office in Salisbury, another male rhinoceros was captured and caged and this time the electrician got his wiring right.

I can still see that rhinoceros's expression of surprised gratification as the switch was thrown. You could almost hear him think to himself. *'Oh Boy! I didn't think this was going to happen to me for at least another three years'*.

Quite frankly, I think political correctness is the worst form of censorship. You're not allowed to speak your mind unless you're black, or unless you're a terrorist, or unless you're an Arab or a minority people. Then you can say what you like. But if you are like a lot of us you are not supposed to say certain things – **WS**

Shepherd by Another Name

Lloyd Wilmot

It was in the late eighties that Richard Fair and his wife Collette had flown to Savuti to be interviewed for a possible job as a managing couple of our Lloyd's Camp. My wife and I were very pleased and impressed with them and it was agreed that they would return to SA until we could get the necessary permit applications through. Before they left, June and I took them on a moonlight walk as a way of introducing them to our bush; a little different from the bush they were used to in South Africa.

Setting off on an elephant path we crossed the Linyanti Plain and found a troop of baboons roosting at what was later to be called

Disaster Pan. The moon was exceptionally bright and the baboons became agitated at our passing. Some began climbing down and running to other trees around the pan. For sheer devilment I ran to the large Leadwood and baboons fairly rained out of it with barks and shrieks. Satisfied with my mischief, I re-joined the others and we continued walking toward Poacher's Pan and beyond.

We followed a narrow road and as we reached the pan we heard the baboons giving alarm barks. They don't bother with hyenas and a leopard would have provoked sharper, more urg+ent alarm barks. It had to be lions. For safety we had to get to an open area. Urging everyone to follow me we ran to where four roads converge and sat down. Within minutes about six lionesses came walking down the road following our trail. The white under their chins showed clearly and it is exhilarating to watch lions advance on you while sitting down. Each of us had bits of wood to throw in defence if necessary and my trusty Maglite torch was ready to shine if needed.

It was Scarleg's pride. Some members were missing. The lions walked right up then paused and flopped down a few metres away to watch us. I whispered reassurance to Richard and Collette and told him to be very alert and ready to throw his wood if the lions made any aggressive move.

Collette was not used to this and her unease showed. From Pump Pan nearby we heard the other members call whereupon Scarleg and two others began calling back. The roars were loud and we were sure this would bring the others. Keeping a close watch we sat and waited, enjoying the whole experience. Soon after, the rest of the pride arrived and we were completely surrounded. With the added support Scarleg made a sudden rush towards Colette but Richard stopped her with a quick throw of his piece of wood. It was amazing how the pride leader had identified Collette as the weak link, as in being afraid and the most vulnerable. With her rush checked Scarleg moved further back, again flopping down to watch.

We stayed a little longer then at a given signal we all stood up together. The lions crouched, some moved back and then I rushed toward a young male we knew as Dopey. He lost his nerve and with a growl he bolted, opening a gap in the circle. We started walking toward camp whereupon the whole pride sprang up and began to follow. I brought up the rear and watched that they didn't try another rush. Emerging in the open Linyanti Plain we experimented where one of us would walk with a slight limp. This immediately got the full focus of the lions. Then one of us would separate and lag behind a bit and again the lions would focus on that person. They 'frog-marched' us all the way to camp. Each time they got too close I would turn and face them while the others kept walking. By checking them thus we reached camp and the lions gave up.

When Richard left, he wrote in our Visitor's Book *'If Lloyd is my shepherd, I Wilmot want.'*

Africa – You can see a sunset and believe you have witnessed the Hand of God. You watch the slow lope of a lioness and forget to breathe. You marvel at the tripod of a giraffe bent to water. In Africa, there are iridescent blues on the wings of birds that you do not see anywhere else in nature. In Africa, in the midday heat, you can see blisters in the atmosphere When you are in Africa, you feel primordial, rocked in the cradle of the world – **Jodi Picoult** (American author)

Wake-Up Call

Greer Noble

This is not my story but a true story, nonetheless, about an injured Spotted Eagle Owl that was nurtured back to health by a kind South African farmer. What struck me was how this loving caring bird, when released back into the wilds, kept coming back and bringing gifts of bats and rats to the people or persons who helped him, even bonding with the one family cat, yet had no time for the other cats, acting aggressively towards them. Another injured fledgling owl was brought in and the owl then took responsibility for that owlet too, bringing it two rats every night. The farmer placed a box in a tree where the owl would sleep during the day. It also brought his wife a rat or bat for 'breakfast' in the hour just before sunup!

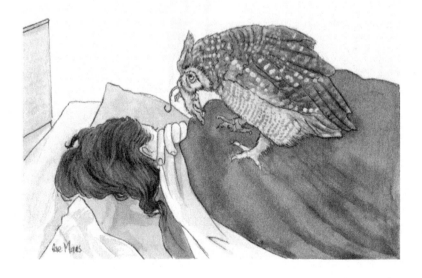

It is my hope that the intelligence of these beautiful caring creatures touches the hearts of many who read this, especially those who associate owls, as do several African cultures, with death. They believe owls should be killed as they regard them as spirits of the dead and a bad omen that foretells the death of anyone who sees them, an unfounded superstition passed down by their ancestors.

My Most Sobering Moment - Ever!

Jeremy Bentley

I hooked up with two wonderful old friends of mine, Paul and Jenny, who ran the Waterbuck Inn at Main Camp, Hwange National Park, formerly Wankie Game Reserve, in Zimbabwe. This reunion took place after a gap of about 15 to 20 years. I now had a wife and family and was older and... um... supposedly a lot... er... wiser.

It was a momentous occasion to reconnect with such close friends from my salad days and even after such a long time, we immediately picked up where we left off.

As Paul and Jenny owned the pub, that night we partied... er... hard! At about 11.30 my wife said she was going to take the children back to the chalet and get some sleep. I would follow a little later. We were after all on holiday. The chalet was 500 to 600 metres from the pub so off they went in the car. No problem I would walk back.

At about 3.30 a.m. and very nicely oiled, I said '*Good night*' and staggered out of the pub to go and find our chalet. That was when I realised there were no street lights. It was pitch dark. About halfway I stopped or rather was stopped in my tracks... as this thunderous, awful withering roar let rip.

It was so loud and unmistakeably threatening that anyone hearing it at such close proximity would become possessed with a frightful overdose of adrenaline. It's not the sound you want to hear emerge from a few feet away from all around you in pitch blackness, without a weapon, not even a stick.

I was in the middle of a pride of wild lion. It was the fastest I have ever sobered up!

I started thinking... So this is how it happens! I steeled myself and... shouted.... no sorry, stet that - screamed, '*Footsaaaaack'*!!!!!

Incredibly the sounds paused for say three very long seconds... then I walked, or rather groped my way on midst the loudest cacophony of thrashing grunts and growls, roars and snarls so unimaginably close I

46

was pale with fear. Eventually I got to what I thought must be my chalet, and decided even if it wasn't I was going in any way!

'*Thank you God!!! Thank you!!!*' There was my wife in bed listening to the bedlam outside, half terrified herself. She said, '*Do you realise that those are lions outside?*'

Peeking out I watched two lionesses slip into the shadows. They had 'escorted' me to the front door! '*No just little puddy cats!*'

The next day we found that I had wandered through a pride of lion that had made a zebra kill between our chalet and the pub and had continued to favour the zebra even though a couple of them had accompanied me back to the chalet.

*Footsaaaaack – spelt '*voetsek*' – Afrikaans for get lost/buzz off

'*Nothing but breathing the air of Africa, and actually walking through it, can communicate the indescribable sensations.*' **William Burchell**

Serious Cistern Queue

Greer Noble

We'd only just arrived at Savuti Camp in northern Botswana, when my other half made a dash for the ablutions while I set about unfolding our camp chairs. But within seconds he was back, breathless, asking for the camera, quickly exchanging it for the toilet roll.

'There's an elephant... trunk in the cistern... drinking!' he managed excitedly as he sped off again.

I started following but then thought better of it and watched instead. The ablutions were only a stone's throw from our camp site and I did not want to unnecessarily alert them for this was so unbelievable. To be able to capture this on film would be very special indeed.

He neared the ablution block and was about to enter again when a young bull came shrieking around from the back, it's ears flapping menacingly, a warning sign to back off. Water was scarce and this find, the teenage elephant made abundantly clear, was theirs. The feisty sentry scraped the soft sand threateningly with his front foot to show he meant business, gave another shake of his massive head and ears and stood watching suspiciously. Needless to say my husband beat a cautious but hasty retreat. The young bull, once satisfied that the intruder was far enough away, disappeared around the back once more.

Wasting no time, we cautiously crept around the far side of the ablutions, albeit at a safe distance. To our amazement we saw three of them queuing, patiently and politely waiting their turn at the toilet window to get to the cistern while the rest of the herd, evidently having had their fill, congregated further back under an old leadwood tree. It became obvious that they would suck up the water they needed from the refilling cistern then make way for another in the queue.

48

Thwarted, my husband headed off, spade in hand, in the opposite direction.

Unhappily for elephants Savuti Camp's ablutions are now built like Fort Knox though I have no doubt that in desperation, elephants would find a way to break into that as well. Though with the Savuti River now flowing for the first time in decades, these serious cistern queues no longer occur... there.

To safari in Africa is addictive – you will find an irresistible yearn to return to all those magical places and familiar faces, a sense of belonging, a need to nourish your spirit, your soul... for to experience the wilds of Africa is to experience the most exciting, the most unpredictable life on earth! – **GN**

Covert Cotton Pickers

Ken Tilbury

Baboons, for farmers in Africa are the most intelligent, tenacious and dangerous pests. They move in large troops, are very disruptive, cause untold damage to crops and can easily tear a large dog to pieces. When I was farming tobacco in the Goromonzi district east of Harare (or Salisbury as it was then) the baboons and I had an ongoing war. When it was time to plant the tobacco seedlings I would have to employ crop guards to keep them out of the crops.

Some of the lands were located in among the rocky hills. The baboons who lived on these hills where there was an abundance of fruit; marulas* and masanjes*, loved to watch the planting operations. They would sit on the top of the biggest granite boulders barking orders and advice down to the workers below.

As soon as everyone left the lands at the end of the day, the baboons would jump down from the rocks to go and inspect the work that had been done. The crop guards had their time cut out keeping the baboons away. If they did manage to get into the lands it was devastating. They would wander down the ridges pulling the tobacco seedlings out and after smelling the fumigant, discard them. Every morning the damage had to be repaired before any new planting could be carried out.

When the maize cobs were nearing maturity, the baboons would know exactly when it was safe to raid and reap armfuls of juicy young cobs, damaging just as many as they took away with them. It was almost impossible to keep them out of the lands, in spite of employing more crop guards. The only thing that worked was to give the crop guards shotguns to fire at the baboons when they came near the crops.

When I moved to the lowveld I had more problems with these almost human pests. One Sunday morning I saddled up and went off to check the irrigation around the farm. It was a pay week-end and there was a strong likelihood that one or two irrigators were still under the weather and might not have pitched up for work. As usual my two dogs, an Alsatian male and a Bull-mastiff bitch, accompanied me as I cantered off. After inspecting the farm, and satisfied that all was in order, I decided to ride home via the cotton fields along the Lundi river, where we had started picking that week.

As I rode down the hill towards the river, I was surprised to see a line of cotton pickers' heads sticking up above the cotton plants working in the field. Surely I had not authorised cotton picking on a Sunday? I asked myself lifting my horse into a trot - I had to speak to the induna.*

As I got nearer to where they were working, the dogs got very excited, started barking and tore off into the cotton fields towards the line of cotton pickers who, as I got nearer, appeared to be a lot smaller that they should be.

With the dogs barking and closing in there was a flurry of excitement and with a great deal of rustling, the dark heads disappeared from sight under the foliage. Seconds later a troop of baboons galloped out of the field making for the safety of the river. The cotton pickers I had seen were baboons.

Earlier in the week they must have been watching the labourers picking cotton from across the river and had been emulating them – picking the mature cotton bolls and tucking it under their arms instead of into bags. When they couldn't hold any more they just dumped their pickings on the ground and picked more.

It was winter so the river was shallow and easy for the baboons to cross the wide sandy river-bed, climb into the trees along that bank and, thinking they were safe, sit in the branches barking abuse at me and my dogs. Highly excited, the dogs looked back at me briefly before charging off across the river in pursuit of the baboons. I whistled and called to them but they were far too excited and took no notice of me. Worried that the baboons would kill them, I followed them on horseback across the river to try to bring them to heel.

Once there I saw the baboons scampering away under the mopane trees looking back at the dogs chasing after them. At last, satisfied that they had seen the baboons off, the dogs heeded my whistles and turned back. As they did so the baboons stopped their flight, turned and chased after the dogs. The dogs now realising they were the ones being chased, turned back again to confront them. As soon as I caught up the dogs targeted a large male at the rear who had separated himself from the rest of the troop, and was loping away from them towards the reeds along the banks, barking to attract the dogs' attention as he went.

I knew this was a deliberate ploy to lead the dogs into an ambush while giving his troop time to make their escape. The dogs, too excited to see what was happening, charged headlong into the reeds after the baboon. This was not good. The reeds were too dense for me to ride after them and so I quickly dismounted, tethered my horse and ran after my dogs hoping I was not too late to save them from certain death at the hands of the big baboon. As I pushed my way through the reeds I could hear the dogs frenzied barking up ahead and the loud grunting of the baboon. As I got closer one of the dogs yelped and I feared the worst. But emerging from the tunnel in the reeds I was amazed at what I saw. The dogs had caught the baboon and had it on the ground, the Alsatian by its throat and the Mastiff by its testicles. There was no point in trying to get the dogs to release their victim until it was dead. When they did release their hold they wagged their tails and looked at me proudly with their tongues hanging out.

The labourers were not happy to have to clean the mess left by the baboon pickers but they had new respect for my dogs and we didn't have any trouble from baboons for the rest of the season.

* marulas – succulent fruit resembling plums
* masanjes – wild loquats
* induna – foreman

Footnote
The end of this story may sound vicious but more often than not it is the baboons that do the chomping. As a 12 year old boy my father was attacked by a troop of baboons. For the rest of his life he wore long trousers to hide the scars on his legs. This was practical in any case in the bush what with thorns, snakes, tics, mosquitoes etc. He always looked very handsome in the evenings in his longs. **GN**

'The wise sage laments neither the living nor the dead as both are eternal and appropriately placed in Maya.' **Vedas**

Deadly Peck

Tom Lang

This true story took place in the fifties. I was born on a farm in Rhodesia at Umvuma near the Shashi river. In those days many of the farms in the country had no electricity - it was candles and two candle-watt power hurricane paraffin lamps. There were no boreholes, just wells. And many a time when you winched up a bucket of water there would be a damn snake hanging on so you would let go and run like hell, wait for the snake to slink off then start again. You bathed once a week or so in a galvanised tub in the kitchen. The eldest bathed first and in those days families were big so if you were the youngest you joined the buffalo in a cold mud bath 'cause some bugger had used all the hot water. But at least you got wet and that was classed as a bath.

The toilet was called a long-drop, about fifty metres from the house because of the flies. It was a hole about ten feet deep, bricked up around the sides with a large board seat. You never opened your mouth in there for fear of swallowing a few flies. Once we had to dig out one of our mother pigs and her brood of piglets. She had taken refuge underneath the seat, pushed the wall down and fell into the shit with all her kids - what a mess.

Good old Xmas came around and we were invited to our neighbours for a party. Off we went in my dad's old model T Ford with spoke wheels and thin tyres - if a cow pissed in the dirt road the T got stuck. With one squealing pig for the braai* we hillbillies finally got there. That night fires were lit, boere* music was played, people danced and drank and the party went on and on until all hell broke loose. Somebody said a guy had been bitten by a snake in the toilet. I ran to have a look and there some others were inspecting this guy's backside. He was breathing fast, his wife was kissing him good bye, telling him she would look after the kids and the farm and that he must pray etc. etc. Some guys in their drunken state were trying to think of a way to get him across the swollen river to a doctor.

A young guy offered to swim the river there and then and go for help but was stopped by an old timer who said that we'd better find and kill the snake first and let him take it to the doctor so he would know what serum to bring.

Back at the long-drop we found that the victim had used the old drop instead of the new one next to it. By now it was daylight, so the old timer, armed with a big stick, went in to kill the snake.

Suddenly there was a mighty roar from the old timer who came out laughing so hard he couldn't talk for a moment or two. Then, still chuckling, he explained that the victim had gone in with a candle and sat down, nearly sitting on a broody hen on eggs which pecked him on the backside. I believe that to this day his wife continues to milk him by keeping silent about the peck.

*braai – barbeque
*boere – Afrikaans speaking South African farmer

There is nothing which at once affects a man so much and so little as his own death – **Samuel Butler**

Weird Adoption!

Trish Jackson

My husband David worked as the group geophysicist for a large mining corporation in Rhodesia. One of his duties was to travel to remote areas to investigate private gold mines being offered for sale. One such trip took him way into the middle of nowhere, where a farmer named Bob had a mine for sale.

In keeping with the Rhodesian penchant for hospitality, Bob invited David to dinner with himself and his wife at their home that night. David accepted and looked forward to having a home-cooked meal rather than the unappetizing fare offered at the local hotel.

When he arrived just in time for sundowners, he did a double-take. Two adult baboons wearing skirts rode tricycles around the lawn. Bob came out to meet him and they stood and watched while Bob explained that he and his wife were childless, and to fill the void in their lives, they had 'adopted' three baby baboons several years ago. Bob led David into the house to the bar adjacent to the living room and offered him a beer. The baboons ditched their trikes and followed. Bob introduced his wife and their 'daughters', whose names were Anabel and Mary-Lou.

'Anabel is old enough to drink,' Bob explained while handing her a beer, and David watched her put the bottle to her lips and glug the beer down.

'We have to chain Mary-Lou to the couch when she watches TV,' Bob's wife said. *'She gets a little over excited during fight scenes and attacks the TV.'*

While they enjoyed their drinks, the hosts showed David the photograph albums of their 'children' growing up. They had alas, lost their 'son' Peter, the third baboon they adopted. When David found out the baboons slept in beds in the bedrooms and used the toilets just as any children would do, he was very thankful he had declined their offer of accommodation.

At dinner time, sure enough Bob and his wife sat at either end of the table, and the baboons were seated across from David. The cook served everyone including the baboons, which had a special diet, and had better table manners than some human children. However, they were uneasy at having a stranger at the table. Although they had had their canine teeth removed, they were still big, ugly, and hairy, and every time David looked up as he lifted a forkful of food to his mouth, the baboons ducked their heads at him and wa-hu'd which made it difficult to stop his hand from jerking.

After dinner they all retired to the bar again. Suddenly they heard a commotion in the kitchen. A huge 300 pound bush pig charged into the lounge and dove onto the couch. The cook had left the door open—big mistake! Bob tried to call the bush pig off but to no avail. Eventually he had to get something sweet to entice him off the couch and back outside. It turned out he had been bottle fed on the couch as a baby and had never lost the desire to lie on it. Apparently they had had to replace several broken couches.

Needless to say, David declined the next offer to have dinner with them.

If there's one thing I've found, living in the wilds ~ not a day goes by that something doesn't surprise you – **GN**

A Desperate Act

Lloyd Wilmot

At Savuti in May 1990 we had a three day gap in the Lloyd's Camp bookings and decided to go camping. I had seen some large pans in the Mopani forest on the eastern side of the marsh from the air and by following certain elephant paths we reached one. There were fresh lion and buffalo tracks around it which gave a certain edge to our surroundings.

There were two vehicles and our party consisted of my four year old son Ashley, his mother June, my sister Daph and two other women. We parked the vehicle in such a way that with some logs and branches we had a secure enclosure for our bedrolls. Just after darkness fell the lions arrived and walked around our enclosure. We watched them in the torchlight and took a few flash photos. Not finding a way in they lost interest and wandered off to drink before flopping down on the hard clay. We fell asleep and by next morning they were gone. I took three women with me tracking the lions westward on foot until they crossed the eastern road about two kilometres away. We headed back and packed up camp.

Ashley, my son, accompanied me in the Hilux carrying the camping gear whilst the women followed in the game-viewing vehicle. We agreed to meet where we had last seen the tracks crossing the road. Reaching the spot, there was no sign of the other vehicle. Before me lay a belt of Mopani trees and I felt sure the lions would have gone through this to hunt in the marsh. On the other side lay a parallel game path so I drove round and parked the car to wait. Eventually I decided to get out and look for tracks. If the lions had entered the marsh they would have left ample evidence on this path. Ashley followed me and after about 250 metres distance, went a few paces ahead of me when I stopped for a pee.

Suddenly he turned and came running back in a panic. Looking up I was horrified to see two lionesses loping after him with an easy gait. Beyond them more lions were emerging from the forest with a big male bringing up the rear.

Ashley leapt into my arms and I hurried backwards desperately casting about for some wood to defend ourselves. Seizing a piece of dry wood I flung it at the nearest lioness about two metres away. With Ashley trying to climb on my shoulders my aim was off and the wood bounced past the lioness. It distracted her in that she lunged after it and took it in her jaws. The second lioness thought she had something and stopped to seize it too. In this confusion I backed off as fast as I could with Ashley half crying, half whimpering in his terror.

The pause was momentary. The lionesses converged again, coming on quickly with others giving them support. Realising I wouldn't reach the vehicle I forcibly put Ashley down behind me. Picking up a decent branch I lunged toward the nearest lioness and hit her hard across the face. It was a desperate act of defence. She sprang backwards with a burst of a growl crashing into the lioness directly behind her.

This stalled all of them. Grabbing Ashley I backed towards the Hilux as fast as I could. The other lions were now excited and took up the chase again but I had reached the door. Ash scrambled through the window then I jerked the door open and jumped inside. Both of us were shaking with adrenaline and very relieved. There were thirteen lions in all and they milled around the vehicle wondering what had happened to the easy prey that was almost in their grasp. Ash could barely bring himself to look through the closed window before sinking low in his seat again.

I started the Hilux to drive back and see what had become of the others. Finding them headed towards me on the road we stopped and my wife explained that they had watched wild dogs kill a steenbok. Then she noticed something was amiss when Ashley wanted to get into her vehicle. She could see from his tear-stained face that he was agitated and asked what had happened. When I said "*We nearly lost our son*" and told her, she burst into tears whereupon the other women began crying too.

Choose a job you love and you will never have to work a day in your life
Confucius

The Scratching Post

Greer Noble

Nights were hot in Bumi so we'd carry our beds outdoors and sleep under the stars. But be warned - if you ever do this it can become addictive for there's nothing else like it. The night sounds; the lion calls; some early mornings, pre-dawn, you'll hear a leopard cough. Sometime during the night you'll be dreaming of some confounded noise, some chafing... what is that, is someone sanding a door, a table? Then it wakes you and you realise you're not dreaming. Now you can smell something pungent, wild, earthy! Lying on your stomach, you lift your head and look around carefully. Your eyes become more focussed... and then you see it! A huge burly grey shape a few metres from you! The corner of the building, the corner of *your* cottage has become a scratching post – a rhino scratching post. How awesome, there he is having a glorious scratch. You turn over and go back to sleep feeling very privileged; greatly honoured. *(Bumi is a magic plateau overlooking Lake Kariba, Rhodesia/Zimbabwe).*

Shorty's Shortcomings

Greer Noble

In the 1950's my father hunted there with his friend, Tony Nerantzoulis. Loveable characters, Tony and his wife, Koula, with her amazing flair for cooking, had a beautiful farm not that far from what was then and is once again the Gorongoza National Park. Carved out of virgin bush along a river bank, they grew vegetables that would have put Texas to shame. They were completely self-sufficient. Far from any semblance of civilization, they had to be.

A Greek taxi driver in his youth from the port city of Beira in Moçambique, Tony gave up the bright lights for that farm where he brought up his charming family.

We'd sit around a long table under a huge mango tree with Tony enchanting us with his endless repertoire of bush stories while enjoying Koula's sumptuous meals. I've yet to come across such hospitality. The only pity was that our Portuguese or Greek was as non-existent as Koula's English.

One of the most extraordinary incidents told to us by Tony involved his eight-fingered gun-bearer, Shorty. He'd shot off his own fingers, poor fellow, in using a double-barrelled shotgun as a leaning post. With both fingers in question hooked into the double barrels, he'd accidentally pulled the trigger. But it was the sequel to this that really had us spellbound.

Tony, often too caught up in his farming to go hunting himself would give Shorty two cartridges and send him off into the bush to bring back an impala or kudu which his family and staff would live off. It varied; at times it was game birds or a warthog but always for the pot. In the case of a large animal like a kudu, Shorty would cover it with branches and hot-foot it back to Tony who would immediately send out extra muscle with tractor and trailer.

Only one day, nightfall came and Shorty had still not returned.

Tony and Koula were worried. Even though it was wild, wild country Shorty, closer to a San bushman than a local, could easily hold his own. When he still hadn't returned after dinner Tony, with a couple of his best trackers, jumped into his old battered Bedford and drove along the farm track as far as the road went before heading off on foot. With torches and a spot light they spread out and searched throughout the night, firing intermittent shots in the air, calling his name... but to no avail.

It was at first light when one of the trackers found Shorty's shirt. He fired three shots in succession, the signal should any of them find Shorty. Rushing to the spot Tony arrived first, followed some minutes later by the other tracker. With renewed hope they intensified their search in that area. The sun was climbing fast, evaporating any dew that had fallen during the night when Tony spotted something high up in the branch of a dead tree. The younger tracker climbed up and retrieved it. They were Shorty's trousers. Not a good sign.

"Elefante," announced the older tracker.

Sue Maas

Tony nodded slowly. Yes, for Shorty's trousers to be tossed that high in a tree it could only be an elephant. Despondently they set about searching for Shorty's body... or what was left of it, until midday. Fearing the worst, they finally gave up. Very subdued and dead on their feet they made their way back to the truck. There was no doubt in anyone's mind about poor old Shorty's fate. He'd been attacked by an elephant which had probably tossed him around like a rag doll. As there was no sign of blood on his clothes had he been gored, he must have been crushed by the elephant kneeling on him, as is their way. Then during the night hyenas would have finished him off. Tony drove back with tears in his eyes, praying that Shorty was at least well and truly dead before the hyenas arrived.

Koula, hearing the vehicle, rushed out to meet them, a huge expectant smile on her face. Tony tried to tell her but the words would not come. She took him by the hand and hurried him into the kitchen. Tony almost fainted. There, sitting at the table wrapped in a large cotton towel, was Shorty sipping a mug of steamy soup. With two grinning trackers at his side an unbelievable story unfolded.

Yes, Shorty was attacked by a huge bull elephant in musth. It first grabbed him, curling its trunk around his chest but he managed to wriggle out of his shirt. It then charged after him and whipped him up again, this time wrapping its trunk around his torso, swung him to and fro in the air as if deciding how to skewer him. But Shorty, undoing the buckle of his belt, again miraculously managed to wriggle out of his oversized trousers... only this time he knew better than to try and run for it. Instead he slithered as fast as he could into the nearest bushes. He knew his human scent would soon give him away so he stretched out and gathered fresh dung from an earlier herd, quickly smearing it all over himself. It seemed to do the trick - after sniffing around for what seemed like an eternity the angry bull gave an electrifying screech, attacked a nearby tree and went on his way. Pretty shaken Shorty limped home in a sorry state of undress. He'd miraculously escaped with his life and probably the only thing bruised was his pride, the injuries he sustained being minor.

'More vino anyone?' Tony smiled, bringing us all back to earth.

Surfing Safari

Angie Gullan

Standing on the beach at sunrise, Captain Mitchel Niemeyer noticed a local Mozambican man running and screaming feverishly from around the point at Ponta do Ouro. He'd come face to face with a hippo!

We were launching our boat with a French film crew at the time so headed for the point to see for ourselves. There was the hippo which seemed to be wading in the waves. Then he headed towards the shore so we beached the boat and made our way on foot over the dune and rocky point to get a better view.

Sue Maas

After watching for about two hours, the hippo made his way around the point, over the rocks then lumbered into the pounding surf - and disappeared. After about ten minutes he suddenly surfaced in the bay where, not surprisingly, there was pandemonium. Locals were gathering, boats were converging and jet skis buzzed about like bees. Monitors too, from the Reserva Ponta do Ouro, now kept vigil over the hippo, a male undoubtedly from across the border with neighbouring South Africa, forced out of its natural habitat by a more dominant male in the Kosi Bay area, a series of inland lakes.

He stayed in the Ponta do Ouro bay for two days before heading up the coastline to Ponta Mamoli where he was photographed lying on the beach. He looked somewhat lethargic and we feared that he might have died. Relief soon set in as his head moved. Reserva Monitors later reported that the hippo had, during the evening, made his way to an inland lake for a short while then moved back into the ocean.

The next morning he was again photographed, this time on the beach at Ponta Malongane, a few miles further north where he was last seen. From there he probably sensed some small inland lakes a little further north and found new pastures to explore.

A hippo surfing safari? We'd like to think so!

Footnote
Far from looking like the world's most competent swimmers, hippopotami surfing in the sea may seem improbable but as this remarkable story demonstrates, in nature few things are ever impossible. Other known saltwater localities where it is not unknown for hippo to indulge in some boisterous surfing is the Kenyan island of Manda Toto also in the Indian Ocean and, in the Atlantic Ocean, south west of Gabon's Petit-Loango Reserve as well as the Orango group of islands off the mainland coast of Guinea Bissau, part of the Bijagos Archipelago – **GN**

Against My Better Judgement

Lloyd Wilmot

Down the western side of warthog alley in Savuti one can still trace the course of an old road cut by the state many years ago. We used to follow this track because it led to a trio of pans that held water till late in the year. Few people knew about it. We loved going there as the pans were a favourite haunt of buffalo herds in the surrounding mopane forest. And, of course, where you find buffalo, you find lions.

Around March 1987, I think it was we had a group of four Americans, Doug Reiser and his girlfriend plus Mike Costello and Linda Fuller who had come on a week-long safari. These were regular clients who stayed every year. For a change we decided to go camping at these pans and duly loaded a second vehicle with the necessary bedding. My wife June and our three month old baby Ashley came too. We slipped away and by taking circuitous roads ended up at the pan before sunset to set up an enclosure of logs and branches for our bedrolls. There were buffalo tracks and some lion spoor about two days old. We could hear elephants feeding nearby.

After a pre-cooked supper after sunset, we sat talking quietly around a small fire. Ashley was safely asleep in the vehicle cab. To our north we suddenly heard a bellow followed by a commotion. It was a kill. As I urged the Americans to grab their cameras and follow me, growling could be heard as lions began to feed. There was fairly bright moonlight and we hurried thither keeping a maglite torch at the ready to switch on if needed. About 400 metres up the track loud growls indicated we had reached the kill near the edge of a dry pan. Looking through binoculars I established that about ten lions were feeding on a wildebeest.

In whispers I told everyone to double over and follow me. We approached to within about 12 metres of the kill. The lions were so busy they had not noticed our arrival. Some mopane bushes also helped to screen us. Then a young lioness spotted us. I got everyone to sit down on the hard dry clay of the pan and before long she was joined by another as she walked up to investigate. As they got up

67

close I switched on the maglite and the beam blinded her light-sensitive eyes. This checked both of them and after standing undecided for a few minutes both turned and went back to feeding. Taking two clients at a time I led them right up close where we took a number of flash photos. The lions were looking starved; not particularly bothered with us, being more intent on getting a belly filled from the rapidly diminishing carcase. Withdrawing carefully I led everyone back to camp. They were all highly excited and thrilled with the adventure. When June heard the details she was bitterly disappointed to have missed the fun. She begged me to take her too and against my better judgement, I agreed.

June and I had done this sort of thing a number of times but what concerned me was that the lions would probably be finishing their feeding by the time we got there. This would mean that they could devote their full attention to us. Arriving at the pan I saw that most were lying in the open, near where we had sat earlier. Two lionesses were fighting over the last pieces of the kill. Approaching slowly and doubled over very low, they allowed us to get close. As we tried to head to the kill to photograph the lionesses, I could sense the lions were unfriendly. We began to retreat but this seemed to embolden them.

My instincts had been right and now my fears were realised as they got up and converged on us in menacing way.

I threw a piece of wood at the nearest lion, a young male and he growled as he turned. This was followed by a charge from a lioness which I fended off with a second piece of wood. By now we were surrounded and June and I were standing back to back. Desperately lighting around I broke off chunks of clay from old elephant tracks with my feet. With a shouted warning June fended off a charging lioness that burst from behind a mopane bush. Grabbing pieces of clay, I flung these hard at the nearest lions as I lunged toward them. June did the same on her side.

This checked their enthusiasm and only by showing no fear did we manage to keep them at bay and edge slowly back toward camp. The lions were still full of fight and I had to throw more chunks of clay from time to time while blinding them with the maglite. Now we faced the narrow track through the mopane and the lions used every advantage to stalk and re-engage. Only by careful watching and hurling bits of wood we found, did we manage to reach our enclosure. The Americans were relieved to see us and surprised that the lions had frog-marched us all the way back. We kept watch till late but the lions eventually gave up and wandered away.

The lion's power lies in our fear of him – **Nigerian Proverb**

Out of the frying pan...

Mike Ballantine

Sue Maas

After a leisurely, albeit short, cruise up the Sanyati Gorge we headed towards the middle of Lake Kariba where my wife, son (aged 4) and daughter (20) jumped overboard for a refreshing dip. (Crocs in those days were not that plentiful or so we believed). I was tinkering with the canopy ties when gusts of wind made me look up. What had been a glorious sunny day was gone. Replacing it were ominously low dark clouds announcing the imminent onslaught of one of the lake's unpredictable, treacherous storms where waves from the north and south shorelines clash creating extremely dangerous waters.

'Get in NOW!,' I yelled. *'Ä bad storm's on its way... we must find shelter.'*

All aboard I gunned the 115hp Yamaha engine propelling our cabin cruiser and sped for the shallows between Spurwing and Fothergill Islands. Finding a path through the myriad stumps there I had secured the bow and moved to the stern when the storm broke. It unleashed a deluge of rain, thunder and lightning and mighty gusts of wind which seemed to come from all directions.

Apart from bobbing up and down like corks and riding out the squall in our life-jackets, we were secure… or so I thought.

'That houseboat's heading this way for shelter as well,' Greer shouted above the howling wind.

It was about 500 metres from us. We'd had some experience with houseboats and once had a small share in one called Philippa. She was about 20 metres in length but this double-story seemed larger and was growing by the second… now only 250 metres away … and heading straight for us.

At 100 metres I screamed and gesticulated frantically to the person at the helm. He held up both arms as if to say, *there's nothing I can do.* It then seemed obvious that the boat lacked the power to fight the wind. It was too late to cast off and hope to drift out of the way.

The sight was frighteningly awesome as the huge houseboat ploughed through and snapped dozens of tree stumps as it towered towards us. Frenzied shouts and signals to change course got the helmsman's same helpless response.

Fingers crossed… it missed us… by no more than 3 metres, but left behind one of its tenders that had been caught by a branch and destroyed. . It was eventually stopped by the shoreline several hundred metres from us after having lost its second tender to the stumps as well.

Later we got three versions as to the cause of the runaway houseboat… The engine failed… Gears could not be engaged… The wind took it… Take your pick. .

Drunk on the elixir of the sinking sun, blood red over Kariba… now the night sky, alive with a zillion diamonds – Africa, my home – **GN**

Bizarre Behaviour

Reiko M. Goodwin

I was conducting a primatological project in the Lama Forest of the Republic of Benin some years ago. Living away from my husband it was a lonely life, especially because I could not habituate the monkeys and collecting high-quality data was very difficult. This life became less lonely when two cats started to live with me. Soon they had five kittens.

One morning Nikki, the mother cat, started to gently grab a kitten in her mouth and swiftly moved it to a rear room. Then she moved the others one by one into different rooms. Musofin, the father cat, was not around. I was very surprised with Nikki's behaviour. Why was she suddenly doing this? I could not figure it out. Then I stepped outside into the front yard and found that millions of marching army ants were about to enter the house.

I screamed for help. The villagers rushed to the house and they started to pour petrol on them. I do not remember how long it took, but the army ants changed their course and vanished into the forest.

Nikki had obviously sensed their coming long before we noticed them and instinctively knew that by separating the kittens most would survive an onslaught by the ants.

A Stitch In Time...

Greer Noble

Hours ticked by as Malagasies came and went in their droves as did the planes. Given the poverty of this third world nation we were amazed at how many locals used this mode of transport – it seemed quite commonplace, a necessity to reach the remote settlements scattered all over that vast island and its islets. Antananarivo Airport was what you might expect of one of Africa's poorest countries, though I'd hoped its dingy, seedy interior was not indicative of its domestic aircrafts. This was to be my first adventure alone with my teenage son, to explore the world's fourth largest island of Madagascar.

Relieved, the interminable wait over, we boarded amidst much shoving and pushing. As predicted, the interior was shabby and tatty, the seating in dire need of reupholstering. I couldn't help wonder about the state of the engines. It reminded me of a bus trip I once did across Turkey. All that was missing were chickens and the odd goat. Without further ado the aircraft spluttered into life and hardly waiting for all to be seated, took off, rattling and shuddering to such a degree, I expected it to fall apart at any moment. It was so bad, my son and I looked at each other and collapsed laughing. I think we giggled the entire way, probably partly out of fear.

Excited to see lemurs in the wilds, our first two days in a remote jungle proved challenging – not only did we see nothing apart from a couple of humanised lemurs that hung around camp and a glimpse of an elusive pigmy lemur caught high in the forest canopy by our guide's spotlight, we were also immobilised by a severe bout of food poisoning. With no hope of a doctor (one doctor to every 6,000 Malagasies) we were lucky to have recovered as quickly as we did with our own medical supplies. Keen to move on we headed northwest for the tourist island hot-spot of Nosy Be, confident that things could only improve. How wrong we were.

After relaxing and detoxing on fresh tropical fruit for a couple of days we regained our energy and booked to go diving. In high spirits early the next morning, dressed in swim suits and kikois, we descended the steps to the beach to rendezvous with our dive masters, an Ausie and a Spaniard. These two young men had recently bought the business and inherited a dear little lemur which had belonged to the previous owner. Attached to a long chain from a band around its waist, the opposite end of the chain threaded through a wire strung between two coconut palms, allowed it to move freely along the wire. Without warning it jumped down and started to climb my kikoi. The Ausie assured me it was safe to stroke it as long as I made no sudden movement.

Its cute little face looked up at me appealingly. I slowly bent to stroke it… and it bit me. Its razor-sharp teeth sliced my hand open between my thumb and index finger. The blood shot out like a fire hose. I knew it had hit an artery. Pandemonium! Someone ran for a huge wad of cotton wool and, with that in place, the two young men gently but firmly steered me towards their car, a truly ramshackle, buckled and dented mini. Ushered into the back seat next to my son, the engine started after several laboured bursts. As it reversed, our seat shot backwards and toppled, taking us with it. We both landed on our backs, feet in the air.

In the turmoil that followed it was so surreal I felt I was in an old fast-track Charlie Chaplin movie of fits and starts. The Ausie and

Spaniard jumped out, helped right us while the car rolled forward, scrambled back in to apply brakes and we were off again!

About a mile along a cobbled street we stopped in front of an unobtrusive, plastic-curtained doorway. I was offered the only chair in the small room. Curled up a big black cat took the best part of an old desk. I didn't have to wait long. A tall slender woman in a white jacket entered, apologised for not being a doctor but said she would help me. Before I'd even registered she jabbed a needle into my leg just above the knee. Anti-tetanus she explained. It was left dangling, resting on my bent knee. She proceeded to clean the wound on my hand with everyone still standing around. To my utter astonishment she started to stitch up the wound without administering any form of local anaesthetic. The Ausie whispered in my ear that he thought my son was about to faint.

The woman told me, as she tied the last knot, that I was extremely lucky it didn't sever the artery completely because then she would have been unable to stop the bleeding. Good to know. I asked her about rabies and she told me there was none on the island. I wanted to believe her. The big fat cat had not budged during the whole procedure. The Ausie paid and as if that was her cue, she removed the needle still dangling from my leg. With thank you's and smiles of relief all round, we set off back to our hotel.

Later, over coconut cocktails, tears of laughter streamed down our faces as we related the entire incident to the young New Yorker running the hotel for his uncle. Relieved that I wouldn't have to wait six weeks or longer before being certain that I wouldn't get rabies, I did secretly agonise over HIV/AIDS though – any treatment involving re-used needles could carry HIV and the hepatitis B risk. The cocktails helped convince me she'd used clean needles.

Back to Tana, another night's sleep in the pulsating city of the mother island (nicknamed Big Red due to the red soil exposed by the staggering 80% deforestation), another long wait at tatty Tana airport then onto beautiful Île Sainte-Marie in the East. Famous for its pirates (who would have thought it had been a penal colony for 50 year), and the hope of seeing a humpback and another trip into the forest to spot more lemurs. You guessed right, we gave the lemurs that a miss.

A Croc of a Night

Carol Lyes

Many years ago a celebrity (who shall remain nameless) used to poach crocodiles on Zambia's Kafue River. His method was simple. He would toss a large metal spike loaded with rotted meat attached to a long, strong rope into the river from his small boat and wait until he got a bite. He would then drag the croc close to his boat, dispatch it with a shot from his trusty .45 and haul the carcass into the boat.

One night our celebrity who already had several crocs in his boat happened to glance down into the well. There, one of his 'dead' crocs was preparing to bite his foot (or so he assumed since it had its mouth open right next to his foot). He promptly drew his trusty .45, yelled, '*You think you're going to bite me do you?*' and blasted the crocodile. Unfortunately the bullet also blasted and holed his boat.

Rapidly sinking in the croc infested river, before just making it to a nearby bank, he swore-off poaching for life!

A fool and water will go the way they are diverted – **Ethiopian Proverb**

Esmerelda

Rob Fynn

By paraffin lamp over dinner one evening, I heard a scuffling down the other end of our cavernous newly built gazebo which served as our living room, our admin centre and our warehouse. Picking up a lamp, I tiptoed down to investigate the intruder, suddenly finding myself standing next to an equally surprised hippo. We both jumped and hippo shuffled off. Nothing too unusual about that.

Next evening, same noise, same time. I cautiously re-investigated, expecting and indeed meeting friend hippo again. We looked at each other curiously, and quietly went our separate ways. Every evening thereafter, for the next three years, Esmerelda, came visiting at dinner time.

She became so familiar that I could walk slowly up and greet her with a hand shake to her tusk, when she would open wide her huge gaping mouth, breathing hot sweet hippo breath over me, shaking her head up and down. As construction progressed she adapted to the new situations, arriving as we sat down with our guests for dinner under the stars, to graze quietly, well, noisily actually, on our cultured lawn.

Diners would have this gigantic mouth chomping next to them, and occasionally a huge grinning jaw would plonk on their table, collapsing it under a hippo head weight of some 200kg, leaving a wobbly looking table and guest.

She also took to visiting the harbour at the end of the day when the boats from the afternoon's activities were being rowed ashore from the jetty for the night's mooring. She would slide quietly astern of a boat, open her mouth over the engine, and give it a gentle push to help it on its way, the paddling boatman on the bows chuckling with delight as he slid up the bank. In between assisting the boatmen, she would frolic about, lying on her back in the mud, paddling her stumpy legs in the air to the cheers of onlookers gathered for our daily cabaret.

This clearly had its risks and we were at pains to warn everyone that she was indeed a wild hippo, and that they should avoid approaching or feeding her. My wife Sands was a good and bad example in this respect. When she noticed Esmerelda approaching during dinner, she would quietly collect her plate and glass of wine and make smartly for the stairs leading up to our look out bar. Most of the guests took this as their cue to do the same. A mass exodus would follow, leaving just me and my immediate dining companions who I'd managed to restrain and one hippo, all peacefully continuing our meal with the peanut gallery audience above us.

A group of German visitors arrived, celebrating a birthday, for which they'd specially brought a keg of beer. We consumed this in one evening. We were regaled the next morning with stories of weaving young men finding Esmerelda asleep on a sandpit near the path on their way home and deciding to take pictures of each other reposing on her, which they showed us. Whether she was asleep or just tolerant I don't know, other than they were very lucky young men.

She must have been the most photographed hippo in the world.

One day we received a letter from a lady in Canada who had just read about and seen pictures of Esmerelda in a Toronto newspaper.

She related her strange story of how she had been working on a rhino project in the Matusadona two years before. Her favourite evening activity was to sit on the high ground at a point behind Fothergill and watch the sun go down.

'One evening,' she wrote, 'an extraordinary spectacle played out before me. A big cow hippo started running up and down the shoreline, enraged and bellowing. Catastrophically, it ran on to one of the many sharp, spear like stumps that stood amongst the grass, impaling herself, where she died in roaring agony.

'Aghast and dumbfounded, I walked down to inspect the carcass and seek the cause of the commotion, which I never found – maybe a croc after her baby? What I did find was the baby hippo nearby, which after a while overcame its shyness and approached its now dead mother and me. An adoption process took place and I walked back to the camp with a baby hippo following.

'We now had a 'no options' camp pet, whom we named Hey You. We had to feed her mealie meal (the staple diet of everybody in Africa, including Hey You). This rapidly became a somewhat hefty and unexpected increase in the food budget. I encouraged the cook to add grass in an attempt to wean the young lady off the mealie meal. No ways. Mealie meal was tastier. One day the cook, whose grass cutting duties were becoming quite onerous, suggested we pour the mealie meal onto the grass! Reducing its quantity daily, we finally persuaded Hey You into being a grass eating hippo.

'She would walk with me, and we swam in the lake together, she keeping the crocs at bay, I hoped! She was a great companion. We bade a sad adieu after six months, returning again three months later to check on her. We boated round the bays I knew so well calling her name. There was a particular hippo that seemed quite friendly but we didn't want to presume on the reunion, in case it was somebody else!'

Our Canadian friend posed the question whether Esmerelda might be their Hey You, describing that Hey You loved chocolate mousse, and could we try her on it? We didn't, but I did notice a particularly brown set of hippo teeth. It was possible, and I passed on her best love.

We referred to Esmerelda as 'her', for that's who we thought she was, until one evening we were amazed to see 'her' with a full and unashamed erection. It is very difficult to sex a young hippo, their genitals being completely hidden. Poor Esmerelda, in this delicate state, was greeted with hoots of laughter from all her onlookers.

Soon after this, clearly the beginning of her manhood, she came unwittingly into competition with two territorial bulls, which chased 'her' off Fothergill to Long Island, some 5km offshore. There she seemed to settle down until a sad episode with some campers ended in her being shot dead, so often the tragic end for wild animals that become too familiar with man.

Animal antics in the wilds are never without humour. 'If life is a cabaret...' then it applies as much in the bush as it does in cities –   **GN**

Mugabe's Elephants

Anonymity Requested

The rainy season started late and brows and graze feed in Zambia's National Park and the bush surrounding the nearby town of Livingstone were still in short supply. The town itself was invaded most nights by herds of elephant searching for food. They'd walk right up the main road then fan out into the residential suburbs looking for such delicacies as paw-paws, mangoes and guavas.

Then before sunup they'd move back to the Zambezi and, under the shade of a Natal mahogany, 'discuss' and 'plan' the next night's foray into the town. Having crossed the river some months before from Zimbabwe where they'd been behaving as badly for years in Victoria Falls, these elephant are referred to as 'Mugabe's elephants' due to their total disregard for fences, gates, humans, dogs or even land rights!

A wealth of beautiful memories is more valuable than material wealth, and that is our heritage, our treasure, which no goon can ever take – GN

A Scary Calculation

Lloyd Wilmot

It was late August in Botswana and Savuti had been hot. The air was filled with the smoky haze from distant fires in the Chobe. As evening fell, a full moon rose and lit the scene of jostling elephant bulls sucking desperately at the outlet pipe in our waterhole. Then just before supper eight young lion came into camp and enjoyed a long drink from the bird bath next to our hide. Taking the clients into the hide, we had watched them from close quarters until they had drunk their fill and jumped down the steep bank to go sprawl on the cool sand about 60 metres from camp.

For certain special clients we used to park an old Land Rover in the dry river bed between converging elephant paths and let them sleep on the roof. This gave them the unforgettable thrill of watching elephant passing to and fro at close quarters almost all night. Now with lions and elephants they would have a really interesting night.

I had already agreed that two of our regular clients could spend the night there on the Land Rover. After supper Peter, our camp manager, said I could go off; that he would escort the clients to the Land Rover and close up camp. Bidding everyone goodnight, I turned to leave when Gerhard, a young South African friend of Peter's came up to speak to me about some matter. I then invited him to accompany me to go park the vehicle to which he agreed with some hesitancy.

'Go Gerhard' Peter encouraged him and he got in.

I drove round the back of camp down into the riverbed, pulling low ratio to get through the heavy sand. The lions were lying on our usual parking space so I crept up gently and parked among them. The lions were youngsters about three and half years old, five males and three females. With lions on either side, Gerhard asked 'Wat nou*?'

'Get out on your side,' I hissed at him and began to shift over to follow him as I had four lions very close on my side. As he gently climbed out and I joined him at the door, the lionesses lost their

82

nerve and went round to join the males. *'Do exactly as I say and do'* I whispered to Gerhard.

Clutching three stones and my flashlight I doubled over and walked slowly toward the drinking elephant bulls closely followed by a nervous Gerhard. The moment we emerged from behind the vehicle into view of the eight lions, they fixed us with their full attention. Signaling Gerhard to walk ahead of me we set off as I kept a careful watch on my back. Hardly had we gone six paces when the lions got up as one and began stalking us. Gerhard was noticeably uneasy but I urged him to keep moving. There was no need to use the flashlight as the moon was very bright. The lions came up rapidly and I had to wheel round and confront them. This stopped them in their tracks and I turned to follow Gerhard.

Within a few paces the lions had gathered their wits and came on boldly. At the last moment I wheeled again and threw a stone at the nearest lion, a cheeky adolescent full of himself. Shocked at being hit in the face, he gave a burst of a growl and broke away. The confusion was brief. Immediately the others came forward eager to engage.

Realizing the situation was getting out of hand and turning nasty, I calculated that if we headed straight for the elephant we could get some protection. Taking the lead, I walked up to the bulls with the lions right behind us. A large bull elephant reversed out, still pouring water down his throat. As he saw us, he turned and charged and I threw my stone hard, hitting him squarely on the forehead as he kicked sand all over me.

The lions scattered. In the ensuing dust and confusion I shouted "*Gou*!" and the two of us sprinted past the remaining bulls and reached the steep bank in front of camp. Telling Gerhard to climb quickly I threw my last stone at the nearest lion and succeeded in stalling them long enough to scramble up after Gerhard. Fear lent me wings and with hands and feet I managed to reach safety at the top.

Gerhard was breathless with excitement and could hardly relate to Peter and the remaining guests what had happened. They had heard the elephant trumpet then seen us burst into camp looking relieved.

Leaving Gerhard to explain, I slipped away to my cottage some distance away.

*Wat nou - What now
*Gou –   quick

Only those who will risk going too far can possibly find out how far one can go – **T. S. Eliot**

Bush Hooligans

Greer Noble

Of all the safaris we've been on throughout Africa, very few hold a candle to Botswana's wildlife reserves. There's a lot to be said for its 'no-tar-roads, no-fence-camp policy' and in so doing, preserving the pristine wilderness of their national parks. You are on your own. If you want to be stupid and walk up to a lion or elephant in camp, or be careless with your foodstuff allowing hyena or baboon to have carte-blanch, it's up to you. And yes, some people have been killed... and so have those who cross highways or swim with sharks. It is not unknown to be attacked, even *in* the confines of a fenced camp.

The laughs we've had are endless. Baboons can be especially mischievous, raiding tents when you're out game-viewing or collecting firewood, to the extent of carrying off big cold-boxes or cooking utensils... and if you're lucky they won't pee and defecate in your tents because that can be truly disgusting. They are reckless and destructive yet comical in their antics, especially when it comes to grooming each other. They have all the human traits of spite, jealousy, temper, mischief and love; and I'm sure, like any parent, tolerant of their offspring up to a point. And similar to some human communities, they have total disregard for women and can be quite intimidating. They are, without a doubt, the hooligans of the bush.

85

The Dung Dance

Greer Noble

Small things amuse small minds, so the saying goes, but the big five are not the only fascinating creatures in the bush. There's the insect world which, in itself, can hold one spellbound for a lifetime. As honorary officers we were asked by coleopterists to collect the Tock Tock, a rare species of beetle of the Tenebrionidae family, on a trip into the Okavango. They'd devoted decades studying this *one* species. Armed with ethyl acetate, pins, labels etc and a letter to the Botswana authorities we set off full of enthusiasm. But try as we may, we could not find the illusive Tock Tock. What it did, however, was inspire us to look more keenly at entomology. One rather amusing fellow soon caught our attention – the much revered six legged dung beetle. All of five centimetres he, with much dexterity, shaped a steamy pile of elephant dung into a perfect ball several times his size and rolled it away from the pile. An opportunistic hitch-hiker soon clambered aboard. We were not sure if this was hindering or helping, or perhaps it was a means of attracting his attention because she proceeded to do what can only be described as a tap dance, stamping the dung while the ball rolled, maintaining perfect balance. There were a few hurdles along the way when the ball rolled into dongas. Help soon arrived only to turn into rivals and the odd skirmish ensued, but our little chap remained victorious. He eventually found a suitable soft spot to bury the ball. The female wasted no time diving in, hotly pursued by the male who, up to now had totally ignored her. The ball breeding chamber was now occupied and with an endless supply of fast foods; nutritious bits of undigested vegetation passed down by the elephant. All on video, we had many a laugh, escalated by my husband's eye-watering commentary, making out as if it had taken place over several days!

Footnote: Africa's nocturnal dung beetle is the only known non-vertebrate to navigate and orient itself using the Milky Way. The world's strongest insect, it can pull 1,141 times its own bodyweight – akin to a human dragging 6 double-decker busses! Known as the *scarab* beetle among ancient Egyptians, it enjoyed a sacred status. Believing it to be only male in gender, reproducing by depositing semen into a dung ball, its supposed self-creation resembled that of Khepri the Sun God who created himself out of nothing. **Dr Rob Knell, researcher, University of London.**

An Unholy Feast

Rob Fynn

A missionary who had spent the evening in the dining area of Fothergill Island camp on the shores of Lake Kariba, extolling the virtues of prayer and faith as the best weapons against fear, had a lion kill right outside his chalet that night.

The pride had chased a buffalo herd straight through the camp, killing one, and our missionary and his wife passed the night listening to the pride eat and fight over the carcass two metres from their bed. Only a low wall topped by a reed mat separated them from the grizzly feast.

We learned of their ordeal when the kitchen porter brought them early morning tea, promptly dropping his tray and running for help.

Chasing the lions off, much to their chagrin, we pulled the buffalo carcass out of camp to ensure our guests' slumbers the next night.

Our missionary assured me he had slept well after pushing the dressing table against the doorway. His wife looked less confident.

The wolf cometh in all forms... the Lord hath a sense of humour I see. **GN**

. Oddballs

Greer Noble

I'm addicted – I've been drawn back to the Okavango time and again, ever since I was a child, accompanying my father. To fly into the swamps is the best way to explore the islands in style. On one occasion we slept in the open in our sleeping bags on an island camp called Oddballs. I can't recall if it was because they were full or not... only that it was *awesome*. Refreshed the next morning we set off deep into the delta in mokoros (dugouts), expertly poled by local tribesmen. The water, cool against the intense sun, was crystal clear. In fact so pure we scooped it up and drank deeply.

We were a party of five, including Richard's and our son. The silence was ethereal, broken only by the odd honk of a hippo as we bravely edged past, or a flash of colour as a bird glided by. Sheer bliss! But that night, camped on a nameless islet, we were hijacked by mosquitoes, clouds of them. They were murderous. Like me, Richard couldn't sleep. Puffing cigarettes furiously, sleeping bag up to his chin despite the sweltering heat, he'd placed three empty beer cans around his head, each with a burning mosquito coil. I had to stifle a chuckle. It looked as if he was worshipping some sort of swamp spirit. I couldn't take it any longer and opted for the tent where I spent a mosquito-free night with the boys. At some ungodly hour a nudge and a loud sniff from the outside of the pup tent woke me. A hyena, most likely. Then back to Oddballs for another (safer) glorious night under the stars.

Three Big Brave Men!

Adele Barton

It was the end of a glorious day's fishing on the banks of the Zambezi, in Mana Pools. The sun had just set and we were sitting around a fire chatting about the 'one that got away', when I heard a lion roar. Being my first time in 'wild' Mana, I was a little nervous but my friends assured me that the lion was far away, in fact across the river and that I needn't worry.

After dinner we all went to our make-shift beds under a few mozzie nets thrown carelessly over low-slung branches and slept as one can only sleep in the bush.

At about four thirty in the morning I was woken by the sound of someone, or something hissing. I peered through my net and saw one of my friends near the vehicle.

'Adele, don't move,' he said almost robotically. *'There is a lion right by you.'*

I slowly turned to my left and saw her. She was about ten metres from me. It could have been a bit further but hey, it felt like she was in my net. I could hear the male calling for her but she was nonchalant, licking her great big paw. I got the distinct feeling that she knew exactly where I was too. I could feel my heart pounding. I held my breath. Not daring to blink I kept her in my sights. My mind raced. What would I do if she decided to pounce? I felt trapped, like a cornered mouse.

Then, out of the corner of my eye, I saw my friend climb stealthily into his pickup and start the engine. The lioness stopped grooming in mid-air, also distracted by the sudden movement. She was now showing more than a passing interest.

My friend slowly manoeuvred his vehicle between Her Majesty and me and, much to my relief, I was able to ease myself into it and close the door. Whew, never have I felt such relief. The lioness gave one look of disdain, blinked and, with the flick of her tail, sauntered off into the bush.

The next day we spent fishing again. Then back at camp, after a good scout around to make sure the coast was clear, we settled around the camp fire to enjoy yet another meal of our day's catch. Then I froze. Out of the darkness came another roar.

'Oh Adele, really they are far away, they don't hang around, they are long gone.'

That was it; I announced that I was sleeping in the vehicle. I got all the comments, *'Don't be such a wuss'. 'This is what you come to Mana for.' 'Please... you're such a girl.'* I was having none of it, I was spending the night in the back of the pick-up and that was that. I went to bed.

In the morning I awoke with THREE grown men crammed in beside me. Their story was, they didn't want ME to be scared! Haha!

There's something so thrilling about the scent of a lion at close range. If confronted, the consensus is not to make eye contact but to play dead. In theory, as we're not on their menu, they'll lose interest and move off...mmmm? **GN**

Dicing with Giants

Greer Noble

Kariba was my home, my life, my love. Our hotel which we built and ran nestled in our own private little bay – we being my parents, my dear little daughter and her father. This 42 acre setting was kissed most evenings with the most glorious sunsets on earth which never failed to make up for some of the hottest days on the planet with temperatures often reaching 46 degrees *in the shade.*

But it was on a rather rainy evening when we got news from incoming guests that my father had broken down between Makuti and Kariba, Makuti being a good hour's drive from our hotel. Their vehicle filled to capacity with kids, granny and baggage; there had been no room for a mouse, let alone another passenger. My husband being enlisted with PATU (Police Anti-Terrorist Unit) was out in the bush on call-up, there having been reports of more terrorist insurgents into the area.

So wasting no time I leapt into one of the little Renault cars we had for hire, topped up the tank and sped off into the night. The tarmac was wet and visibility poor as the rain had started up again and now came down in sheets as only it can in the tropics. This did not deter me as I knew that stretch of road like the freckles on my face while concern for my father's safety kept the adrenalin flowing. At least the ters (terrorists) wouldn't be trying to ambush anyone on a night like this, I convinced myself.

The downpour had stopped as suddenly as it had started, as if a big tap up there had been turned off. I had reached a fairly wooded area where, with the rain now down to a fine drizzle, all sorts of shapes jumped out at me from either side of the road. It was quite eerie so I put my foot flat on the pedal, my heart pounding. Even with the rain the night was hot and muggy and in my haste, as luck would have it, I'd picked the only car with malfunctioning air-conditioning. I opened the window to breathe in some much needed fresh air but the rush of it and the drizzle hit me, stinging my face, so I quickly closed it again. The blast was refreshing nonetheless and I was busy wiping my eyes when I caught sight of an obstruction in the road ahead.

Quickly refocusing my eyes I couldn't believe what I saw. My heart missed a beat, my throat constricted. *Elephant!* Oh God I was going to sail right into a herd of elephant. So intent was I on getting to my father I'd completely forgotten about them and how that specific stretch of road was notorious for that very reason. The tarmac was slippery and I was going far too fast to stop. These huge, unmistakable grey shapes loomed ever closer. The road cut through a hill with steep banks on either side which ruled out veering off into the bush. There was nothing left but to keep to the centre, heading straight into them... and pray.

As a collision became inevitable I must have closed my eyes and hoped for the best. When next I opened them that little Renault and I were in the middle of them. Tall trunk-like legs everywhere. And then it was all over.

As if the Renault was in self-drive it kept going. To this day I couldn't tell you whether there were three or five elephant, whether they politely stepped aside to allow this annoying little intruder through or whether I actually went through their legs. But at least I found my father and brought him home. Thankfully these gentle giants were no longer around on our return.

A mind that is stretched by a new experience can never go back to its old dimensions – **Oliver Wendell Holmes**

Shifting Grasses

Greer Noble

Being the last fuel for many miles, we topped up our tank at Tsumkwe using the old-fashioned hand-pump until not a drop remained. *'Pity the next poor devil that comes along,'* my husband commented.

At last we were in the land of the San bushmen. After passing a few villages we branched off in the direction of Katimo Malilo and unexpectedly came across a natural forest of baobab trees, something I'd never imagined possible. The giant of them all was 32 metres in circumference!

We soon reached the Khaudum game reserve post and weren't sure they'd let us through. Due to the desperate remoteness of the area, there had to be a minimum of two 4 wheel drive vehicles. We had a story made up that our (imaginary) friends were following. As it turned out the place was deserted so we deflated our tires to best cope with the thick sand and happily ploughed through.

Just before nightfall we met an old man at a deserted camp on a hill top, with its neat rows of bungalows but no campsite so we continued on until we found an appropriate clearing. After dinner, our son and I climbed into our mosquito-free roof top tents and watched the embers of our campfire. Soon our son slept. My eyelids were heavy and I too was about to turn in when I noticed the elephant grass moving in fits and starts as it zigzagged closer and closer. Lion? Hyena?

'Mike!' I hissed but my husband had fallen asleep in his camp chair. I threw my pillow at him and he woke just as two huge hyenas emerged from the thick grass. As soon as he stood they loped away. I still shudder at what might have happened had I too nodded off.

If there were one more thing I could do, it would be to go on safari once again. **Karen Blixen**

Licked by a Chick

Lloyd Wilmot

Sue Maas

W ith a whoosh of air the tyre went flat. There were no more spare wheels. Switching off the heavily loaded and now boiling Chevrolet truck, my father called a halt. We had spent the morning driving through heavy bush from Mababe to the Tsantsara Valley in Botswana, following elephant paths from pan to pan as there were no roads in those days. Father was en route to the Savuti Channel via the Tsantsara Valley - the only route to get through the fossil dunes of the Magikwe Sand Ridge.

As a 13 year old on holiday from boarding school, this was all a great adventure for me. Father and the staff set about repairing the punctured wheels so I went exploring. We had just reached the point where an ancient river course cut through the sand ridge and there towering above the sand stood a large Mogonono tree. I could climb trees like a monkey and despite having no branches for a good way up, I figured I could reach the top for a grand view of my surroundings. As I approached a vulture flew off and I saw the nest. A friend at boarding school collected eggs and I knew he did not have that of a Whiteback vulture.

With steady effort I gained the uppermost branches but to reach the nest I had to cling, hanging with legs and arms. The drop was over 50 feet and I was afraid the branch might break. With a last reach I was able to peer over the edge of the nest. Instead of an egg there crouched an almost fully fledged vulture chick against the far edge. My disappointment turned to alarm when the chick ambled over and vomited directly in my face. I clung desperately as the most putrid remains of some past kill ran down my face and neck and into my shirt.

Scarcely able to see I concentrated on a careful retreat with no thought of the grand view of my surroundings. Back at the truck my embarrassment was heightened by everyone's derisive laughter. It was a lesson well learned. Despite the soap and Dettol the smell clung for days.

A bird in the hand was worth two in the bush, he told her, to which she retorted that a proverb was the last refuge of the mentally destitute
W. Somerset Maugham

The Intrepid Dhow Race

Greer Noble

What salad days those were – oysters on the house washed down with chilled Bloody-Marys at the Boat Yard, languidly gazing out at white yachts static at their moorings, brilliantly contrasting against calm turquoise waters – quite mesmerising. Bursts of laughter filtered intermittently through low murmurings of lazy locals. Only today was different – there was an air of excitement, of anticipation, for it was the annual Kilifi Dhow Race. Boats of all shapes and sizes started gathering in front of the Boat Yard. The atmosphere was electric as we all bundled into one of the bigger dhows, taking up our positions, our tickets contributing to the prize money although I suspected it was more a matter of national pride for these Kenyan fishermen, just to be competing.

A shot rang out and we were off, not all to a good start; some colliding and one started to immediately sink, a small craft with only a two-man crew. They struggled gallantly but we were already out of sight to see what transpired. A colourful spectacle as we swept by, our sails expertly handled, we overtook competitors swiftly and with ease. Soon we rounded the furthest islet inland to head back again up the creek towards the open sea when our sister dhow sank, utterly and completely, so fast it was unbelievable. The safety vessels soon rescued all passengers and crew. 'Our' dhow didn't win the race but it certainly proved to be an experience of a lifetime.

Stumpy and Patches

Rory Young

Stumpy and Patches were two elephants that used to hang around camp on an almost full time basis. It was as though they knew they were safer from poachers there. Both were large bulls in their prime. Patches got his name from pale discolouration on his skin. He was unusually tall for the area, with a perfect set of evenly matched tusks. Stumpy was named from his stocky build and short thick tusks.

Patches was a menace. He would insist on staying close to man yet would charge anyone at the slightest scent or sound of someone passing nearby. Had these charges been mild mock charges it wouldn't have been too much of a problem. Instead though, he would fly into a screaming and trumpeting rage every time and charge like a runaway train. Scouts and workers became adept at sprinting for the cover of buildings and on a couple of occasions were forced to jump into the crocodile infested Zambezi.

Stumpy on the other hand was much more laid back. We spent a lot of time trying to keep him out of the vegetable garden. In the end the only thing that worked was to post a game scout on permanent duty to fire a shot in the air if he came too close. If the game scout went away for a minute Stumpy would be into the veggies within seconds. Unfortunately he would knock down the kitchen trying to get at marula fruits that had fallen through the windows, but that was just clumsiness not maliciousness.

One day Stumpy approached me, waggled his head and then stretched it down and forwards towards me with his trunk wrapped over his tusk. I was dumbstruck. Elephants do this to other elephants to invite them to play. He wanted to play! I couldn't exactly go and wrestle with him, so I made some noise and threw some dust in a mock display and he happily joined in. Thereafter, when I saw him he would waggle his head in invitation and kick or throw dust or sticks at me and I would do the same.

A most amazing thing happened when I had a bad dose of malaria (we used to get it regularly in those days) and was asleep on a mat in the shade of a large tree in the middle of the camp. It was an ideal spot as the breeze off the river and the shade of the enormous tree combined to bring the oven-like temperature down a notch at least.

No one had noticed that Stumpy had wandered in to feed on the same tree. When they did it was too late. Unbeknown to me he was feeding whilst standing over me. He had literally walked carefully over me and then stood happily reaching up to pluck leaves while I snored away under his belly. There was a bit of a panic. No one could do anything as they were afraid to scare him in case he stood on me. So they waited and eventually he finished his sampling, put his trunk down, sniffed my face all over and then stepped his back feet over me and wandered off.

My relationship with Patches was a whole different story. We did not get on at all. He would wait outside my hut and charge as soon as I came to the door. There was nothing friendly or fun about it. These were extremely aggressive and close to full charges. We had some really close calls. He almost squashed a Singaporean visitor who decided not to wait for the obligatory escort and strolled from his hut to the dining area. Patches missed him by inches. Fortunately this fellow turned into a really good sprinter at really short notice and made it into a building just in time. There were many close calls with the workers and there were more and more calls to have him put down.

Eventually Patches almost got me too. I was at a different camp a couple of kilometres downstream collecting supplies. I walked out of the warehouse and didn't notice Patches standing quietly nearby. Once I did it was too late. He had been next to the building and then walked in between the building and me before charging. I couldn't run back into the building and it was too far to the river. I was stuck and he was coming at me like a giant cannon ball.

Something clicked in my head and I let him have it. I screamed the most foul abusive stream of the most vile and filthy language at him and told him exactly what I thought of him. At the same time I walked towards him.

I have stood down many, many mock charges from elephants and have learned in detail the art of interacting with them. However, this was different; it was what anyone would only describe as a full charge. His ears were back, his head was down, his trunk was curled and I was unarmed. I usually had a side arm for emergencies and when out in the bush always carried a rifle. However, right now I had nothing. I actually had no choice really so I just had to call his bluff and otherwise hope I would go quickly.

He stopped about ten metres away from me just as the last, most disgusting insult came out of my mouth. Then he raised his head, shook it, spraying me with snot and then walked away slowly at an angle keeping one eye on me. I walked back to the warehouse. My friend and colleague Rolf Niemeijer was standing there with a bunch of workers.

'*Young*', he said, '*you are completely and utterly insane,* and then turned and walked away. Right then I found it difficult to argue with that. At least there was method in my madness I suppose. Anyway, it worked.

Not too long after that I returned from time off to be told by Lew Games, my boss, that I needed to shoot an elephant.

'A bull has a cable-snare round his leg. Probably meant for kudu, but it went bad. ZAWA* called in a vet but it took three days for them to get him here. It was already too far gone then, now the poor bugger is on his last legs and in agony. The vet just confirmed he needs to be put down ASAP. ZAWA asked if you could do it.'

I set off with a couple of scouts from ZAWA and a colleague called Peter Caborn who had asked if he could tag along. It was no great hunting expedition. The poor old fellow was only a kilometre from the camp. When elephants injure a foot they can't go anywhere and quickly starve as they cannot get the variety of nutrients they need in such a confined area.

His foot was swollen literally to the shape of a football. He was emaciated and clearly on his last legs, poison coursing through him. It was Stumpy.

Patches was standing quietly nearby. I put all thoughts and emotions out of my mind. The kindest thing I could do for him was to take away his pain as quickly as possible. I shot Stumpy through the brain.

Patches continued to stick around and although he was still aggressive to everybody else he never charged me again. I would often see him from a distance standing at the spot where I shot Stumpy. Elephants do visit the remains of dead elephants. They are also believed to be empathetic like we are.

*ZAWA – Zambia Wildlife Authority

The greatest strength is gentleness – **Iroquois Proverb**

Big Boy and Little Boy

Greer Noble

It was on one of his fishing trips on the Kafue River in Zambia that my father, Eric, decided to make a detour and pay a visit to his old compatriot, Norman Carr, and one of his favourite game reserves, the Luangwa Valley. Wise in the ways of the wilds, Eric was not a person who was easily surprised. His 'playgrounds' included the Maasai Mara, Okavongo, Gorongosa and Matusadona where he lived for several years, which, incidentally, earned him the name of Gora – meaning Vulture, '...*because he works us to the bone,*' his staff would joke.

Once in the reserve Eric and Phineas, his manservant, made straight for Kapani where he knew the Carrs would be. En route, in a trusty 4x4, they stopped to look at what seemed like a leopard running across an open plain.

'*Hand me the binoculars, Phineas.*'

While Eric was scrutinizing the area, Phineas suddenly let rip…'*Hiiiiyeee!*'

Eric looked at him, bewildered. Phineas' eyes, about to pop out of his head, had enlarged to the size of golf balls and seemed to be looking right through him. Just then Eric felt a hot breath in his ear and turned… right into the face of a young lion only millimetres away. Instinctively he slid the window slamming it shut.

Alarmingly, another young lion jumped onto the bonnet. Way too much for Phineas, he squeezed himself under the dashboard. Eric later commented that he would never have believed it possible to hide oneself in such a small space, especially in a short-wheel base Land Rover. But Phineas had all but disappeared!

Gradually pulling away, number two jumped off the bonnet, almost in disgust, Eric thought with amusement. The leopard they thought they'd spotted was long since forgotten.

102

Only when they got to Kapani did they learn that these were Norman's adopted lions, Big Boy and Little Boy. Their mother had been shot in the Kafue Game Reserve when she charged a ranger. He'd found the three newly born cubs she'd been trying to defend, kept one for himself and took the other two to the local mission. These were the two Norman adopted. The ranger's lion later had a roll in the film Cleopatra, featuring Elizabeth Taylor.

Footnote

Talking of Zambia, while lunching at the Holiday Inn in Lusaka, waiting for our vehicle to be repaired, a tall, elderly man approached us. *'Welcome! I hope you are enjoying yourselves?'* he asked, offering his huge hand. What a surprise – it was none other than Dr Kenneth Kaunda or KK as he's better known, former president of Zambia. Another famous doctor in time gone by flashed through my mind, *'Dr Livingstone I presume?'* Perhaps the time and place had something to do with it! Similarly, *'Scenes so **lovely** must have been gazed upon by angels in their flight'* reminded me of the many ***spectacular*** scenes in that magnificent country, not the least of which is Luangwa Valley – **GN**

Driver's License a la Africa

Greer Noble

What it was to be 18, single and living in one of the hottest, wildest spots in Africa! Intoxicated with life, driving around in an open short-wheel-base Land Rover, air buffing my face like a giant powder puff (who needed air-conditioning?), it is little wonder I enjoyed driving so much. The thrill of stopping for the odd elephant to cross the road; headlights catching a leopard on my way home at night after watching an open air movie under the stars from the terraced hill-side (where it wasn't unheard of to be distracted by the odd lion strolling across the concrete stage below the screen), the last thing on my mind was the fact that I did not have a driver's licence.

Our community was small, intimate. Everyone knew everyone. And so it was, one day, when one of our British South African Policemen, as they were known back then, young men in their twenties fresh out from Britain, asked me when I planned to get my licence. I laughed and shrugged. Silly man, I'd been driving for years... started on my father's ranch when I was twelve.

He was a decent sort, only trying to help. *'Greer, we all know you don't have a licence so please, I'm asking you, for your own sake... do something about it.'*

What a bore. Oh well... I knew it would come to this eventually. So I took the plunge and booked my test.

'You'd better take my Mini Moke,' offered our neighbour. *'Your old heap doesn't even have a rear-view mirror... they'd fail you before you start.'* So the Mini Moke it was.

As I whizzed around a bend, the huge inspector beside me, holding onto his very bad quality hairpiece as if his life depended on it, I caught sight of my mother at the filling station. One look at her face and it wasn't hard to imagine her cracking – she confirmed having done so afterwards. The sight of me careening past in this funny little white car, my long hair flying out the back, with the terrified inspector literally overflowing in the seat next to me, doing a sort of balancing act between holding onto his toupee and the bodywork of the car.

Sue Maas

I didn't know who this stern inspector was, apparently up from Salisbury. Just my luck… I'd imagined it would be a mere formality with one of the policemen we knew.

Back at the police station – the village was too small to have a traffic department – I was marched into the office where several young policemen sat at old worn wooden desks, fidgeting on tatty typewriters that had definitely seen better days.

Inspector McBride fondly twirled his ample moustache and indicated with a flash of his dark eyes and a twitch of his heavy bushy eyebrows for me to be seated. '*Let us begin,*' he announced with the severity of a murder trial. '*What is the most essential component of a vehicle's engine?*'

My mind raced, willing the tapping keys to be some sort of Morse code, giving me a clue. '*A carburettor?*' I blurted self-consciously.

'*Mmmmmm…*' the inspector pondered, giving no indication as to whether my wild guess was right or not. '*Lights,*' he continued in his thick Scottish brogue, as if the questions themselves weren't bad enough. '*How many lights should a vehicle have?*'

Well that's easy enough, I thought. '*Headlights, tail lights, indicators, brake lights, parking lights*', I rattled off, relieved.
'*And?*' his bushy eyebrows quizzed.

I frowned, wracking my brain... '*A torch? In case of a breakdown?*' I tried foolishly, groping at straws. I was sure I'd heard a snigger.

The inspector's eyes rolled as he said, '*Number plate lights, lassie, number plate lights.*' He continued without a moment for me to gather my wits. '*When should one use hand signals?*'

Hand signals? Was he serious? '*To wave down traffic in the case of a breakdown... or accident I suppose?*'

As before the inspector ignored my answer.

'*...should the indicator malfunction?*' I added as an afterthought.

McBride snorted.

Was that a yes?

'*How many revolutions does your steering rod turn to enable functionality in four wheel drive?*'

More sniggers. '*Is that two or all four tires?*' I ventured, my mind in a flat spin.

'*That's na what I asked, lassie... please answer my questions.*'

Worse was to come.

'*What angle should yer accelerator be when travellin at thirty miles an hour?*'

My mind simply went into freeze mode. Please God let this be over. '*Please could you repeat the question, inspector?*'

'*Ye either know the answer or ye don't.*' With that he stood unexpectedly, tucked his file under his arm and abruptly indicated for me to follow. Once outside he told me very firmly that I was to precede to the police pub some forty metres away. He would see me there shortly with my results.

The place was abuzz, not unusual for that time of day, and I was soon among familiar faces. I was offered a drink. Known as the Jam Jar, it was a favourite water-hole among locals, police reservists and Selous Scouts as well as young customs and immigration officers and nurses from the nearby hospital.

I waited in trepidation, believing I'd failed dismally. I was half listening to a conversation when in walked the inspector... stone-faced. The rest of the young policemen in the office had, in the meantime, drifted in. Suddenly there was complete silence.

'*Well, young lady,*' he boomed.

I could feel my face burning. Surely he wasn't going to embarrass me in front of everyone.

'*I should na be givin you yer licence,*' he winked at the others, '*but I suppose I'm goin to ha to.*' With that he beamed and, as if that was his cue, everyone in the pub burst out laughing and clapped.

Was my face red! The whole thing had been a setup, a charade, even the ridiculous questions had been cooked up by them. But when I learnt that my entire oral test had been piped through to the bar on the public address system, I was mortified.

That was then... my driver's licence a la Africa! Today it's a lot easier in some of the continent's countries – you can simply buy your licence!

You're never too old to learn something stupid – **From Paraprosdokians**

Sadler's Wells Candidate

Eve How

At 6.30 one hot summers morning in December, on our Eastern Cape farm, my aunt Tinka arrived breathless from their next door house. *'There's a puffy in my studio,'* she exclaimed excitedly. *'It's STANDING at the glass sliding door.'*

I ran to get our snake gun (special modified .22) without registering anything but the word *'puffy'*. However, as things go with snakes, by the time we got there, there was nothing to see.

My sister Paula and I searched the studio, gun at the ready with no results. We closed the door. '*It will come out of hiding sooner or later,*' I said.

Half an hour later a phone call revealed the snake had indeed re appeared, *standing up* against the glass door. '*It's standing on the tip of its tail!*' shrieked my aunt Tinka in disbelief. '*How can it do that?!*'

My father, Noel, alias 'Smoke Finger' (therein lies another tale) arrived to observe that the puffy was indeed standing on *tip tail* up against the glass.

If one could lip read snake language I am certain it would have been saying, '*Help!! Let me out of here!*'

Smoke Finger, slowly, with caution, opened the door and let the puffy out of its life.

The twist to this little tale is that ordinarily we would never demise a snake, poisonous or not, for hunting rats and frogs but puff adders pose a grave danger when they come into our human domains, resulting in serious consequences on either side.

Footnote: Tinka Christopher, a renowned artist, presented this Christmas card to my brother Noel, her brother in law, so very typical of her beautiful sense of humour – **GN**

Hairy Hijacker

Trish Jackson

W hen we visited South Africa we took my mom, then 80 years old, to have lunch at Cape Point, the southernmost tip of Africa where the Indian and Atlantic Oceans meet. On the way one drives through a nature reserve.

We had a wonderful meal only mom couldn't eat everything so she took a 'doggie bag' when we left. We stopped at a minor traffic jam and David, my husband, wound down the window of Mom's little car to find out what was going on. We were told that a baboon had jumped into a German tourist's vehicle. David went to investigate and, sure enough, there was a van with a child sitting in the back and a baboon sitting with the child, baring its fangs. Baboons have a way of recognizing a person of authority and it wasn't too difficult for David to get the baboon to exit out of the back door of the van.

While everyone was thanking him, it loped casually over to our car, jumped effortlessly through the open window, and sat beside my Mom on the back seat.

'Just sit still.' I whispered. *'Don't move.'* I had no idea how we would get the baboon out but didn't want it to get scared and bite my poor mother.

'I won't move,' came the calm response.

Just about then David realized what had happened and started heading toward us, rapidly. The baboon coolly grabbed the food box, hopped out of the window and took off down the road.

.

*A **baboon** in a forest is a matter of legitimate speculation; a **baboon** in a zoo is an object of public curiosity; but a **baboon** in your wife's bed is a cause of the gravest concern –* **Winston Churchill**

Don't Tangle With Cats

Mike Ballantine

My wife is a Leo – she's soft, cuddly and purrs when spoilt; but does not suffer fools lightly and shows it by extending her metaphorical claws every now and again.

We were on our way from Savuti to Kasane along a little used track off the main route when we had to stop for a stationary vehicle with trailer, in the middle of the road. The owner (who we shall name Slim), very relieved at seeing us, explained that his timing chain had broken. No wonder! His small 4-cylinder, 2-wheel drive, low-clearance car had been towing (and often dragging) an over-loaded trailer over that rough dirt track with a very pronounced *middel-mannetjie* (centre ridge) along many stretches. His nephews, two youngsters in their early teens, were with him.

They had been stuck there for only a day before we arrived – lucky for them we had taken that diversion or they might have been there much longer! Never mind that Botswana's National Parks require 4x4 vehicles (preferably accompanied by another vehicle) to be used, Slim believed he'd make it, having traversed some of the park's other dirt roads without undue difficulty.

After warning him that we could damage his car by dragging it at times over the ridges we proceeded to tow vehicle and trailer towards Kasane, a few hours away – that is, until I noticed the claws appearing. Greer felt that Slim had put the youngsters' welfare at risk and wanted him to pay for it.

'*I want a mokoro,*' she said emphatically.

'*After towing Slim to the Chobe workshop, we'll ask around,*' I ventured.

'*Today, before we drop him off,*' It was a command, not a proposition.

The penance Slim paid for hooking up with us was to be towed for 5 not 3 hours to a half a dozen small villages in the flood plain area until we found a suitable mokoro. And after taking half an hour to beat the villager down from 20 to 15 pula (10 pula to US$1), he eventually got his 20 as I didn't have change.

The cat had a smug look as we turned into the workshop – Land Rover, crowned by a 5 metre long mokoro, towing a car, towing a trailer. But in all fairness I had promised her one for the eight years we'd been exploring the Okavango.

PS We were to keep the mokoro for some 20-odd years, taking it to our bush retreat in the eastern Transvaal from our coastal resort in Natal.

Footnote
Volumes could be told about this mokoro and its passage of time skimming the delta channels? How old would this once majestic tree have been? Who carved it and how long did it take with their primitive tools? What did it and its passengers encounter? How was it holed? Then a cattle trough in the tribal village... until purchased by these mad wazungu. It became a swing-seat at our beach cottage and later a much admired 'dresser' for serving salads at our little beach resort! What fascinating stories will its next 20 years bring? – GN

Old Brogues For A Young Ghandi

Greer Noble

On 2nd October, 2003, the City of Johannesburg marked Mahatma Gandhi's birthday by unveiling a bronze statue of him in Gandhi Square in the city centre.

But what is also interesting is the very human story behind it. My brother's sister-in-law, Tinka Christopher, tendered to the adjudicator at the Johannesburg Art Gallery to sculpt the two-and-a-half metre statue of Mahatma Gandhi and won. Not surprising since she already had several works to her credit around the city: a two-children sculpture in Bank City; a fish eagle at Midrand's corporate offices and a stallion at Toyota's offices in Sandton to mention a few.

At first Tinka was a little disappointed at having to do Gandhi as a young lawyer as the artist in her yearned to do the much older Gandhi. However, having little say in the matter, she set to work throwing her heart and soul into it. When it came to the robe over his suit, to create movement, she sculptured it as though it was caught by a breeze, blowing it to one side. For some reason, on one of the intermittent inspections, this was frowned upon but determined to have her way this time, she stood her ground.

But the funny part, which probably very few people know about... let's say a family secret and one much laughed about... was when it came to Gandhi's feet. It just so happened, around that time, Tinka's husband had thrown out a pair of old brogue shoes which their gardener wasted no time in claiming.

Damn, Tinka pondered, *they would have been ideal.* It kept niggling her until she could stand it no longer. She bought them back from the gardener. Astounded at this unexpected windfall, he kept shaking his head. Who would want to pay good money for such a worn out pair of old shoes? If the madam wanted them why didn't she just take them back? Totally bewildered, he strongly suspected something wasn't right in his madam's head.

No mean feat, it took three months of working ten hours a day, seven days a week to complete the sculpture in time for the unveiling. I'm sure Mahatma Gandhi had the last smile though as those self-same shoes are, of course, now firmly bronzed, forming an integral part of the statue forever more.

And so it is that a young lawyer gazes determinedly into the centre of Gandhi Square for all time, where Gandhi practiced as a young attorney at the Johannesburg Law Courts in the early 1900s, returning to India in 1914, after having shaped and established Satyagraha, his policy of passive resistance.

I cried because I had no shoes until I met a man who had no feet.
Saadi Shirazi

Knickers in a Knot

Eve How

Sue-Maas

It was in the late sixties in what was then still Rhodesia. I was 13. My family and I and numerous friends headed off as we usually did in school holidays to our favorite spot, Mana Pools, on the banks of the Zambezi river to fish, game view and relax.

In those good old days Mana was wild, there were no fenced areas for camping, let alone toilet blocks for civilized ablutions, but we were very organized, even our faithful cook was brought along. We chose a suitable spot on the banks of the river with a good view over the fast flowing water and set up camp under the tall shady Tamarind trees. A little way down stream, a good 20 metres in so as not to pollute the river, we dug a long-drop 'toilet' and screened it off with a wall of thatching grass. Bathing was done in the river keeping a wary eye out for crocs.

We settled in and as afternoon gave way to evening we noticed a herd of elephant come down to the river for a bath and drink right in front of our camp. We gathered to watch their antics but it soon became too dark to see well enough. Someone in the group moved a vehicle to the bank and turned the lights onto the elephant. At this point I needed the loo, so I wandered across to our long-drop. No sooner had I sat myself down when all hell broke loose. In the river, much splashing and trumpeting from the elephant and shouts from the people on the bank.

Next thing I knew, my father had burst into the long drop, grabbed me by the arm and was yanking me through the door. I, having no option but to follow, running with tiny steps like a Chinese lady with my knickers around my ankles, was suddenly swooped into his arms.

It transpired that the elephants had taken offense at having lights shone on them and a large bull elephant had charged up the bank heading directly toward the long drop hence the rescue by my knight in shining amour, dad. I, however, would rather have been stomped on by a raging elephant!

The bull elephant decided that discretion was the better part of valor and side stepped the long drop leaving it standing as he trumpeted off into the night.

The last laugh however was not on me. When things settled down in the camp and the nervous giggling had quieted someone said 'where's cookie?' After much calling we finally heard a muffled sound coming from the boot of one of the vehicles. Our cook had been so terrified he had jumped in and slammed the boot shut.

Footnote
Mana pools is definitely a place you want to add to your bucket list. Having explored many National Parks throughout Africa and having lived in the wilds for extended periods, this section of the great Zambezi stands out as being particularly special. **GN**

The Voyeur Boys

Greer Noble

Have you ever had the feeling you're being watched... especially swimming in your birthday suit?! Well there I was having a glorious wallow in the privacy (or so I thought) of our little private bush lodge pool under the hot African sun in my altogether when I got the distinct feeling I wasn't alone.

I turned slowly and there, as blatant as can be, were two peeping toms in striped pyjamas – two very curious zebra, so bold they then proceeded to *drink* out of the pool right under my nose.

I was enchanted and very tempted to stroke their velvety noses but refrained in fear of retribution, having seen them powerfully nip each other... and *their* hide is thick.

This became a ritual and almost every day they would come by for their daily 'pint'.

Malawi Gold

Rob Fynn

I had taken up a position in Malawi on the Sucoma sugar estate installing the irrigation system for a 2,000ha extension. The irrigation company's new MD came up to inspect the project. I lined up an aeroplane from the local club to fly him in. The entire hierarchy of the company had been wiped out in a light aircraft accident a year earlier and a blanket ban had been stipulated for directors in small planes. In deference to my navy training and he being an ex RAF pilot, he agreed.

Arriving at the airport on Monday morning to pre-flight the aircraft after a particularly whacky weekend, I was in a strange state of mind. I was back in the bush, on the Shire River, where I had found my lovely Mauritian girlfriend, Odette, the daughter of one of the managers. My attention span appeared limited to seconds. I went up to the control tower for a briefing and walked out not having absorbed a single word. Feeling very anxious and battling to make the simplest decision, I met the boss's international flight.

'Nice to meet you, Rob. I'm really looking forward to seeing how you've handled that No 4 pump station intake.' He was straight into the job, as expected.

I picked up his case off the conveyor and abruptly walked out to our plane, fighting the mental agony of knowing something was dreadfully wrong with me.

We climbed in, started up, and I called for taxi instructions. All I could pick up was the runway to use. I started to taxi round the perimeter of the airfield, looking at the numbers marked on the ground at the end of each runway. To my great relief, I found them, and expressed this to my boss in the seat next to me, who, by now, was beginning to look at me in a strange way.

I called for take-off, couldn't decipher the response, stowed the microphone, and opened the throttle. Boss gripped the side of his seat and started to curl up his legs as if preparing for a crash. I was fully engaged in trying to read my instruments which to my considerable concern were indiscernible.

A blur of movement ahead appeared as a large aeroplane landing straight across our take off path. Much squawking was filling the radio, all of which I ignored. I still couldn't read the instruments, seeing them clearly enough but unable to make out what they were recording.

Shaken in the turbulence of the large aircraft, we were airborne, the stall warning immediately screaming. I pushed the nose down to pick up flying speed. Our awful predicament was rapidly dawning on me. I was in command of an aeroplane without any ability to assimilate what the instruments were telling me and had no idea how to deal with it.

I frantically sought a solution, not daring to say or do anything but simply fly straight ahead. Then, flying over the escarpment into the Zambezi and Shire valley, the dry veld stretching into the distance, I could make out the great river when suddenly I spotted a patch of green on the horizon.

'The estate! It's Sucoma... there, do you see!' I pointed excitedly, like a child seeing for the first time. The boss quietly nodded. Instant relief for me. Solution found - simply fly towards it and land. No more problem.

The boss, valiantly attempting to converse, convincing himself this wasn't happening, pointed out features he recognised. Ignoring him, I concentrated every effort on getting there and landing.

'Maybe we could fly around a bit to have a look at the pump stations, Rob?' He suggested.

I simply pointed the aeroplane straight at the end of the runway. I noted the airspeed was much higher than it should be but had no idea how to correct it. Hold the nose on the end of the runway. Cut the throttle. Hang in. No distractions. Please!

Wheels hit the threshold. Far too fast. We bounced back into the air. On the third bounce well over halfway down the runway, determined I wasn't taking off to fly round again, I stood on the brakes. As the wheels hit for the fourth time the tyres burst, collapsing the undercarriage and we slid on the aircraft belly deep into the surrounding sugar cane.

When all the noise stopped, amidst thick dust and a strong scent of sugar, I calmly undid my straps, opened the door and walked round to the luggage hatch. Retrieving his suitcase, I casually made my way back through the swathe we'd cut in the cane. People were running towards us, the boss was shouting, and I collapsed.

Soon afterwards, in the company sickbay under concerned medical surveillance, I had no idea what was happening to me – nor could I focus on anything other than vaguely remembering the serious party at the weekend and fearing I must have been spiked there.

Cerebral malaria? Some weird tropical river bug? A week of tests and consultations with a psychologist followed as I gradually recovered normality. The diagnosis was uncertain and put down to a mysterious disease of the Shire valley.

The boss also recovered and as a huge measure of his generosity I was allowed back on the job. But not to fly.

I vowed never to smoke Malawi Gold* again.

*Malawi Gold – by reputation, one of the finest cannabis sativas in Africa. According to a World Bank report, it is often referred to as '*the best and finest*' chamba in the world. It is also known as one of the most potent psychoactive pure African sativas

I can resist everything except temptation – **Oscar Wilde**

The Prince, and I

Mike Ballantine

It was in August 1985 that we decided to spend a day or two at Hlane Royal National Park in Swaziland on our way to Mozambique. No sooner had we arrived, early afternoon at the park's Ndlovu camp when a really funny, tatty, one-eyed ostrich latched onto me. Heaven knows how she lost her eye, but she followed me around like a broody hen and wouldn't let me out of her sight.

Trying to ditch 'one-eye' while exploring the camp I found a very expensive camera next to the trunk of a tree but couldn't see anyone nearby. Then, walking towards a communal braai* area with some tables and chairs we came across a small tribal gathering comprising a handsome youngster and four or five pretty maidens in traditional attire, the youth with red feathers in a band around his head, all laughing, giggling, playing, dancing...

I went up to him, held out the camera and asked if it was his. For a moment he seemed confused, looked at the camera, nodded, smiled, took it and thanked me... while 'one-eye' looked on from a distance.

We later found out that the youngster had spent his early teenage years at Sherborne School in Dorset, England and was the Crown Prince of Swaziland. Less than a year later, at the age of 18, he was crowned King Mswati III - the youngest ruling monarch in the world at the time.

Now 46 years old, he is reported to have 15 wives and 24 children, but is unlikely to eclipse the tally of a reported 70 wives, 210 children and more than a 1000 grandchildren, his father, King Sobhusa II, had during his reign.

*braai – barbecue

Footnote
The pillar-box red wing feathers of the African Grey parrot is favoured by the Swazi royal family; the Malachite kingfisher's bright turquoise plumage is reserved for chiefs in other parts of Africa just as ostrich feathers have been coveted by royalty since the Victorian era – **MB**

What Goes Around...

Lloyd Wilmot

Sue Mais

Way back in 1969 I was camped at Samochima in the Okavongo panhandle during crocodile hunting operations. My sister Daph and husband Bernie were building the Shakawe Fishing Camp next door. Ursula, my cousin from Bulawayo, had just come to stay with Daph for a month and Daph suggested, being a city girl, she come hunting with me. We headed to Red Cliffs and in a nearby lagoon we found a clever croc. Each time I came to shoot, the croc would dive then resurface further on. We played cops and robbers back and forth and the commotion attracted a lone hippo. Too curious for comfort it would come right up behind the boat compelling us to move on. This had everyone's nerves on edge, particularly the driver. Not wanting to lose the croc I would wait until the hippo was right by the engine before giving the driver the signal to start. Ursula was visibly scared but sat quietly terrified next to the hookboy behind me.

Eventually the hippo forced us to leave the lagoon and as we re-entered the mainstream I spotted the red eye of a crocodile against the papyrus edge across the river. Grabbing my rifle, I signalled the driver and stood up to shoot as we approached the papyrus.

Suddenly, a mother hippo and her baby turned about and I realised my mistake. The alert driver immediately swung the tiller hard over and we bumped over the waves as she dived. I sat down on my chair and braced for impact. When nothing happened I shone the spotlight backwards to slightly blind Ursula then stomped my foot hard on the deck. Both she and the hookboy shot straight up in fright and I burst out laughing. She'd got a heck of a fright and said she'd get me back.

The following night we were hunting a backwater lagoon nearer Shakawe. Standing in the prow of the boat in my jeans, tackies and serge hunting jacket, I swung the beam back and forth, looking for croc eyes. As I swung the beam to port, there was a terrific bump under the boat and I went sailing into space still clutching the spotlight. This pulled the clips off the battery plunging everything into darkness.

Thinking it was a hippo the driver carried on for at least a 100 yards before stopping. I surfaced in his wake still hanging onto the precious spotlight and thought I was in the company of a hippo too. Taking a deep breath I swam underwater toward the boat as far as I could but my sodden clothes weighed me down. Surfacing again I called out for the driver. Still fearing a hippo he hesitated and I began to founder. I shouted again with urgency in my voice and long minutes went by before I heard him start the motor and head towards me. By now I was desperate and kept sinking and struggling back to the surface. In the utter darkness the driver, guided by my feeble shouts, approached slowly not wishing to run me over. I lunged for the boat and clung to the gunwale. The driver put the engine in neutral to help me aboard. I told him to clip the spotlight back on and continued to cling to the boat like a drowned rat. With the light on I was hauled unceremoniously on board, absolutely spent. The driver then sped off to a safe distance and I scanned the water for any sign of a hippo. There was nothing.

Curious as to what could have caused such a bump I got the driver to retrace our route. On the second pass I spotted it - a large submerged tree that had drifted in the current. The thick broken trunk was facing upward just below the surface, the branches snagged on the bottom. When Ursula saw this she could not restrain her chuckles. I felt truly *paid back* for the fright I had given her the previous night.

Bully Beef

Greer Noble

In years gone by Tashinga was little known – a wilderness area in Zimbabwe which could only be reached by four-wheel drive overland, through a rather treacherous and extremely rocky mountainous pass, crossing streams and culverts, after travelling on equally rugged terrain for many hundreds of kilometres... or by boat from far across Kariba Lake. It's a place which, forever, leaves an indelible imprint on your mind, for its vastness, colours and abundance of game, it's breath-taking, raw beauty and indescribable ambience is unique. A place with no fences and a place where freedom abounds as you are at one with the wildness of the real Africa. It grows on you.

So return we did, time and again. On this particular trip we'd set up camp in the designated Tashinga camping area, within walking distance of the ablutions. The only other person in camp was an old tobacco farmer who was fishing for the pot. He told us when his two deep freezers were full he'd head for home. A rather shy, wiry little fellow he, rather embarrassingly, warned us, no sooner had we met him, to watch out for a lone rogue buffalo.

Shortly after he'd arrived, the camp to himself, he'd set off to the ablutions for his evening constitutional. He had to pass the Ladies, he explained, to reach the Gents. It was in passing the Ladies that he was confronted by this rather unpleasant individual. Charged, he turned and, escaping by the whisker of a warthog, gapped it into the Ladies. But this buffalo, who our son later nicknamed Bully Beef, had found a delicious patch of well-watered green grass right in front of the Ladies so there he remained grazing for the best part of the night. Just picturing this I had to stifle a chuckle. I got the impression that our new friend was just as concerned about being in the Ladies as he was about Bully Beef.

The time came and our new friend duly left, leaving me some much prized fresh yeast. To my family's delight I made the most delicious bread in our potjie,* on the open fire. I'd divide the dough into two; half would be a current loaf, the other half, plain. This became a daily ritual, a luxury (while the butter lasted), and the best bread we'd ever tasted. Then one day I announced that it would be the last of the fresh bread as the yeast was finished. Only no sooner was it ready when a party of 7 (5 teenagers) descended on us, wanting to know the ropes.

'*Wow, what smells so wonderful?*' they asked. Well my husband was so proud of my bread he thought we could sacrifice one loaf for our unexpected guests.

Devoured in no time the youngsters were back for more. My heart sank when I saw our second loaf being demolished. I felt like saying, '*There ain't no shops here lads!*' They'd come by boat so were soon on their way across the Umi River to spend the night at the luxury Bumi Hills Lodge way up on a plateau overlooking the entire lake.

We settled down for the evening and while enjoying a peaceful sundowner my husband suddenly whispered, mainly for our son who at his age was not accustomed to sitting still, '*Just stay where you are. Don't make any sudden movements.*'

I looked around slowly and barely noticeable in the dark blanket of nightfall was a huge lone buffalo a mere three paces from us. It had to be Bully Beef. I wasn't taking any chances. A young man had recently lost his life when he'd returned to 'his' houseboat to get his hat and an American couple had also recently been killed when they followed the path back to their tent, without a torch, on a small island lodge... all by buffalo. They were lethal. I took my son firmly by the hand and, giving Bully Beef a wide berth, quickly made for the safety of our Land Rover some twenty paces away.

That night was spectacular; the heavens studded with a million stars and our regulars, a huge herd of buffalo that passed every day to graze along the lake shore, had returned as usual to head off into the bush but stopped and camped around us instead, as they sometimes did as soon as they heard the lion. Yet another glorious day in paradise. I actually had withdrawal symptoms long after we headed home, not being able to hear the lions calling to one another in the night.

*Potjie - round three-legged cast-iron pot

He who is not everyday conquering some fear has not learned the secret of life – **Ralph Waldo Emerson**

Whacky Patrol Night

Tom Lang

We were doing a patrol along the lower Zambezi river to Chirundu. It's very wild down there, battling with hordes of mopane flies in the day and mozzies (mosquitos) at night. These mozzies are not the run of the mill moz. Let me explain. When the sun goes down you can hear them revving their engines. They come across the Zambezi river from Zambia in squadrons, wave after wave, like mirage jets with their long hypodermic needles fixed in front. If you haven't got your head under a mozzie net, your family is likely to get a note: Sorry, Johnny didn't make it - was in a contact with mozzies.

That night we had our graze (dinner), put our moz nets up above our sleeping bags and settled down. The night guard was posted - all was well. Thinking of home and chicks you were last with and must contact again, bla bla..

You must remember when you sleep in the bush there is always someone awake turning over or can't sleep or just too hot. Well the night wore on and in the far off distance there were some lions serenading the night away. I remember dreaming I was at a party dancing with my lady, very close. The next minute I heard lions and shot awake like I had a fire cracker up my backside. I was looking at the biggest frigging lion I had ever seen. I fired my weapon in the air, blew my moz net to hell. The frigging mozzies attacked. The radio squawked '*confirm contact*' - all our brains were scrambled. Meanwhile the lion had gone and the mozzies were now having a bloody banquet. Morning came and we were having our coffee and licking our wounds with the fattest lips you've ever seen.

About an hour after moving, apart from a lot of ant heaps in the distance, we saw nothing and stopped for our brew and a smoke to chase the mopane flies away. They were already in our ears and up our noses – everywhere. And what blood the mozzies leave behind the damned tsetse fly suck out while the mopane fly want the six pints of water in your body.

On our way again and right into a herd of elephant with babies, a soldiers dread. Now we were in trouble. Those mamas don't like people near their kids and these little shits were moving towards us, trunks in the air, tooting. All we could do was to hold our weapons up and empty the mags, singing '*roll me over, lay me down and do it again*'. Might as well go out happy. Well you won't believe this but they stopped and those mamas gave us a 'guard of honour' as we walked through. They probably thought there was no joy in killing us as we looked just about dead already. And so ended our patrol that day, feeling shagged but with happiness in our hearts. We were Rhodesians.

If you think you're too small to have an impact, try going to bed with a mosquito... **Author unknown**

A Rude Awakening

Heather Clark

It was my first real trip into the bush as part of a Safari organisation. I felt important. There I was on the Land Cruiser with driver/guide at the wheel, eight foreign tourists on the back all clutching at cameras and binoculars, faces aglow with the excitement of being in the wilds of Africa for the first time.

The road was a rough dirt track with corrugations and holes, thick bush on either side. It would take us about three hours to reach the camp. Halfway there a couple of passengers needed a pee so we stopped on the side of the road. I was relieved as I too really needed more than a pee. Something I ate didn't like me and it was trying desperately to get rid of me as soon as it could.

The guide instructed all the men to pee in the front of the vehicle and all the ladies to go to the back. *"Keep together for safety in the bush."*

This didn't suit me, for having had polio I was unable to crouch down on my haunches like the others so I had to make another plan and in a hurry! I left the road and walked a little way into the bush. Aha! There! I found an old tree lying on its side, pushed over by elephants many seasons before. Perfect! It was the next best thing to a toilet seat. Bog roll in one hand, I positioned myself... and voila... what a relief! Mission accomplished. With little shovel in hand I turned to do the right thing... only the load was gone! There was nothing there!!! I stared at the ground in disbelief... shocked... and as I did so, a movement caught the corner of my eye. There, struggling away under the load was a belaboured tortoise! Poor creature must have been hibernating in the leaves sheltered by the tree. What a rude awakening.

Why is it you can never hope to describe the emotion Africa creates? You are lifted, out of whatever pit, unbound from whatever tie, released from whatever fear. You are lifted and you see it all from above –
Francesca Marciano

Ghostly Baboon

Sue Maas

Sue Maas

Baboons had become a real problem as raiders of our beautiful tropical fruit. Then someone in our Kariba village community came up with an idea to keep the intruders away. We tried it out – it was ingenious in its simplicity.

We strategically placed a tempting pile of fruit under a bucket of whitewash in a tree and waited for the habitual arrival of the troop. When one of them was under the bucket we pulled a rope which tipped the contents onto him.

The others hurriedly scampered off and for days the hapless 'white' baboon was seen desperately trying to catch up with his fellow baboons. They would have none of it - his ghostly appearance scared them silly and, paranoid about returning to their stash of tropical fruit, they kept well away.

Adopt the pace of nature, her secret is patience – **Ralph Waldo Emerson**

Avila and Beyond

Greer Noble

Way north of Inyanga (in the then Rhodesia) was a place where few men had ever ventured. Irish nuns had been sent there to stop paganism. They bravely set up a Catholic mission station under the towering Mount Melleray after which the mission was named. Every year young maidens were sacrificed to the rain gods, thrown from the mount to their deaths below. The nuns showed me the 'altar' after a hair-raising climb, a rocky outcrop that uncannily resembled an altar. More maidens would be sacrificed until the rain gods were satisfied. A shudder ran through my young body as I imagined what it must have felt like being one of those unfortunate girls. When the nuns eventually managed to stop these sacrifices the rain, to the villagers' utter amazement, would fall regardless. They put this down to the instigation of their ancestors; the gods must have sent these strange white women who they believed to have magical powers.

These nuns were to be my companions while my father Eric, and friend Roy, went prospecting for gold and other valuable minerals further into what was unchartered territory... wild, wild country.

I shared a simple bedroom with a rather sweet and tolerant nun. One day curiosity got the better of me and out of shear devilment, as she knelt praying, I yanked the veil off her head. That and the fact that I pretty well ran wild until the day my father returned, probably ensured that I would not be welcomed back. I hoped that it would be the first and last time I would be left in that arid red dust bowl.

At last that day came and a mad dash to catch me. To my horror I was bathed, dressed and my hair done. The last part was the worst. Irish nuns, probably from having shaven heads for so long and no children of their own, began the chore of combing my matted waist-long hair without a clue. Fine and thick, it had not been un-plaited for over a week. They started from the top down instead of inching their way up from the ends. I suffered excruciating pain as clump after clump of my hair was literally ripped out.

How pleased I was to see my father and listen with heightened excitement to what had happened to them after they'd left me.

He and Roy, after several hours of following a little used dirt track sometimes difficult to make out as the elephant grass had taken over, came upon hill after hill of mysterious, perfectly built stone terraces. They were reminiscent of the Zimbabwe Ruins. Had they known then that these hills had been terraced by ancient explorers, possibly Egyptian's, for alluvial gold mining, they undoubtedly would have gone no further.

Driving well into the night, bumping along the track in search of the other mission station which Eric's great friend Bishop Lamont had told him about, a voice from the back interrupted their thoughts. It was Phineas, Eric's faithful old gun bearer and general man servant. He'd been sound asleep in the back of the Land Rover and needed to relieve himself. As it turned out it was fortuitous they did stop as they heard dogs barking in the distance and could just make out a track veering off that they would otherwise have missed. Following this track the barking grew louder. Within minutes they found themselves in a clearing with white-washed buildings clearly visible as a pale moon broke through some heavy cloud. Five huge very agitated Rhodesian ridgebacks surrounded their vehicle.

'Mother of God where have you come from then?' came this Irish brogue. The bearer of a lamp, a very jovial, ruddy-faced, middle-aged man with white hair, bushy white eyebrows and piercing blue eyes stood before them. It was evident that he didn't get many visitors, especially in the middle of the night.

'You wouldn't be Father Clarke, would you?' asked Eric. It wasn't difficult to guess they'd arrived at Avilla. A little chapel-like building with a cross gave it away.

'I would indeed,' Father Clarke broke into a big smile as Eric and Roy climbed down and introduced themselves. *'Let me warm up some of Sister Kenneth's soup. You must be needin it.'*

After each enjoying a bowl of broth, Father Clarke quartered them. The next morning the sun was well up by the time they awoke. They were wondering where Father Clarke was when he turned up looking a little worse for wear.

'Top 'o the mornin to you,' he greeted them. They were soon ushered off to an alfresco breakfast served by two bubbly young Irish nuns clothed in crisp white habits.

Over breakfast Father Clarke told them that one of their ridgebacks had been very badly mauled by lion and, in the early hours of the morning he'd had to shoot the dog.

'I want to show you something,' he said as they started to leave the table. They walked over to a small workshop area and there, lying in the shade was a very dead lioness. *'They killed her last night,'* he averred. Eric and Roy were astounded. Could five ridgebacks really kill a fully grown lioness? Reading their minds, Father Clarke nodded, *'It's not the first time. They killed one only a couple of months back.'*

They headed off following the river downstream. The road was virtually non-existent and took them the best part of the day, having to cross the river on more than one occasion as it twisted and snaked back on itself. A series of hippo pools started to emerge, ideal for a spot of fishing and, of course, prospecting.

It was late afternoon by the time they set up camp. Their stretchers made, mosquito nets hung and the flames high in the fire, Eric and Roy settled down to a long awaited Scotch. By their third the fire had sufficiently died down to form suitable embers for cooking. Phineas settled a frying pan into the hot coals and added sausages. A tomato relish was already simmering alongside the sadza/maize meal. Suddenly there was an almighty explosion. The frying pan went one way and the sausages the other while everyone jumped up colliding with each other in the process.

'What on earth...?' Eric and Roy could only assume they'd made a fire on top of an old unused cartridge.

They soon retired for the night. Around midnight, dead to the world, they were rudely woken. There was a commotion around the re-kindled fire where Phineas and the two mission scouts had been sleeping. Father Clark had insisted they take them along to show them the way. One of the scouts had the beginning of malaria and lay

next to the fire wrapped in his blanket, shivering with fever despite the warm night.

He had shaken the other two awake jabbering like a crazed man. They thought he was delusional with fever until they followed his wide-eyed stare.

The biggest snake they'd ever seen in their lives hung from the branch overhead. Eric, gun in hand, immediately emerged, expecting the worst.

'Shoot, shoot,' shouted the fevered scout. Eric would no sooner have shot the python than his own toe. It was quite passive having recently swallowed a very large meal, its distended girth revealed.

They watched as the reptile silently slipped away into the night

Everyone settled down again, except the scout. He shivered his way in and out of fever, freezing one moment, temperature raging the next. This went on until around four in the morning when he happened to look up. The sight he beheld made him paralytic with fear. He leaped on top of Eric shouting, *'Shumva, shumva!'*

Eric grappled through the net for his gun, thinking there was a lion on top of him. Frantically trying to free himself he managed to roll off the stretcher and, gun in hand, jumped to his feet.

There was nothing to be seen.

With everyone now awake there was much debate about the vanishing lion and it was agreed that this time the scout had really been hallucinating. No one else had actually seen or heard a lion. At first light Eric climbed the bank and there above his stretcher were four huge fresh pug marks! He also found the shell of the cartridge that caused the explosion which had probably disturbed the snake and attracted the lion.

Despite the dramatic initiation, Hippo Pools, way beyond Avila, was to become our favourite haunt for many years. Father Clark told us how, in the early days, they would trade basic provisions with the river people for nuggets of gold washed up in the river. We were never that lucky but just being there was better than any gold nugget.

Fill your life with adventures, not things. Have stories to tell not stuff to show. **Anonymous**

Innocence is Bliss!

Rob Fynn

In typically task-focussed fashion, I loaded my three-week-old baby and long-suffering wife with all the paraphernalia into a ridiculous boat, not much bigger than a bathtub, to head back to our Fothergill camp. But an old Kariba character, Guy du Barry, who drank his fair share of whisky and bayed to the full moon, saw this and came whooshing over in one of his big power boats, calling me uncomplimentary names, and insisted on transporting Sands and Katrina who we nicknamed Neem. I wasn't convinced of her safer passage and thought he had a bit of a crush on Sands, but his gallantry left me with a somewhat ignominious crossing, alone in my bathtub and missing the celebration of my new family arriving home.

Sands always had time to attend to her baby but she had a willing helper and minder, old Buhnu, who soon took the apple of everybody's eye under his wing. Neem would spend hours tucked under his enormous arms against his sweaty armpit, like he was carrying a loaf of bread cuddled against his huge hairy chest. She would be sucking one of his delicious home-made buns while he worked away, singing African lullabies, in baby heaven.

The terrain in camp was covered in washed pebbles typical over much of the Zambezi valley, from the river having varied its course down the ages. They were comfortable to walk on, but not so easy for the crawler. Neen developed what we called the Matusadona rock hop – bum in the air, moving on all fours, no knees touching, much like a spider on four legs.

'Kari? Where is Kari?' Buhnu was asking. He had suddenly noticed Neem's absence. Everybody thought everybody else had her. A frantic search ensued, spreading wider, until there was a low whistle from one of the guys behind the bushes backing the tents. Bustling over, we saw Neem in the midst of a small herd of big dagga* boys, six old bull buffalo, one of the most unpredictable and dangerous animals in the wild.

She was insisting they take an interest in the soggy bun she was carrying, pushing it under their noses while they grazed. They would snort, and move away a few steps. We looked on in awe and wonder, floored as to how to retrieve her without casualty.

Her old friend Buhnu came up with a plan. He crept in closer on all fours, keeping a wary eye on the buffalo, holding up yet another bun, calling her quietly.

'*Kari, Come Kari. Bhunu's bun, Kari.*'

She spotted him, and not having much success with the current bun, she waddled across to get a re-supply. The dagga boys carried on grazing, unperturbed.

'*Bhunu, you old scoundrel, don't think you're getting a raise for that,*' I laughed in nervous relief, scooping her up and slapping him on the back. We all had a great chuckle.

*dagga (pronounced duga) – mud
*Dagga Boys – name given to buffalo as they wallow in mud (to rid themselves of parasites).

The innocence of childhood is like the innocence of a lot of animals.
Clint Eastwood
141

A Night of Sheer Terror

Mike Ballantine

Ever known your blood to curdle.. instantly; your eyes to balloon.. instantly; your hair, every last strand, to spike.. instantly; every bone in your body to freeze.. instantly? In Botswana's Chobe National Park is where it happened.

We did what many seasoned adventurers do… venture off the beaten track for excitement. We had often traversed the main dirt road, in places through thick sand, passable only with a 4x4, between Kasane and Savuti. So this time we decided to go via Nogatsaa, a waterhole rarely frequented, yet notorious for being the site where lion had brought down and killed a young elephant.

We had been driving along a rocky ridge without coming across anything remotely campable when through a gap in the bush we spotted a watering hole the size of a proverbial postage stamp. Already passed our comfort code of finding a campsite an hour before sunset, we decided this was it.

A good 30 metres below us, it must have taken us the best part of half an hour to blaze a trail through boulders, shrubs and trees before we found ourselves at this premium site. Flat ground and shade for us late risers. It took no more than 15 minutes to unfurl our roof-top tent, set up our table and chairs and light the inevitable fire, using slow burning leadwood which we tried never to be without. After a couple of beers, some heated food from cans and an ABF* we turned in; and on our backs in the tent spent a while gazing at the night sky and listening to the distant sounds of hyena, lion and elephant before falling asleep.

It was about one in the morning when my wife nudged me.

'*Elephant,*' she whispered.

I picked up the sound of splashing water. Very quickly we realised that an upwind herd of elephant were cavorting in a waterhole we had not spotted and seemingly quite far behind us. But within minutes they were upon us. We felt we could have reached out and touched their huge hulks as they silently filed past. Suddenly they stopped. Their wild scent was strong yet pleasantly pungent, the slight whoosh of their tails being the only sound.

One large tusker, level with and next to our roof-top tent, sensed our presence, turned, raised his trunk and shrieked. An unbelievably piercing, high-pitched screech, so deafening, it was if we had been struck by lightning.

Our hearts stopped, or seemed to. Not a sound passed between us. Nor did we move, except for the involuntary shakes that had taken hold.

Under the stars of that moonless night we could make out a herd about 15 strong, including several babies and knew only too well how very protective elephant were of their young. We were prisoners in our own tent. Boxed in, there was no way of escape. We willed them to move on but quiet as they were now, their soft rumbling sounds confirmed their confusion. Moments seemed like hours, tortuous hours, then just as suddenly as they'd come, so they filed off along the path, up a slight incline then melted, once again, into the night.

Finally, thankfully and noiselessly, they'd moved on. We almost collapsed with relief and nervously began to converse. The ordeal was over... or was it? Was that more splashing we could hear behind us?

Oh no, oh yes, a new herd of elephant were cavorting in the upwind watering hole. There was no way we could knowingly tempt fate again. In a flash we collapsed the tent, threw ourselves into the Land Rover and with headlights blazing, clawed and scrambled our way back up to the ridge. How we avoided the rocks and trees I'll never know. Perhaps we were driven by the fear of having to relive those agonising moments of sheer terror.

We had been very lucky and got away with nothing but very bruised egos and a potentially lifesaving lesson – to make doubly sure that we never again camp next to an elephant path, of which there are thousands, but more especially one that leads from one watering hole to another.

* ABF – absolutely bloody final... drink

Without fear there cannot be courage. **Christopher Paolini**

Zulu Kidnap

Anonymous

In 1975, at the height of apartheid South Africa, I lived in student digs in Umbilo, a middle class Durban suburb. Many of my friends resided high above Umbilo in Ansell May Hall, a grey monolithic men's residence of the University of Natal. Perched like an eyrie on its top floor, was its infamous beer club. From here, late one balmy night, I bade a bibulous farewell to my friends and began my homeward meander on foot.

The intoxicating fragrances exuded by frangipani, jasmine and brunfelsia conspired with the alcohol to give me an exhilarating rush until on reaching a particularly dark stretch of road the euphoria gave way to the chilling realization that I was being tailed by a kombi – the ubiquitous South African mini bus taxi.

After a while it drew up and several burly Zulus spilled out around me. Fight or flight? Neither was an option. Obeying the signals of my kidnappers, I boarded the kombi with heart in mouth. Was I destined for the pot?

Within minutes we had sped through the white suburbs and entered dockland at Maydon Wharf. After five minutes of negotiating his way through a labyrinth of narrow roads, railway tracks, containers, booms and hostels, the driver halted outside a dimly lit, sparsely furnished hall and to my puzzled relief, instructed me to act as judge in a variety show competition.

With a red megaphone, an ironic symbol of the apartheid police, thrust into my hand, I was seated at a rickety table in front of a simple stage, grateful to be alive and wondering what my social anthropology lecturers would make of this strange sequence of events. My un-communicative captors lurked in the shadows near the door to prevent my doing a runner. On hard wooden benches in the gloom behind me were seventy or eighty Zulus, mainly women, many of whom appeared to be either dozing or tending to infants. Some chatted away, but oddly none seemed the slightest bit curious about the longhaired white puppet propped up in their midst.

Proceedings began promptly with a group of Sammy Davis look-alikes in shiny off-the-rack suits dancing their way through a slick routine. Songs, dances and fashion displays followed. In the surreal atmosphere my eyelids became increasingly leaden, but I had to stay awake to announce the winners of each of the interminable categories. Shortly after 3am the show mercifully ended and the hall instantly emptied save for a few somnolent matrons whose infants snuggled against their ample bosoms. My minders emerged and benignly offered to take me home.

As I directed the driver to my digs, he explained that some abstruse apartheid law required a white presence at these regular social gatherings to lend them legitimacy.

A harmless amateur evening's entertainment had required the abduction of a not-so-sober white Rhodesian student (himself, in apartheid immigration jargon, an alien) by Zulu dockworkers to meet a preposterous apartheid regulation.

People from the Zulu tribe are known to be humane, amicable and very warm. **Andile Smith**

Strange Reflection

Rob Fynn

Our remote Ethiopian camps always attracted an uninhibited crowd of spectators, observing our every move, inspecting every item, curious as to what was in each container we opened. Nothing was sacred, privacy just not being in their vocabulary, even lavatorial excursions. Nor was there any thievery.

One young man carefully scrutinised every knob and dial on our impressive machine, fingering the sand mats and our Sahara goat 'water' skin hanging on the side. Sitting in the driver's seat and swinging the wheel, he experimented with everything short of starting the Land Rover and taking a test drive. Suddenly we heard a cry. Another who had been inspecting the front bumper and our good looking rope wound round it, jumped back with a look of astonished surprise on his face. Others crowded towards him. We leapt across. Snake, dangerous insect? Or maybe pressed or pulled the wrong something?

Cautiously moving forward again the tribesman peered into our wing mirror, alarmed to see his reflection. Soon all our spectators crowded around the mirror to get a glimpse of these little men we kept in this small flat thing on the fender.

Top Secret

Greer Noble

Venture Cruises Boatel was once a popular resort on the shores of Lake Kariba, patronised by tourists from all over the world. But as the Rhodesian bush war escalated so did its guests dwindle, until the patronage at the hotel almost entirely consisted of the armed forces comprising: army, air force, Selous Scouts, SAS*, SAP*, PATU* and once a year, roving ex mercenary scuba-divers who maintained the underwater grouting of the mighty Kariba dam wall. So with at least twenty men to one woman there, it was de rigueur that the highest ranking officers should have first pickings!

It transpired that one particular army officer had a crush on a very charming and talented resident. She was all woman, in fact a most beautiful, vivacious lady of Latin appearance with warm dark eyes, silky olive skin and a smile to melt the hardest heart, an extraordinary pianist, an exceptional tango dancer – and a natural flirt!

This officer was hard pressed to fit this enchantress into the small matter of fighting the Rhodesian Bush War. But strategy being his forte he soon devised a daring plan to do so. Having a fair amount of charisma himself and used to getting his own way, it wasn't difficult to persuade the lady to join him, especially when he divulged that he planned to 'kidnap' her! She too had been in the army in a different war and, understanding, she played along, although insisting on being accompanied by a woman companion. After all she was married and her husband was away at the time.

The evening arrived, the venue being top secret on a *need to know* basis! The officer picked up the ladies himself in his personal army vehicle. The ladies were suitably attired in alluring eveningwear as the night was hot and humid. He was dressed in immaculately pressed camouflage.

The drive seemed to go on forever. Uneventful, not even an elephant, they suddenly made a left turn off the tarmac onto an obscure bush track that the uninformed would most certainly have missed. Long elephant grass parted, giving off a strong earthy scent as the headlights carved a path through it. After some distance and without warning they came into a clearing alive with figures darting around, tents, canvas lean-tos and several more army vehicles. The passenger door was swiftly opened by a camouflaged private and they were ushered to an expansive lean-to where the general outdoor mess was located.

Immediately seated among four or five other officers at a candle-lit table complete with white starched linen, silver-serve and lead crystal glasses, it was clearly evident that they'd been expected! They were served hand and foot and treated like royalty. A huge amount of preparation had obviously gone into this three course meal, comparable with any top-notch restaurant. There was much laughter and merriment.

The wine flowed and much to the ladies astonishment, they couldn't help notice that the bottles of beer and wine were kept chilled in an ice-filled metal coffin – standard army issue!

The trek back was made in the wee hours of the morning. What a night to remember!

Now it is true that the strangest things happen in times of war... so please don't let on but the lady in question, and she was indeed a great lady, was my much adored mother, Eva Noble and her date was none other than the great Lieutenant General Peter Walls, Supreme Commander of the Rhodesian Army! A clandestine yet innocent respite amidst the terror of war! May they both rest in peace.

*SAS   – Special Air Services
*SAP   – South African Police – (air-wing) on loan from South Africa
*PATU – Police Anti-Terrorist Unit otherwise known as 'dad's army'

There is nothing like war to push the human spirit to its absolute limit, often inciting recklessness, lest there be no tomorrow – GN

Conniving Kingfisher

Greer Noble

I was very proud of my fishpond. Designed myself, using the natural rock and moulded into the lay of the land, I watched over a local builder reinforcing and cementing it. The result was totally natural as if it had been there forever, complete with waterfall and hidden pump. It soon had ferns and water lilies and cobbled surrounds. Now for the fish. A variety of beautiful goldfish were introduced, lacy- tailed and the more common speckle variety. They too settled in and much to my delight soon started to breed... until...

One day this beautiful gentleman arrived and perched high up on the sundeck overlooking the bay... and my fish pond! He indeed had a birds-eye view. A euphoric mist came in over the sea permeating the air and skin. It was invigorating to breathe in the fine salty haze. Life was bliss... for the giant kingfisher. He ruffled his feathers... and watched...

A sudden dive... then back again... *with* a goldfish! And again, every time a hit. The conniving little blighter, I thought. This became a regular occurrence. It was soon clear that he'd moved in. He stayed and dived into my enticing fishpond day in and day out. When the goldfish were depleted I opted for black bass – his crown feathers absolutely bristling with delight. Struck by his magnificence I couldn't disappoint him so kept him in constant supply lest he leave me. And they say cats have slaves!

Pigtrail Alarm

Chris Goldswain

The caretaker welcomed the party to tiny Stonechat cottage on Zimbabwe's highest mountain, Myangani in Nyanga National Park They were there to do Pigtrail, a nine kilometre hike which ambled along a river to Nyangombe Falls. Could we do it?

'*Yes! Yes! Many people have done it*', he grinned telling his boss's clients what they wanted to here.

Mid-morning the party set off with loo paper, biltong, vitamin C and sandwiches. Being winter, the river had become a rivulet, a mere trickle. Hopping from rock to rock, they deviated, cheerfully following a sign to 'Elephant Forest', had to contend with thick bush, gave up and re-joined the path. An hour later they emerged onto a sunny grassy ledge and collapsed, exhausted, wishing they were back at the cottage – except for their leader. Mesmerised by a sign pointing to 'Ruins' he said '*I won't be long*' and attacked the very steep path. At the top he found an excuse for ruins ...and saw Stonechat in the far distance.

The sun was getting redder as it slipped further west and for the first time alarm bells rang in his head. The trail was far from over. What had he been thinking! He quickly re-joined the party who would be hard-pressed to get back by sunset. '*Let's move*', he urged. The sun sank, leaving them on a very dark path with no road in sight. They suddenly realised they were very vulnerable there.

The leader, ordering himself to stay calm, decided to jog on ahead to get the car. But the jog became a sprint. He ran and ran, ran through the darkness of mind and reality, ran pantingly human, vulnerable and mortal as the tunnel of branches loomed where the leopard in his mind lay waiting. Finally he reached that blessed road, along which he knew the cottage and the car were waiting.

The drive back with the others, silent. It had been a pig of a trail (and I had been the leader!).

For myself I am an optimist - it does not seem to be much use to be anything else – **Winston S. Churchill**

Latin Ruckus

Rob Fynn

Sue Maas

K az was a tented camp on the shores of the Matusadona National Park, Lake Kariba. An Italian family had booked the whole camp arriving like rent-a-crowd. They talked excitedly from the moment they set foot, the level of noise never abating, even on game drives. The children ran unhindered in all directions, exploring and playing happily.

Out on a game drive, I stopped in a clearing where we had surprised a lioness and her cubs resting under a bush. The party on the roof, as usual, was engaged in animated discussion and hadn't seen them. Oz (early morning tea bearer, tent hand, waiter, game scout and major domo), tried valiantly to communicate their presence to the family. Finally, the penny dropped. The sight of the lions acted like fuel to a rocket crash and the noise level increased by decibels, despite our attempts to quieten their fears.

Finally, the lioness could stand it no longer. Her flicking tail straightened, her growls increased, the yellow eyes boring into the offending intruders, and suddenly she charged.

Instantaneously, we had something akin to a soccer stand collapse. Young Italians were sliding off the roof on the opposite side to the lioness, yanking doors in an effort to climb inside.

Papas cursed and Mamas screamed. *'Santo Cielo! Eccheccazzo!'*

No one was paying the slightest attention to Oz's and my attempts to calm the situation. The growling lioness crouched, only metres away, tail twitching, baring her teeth murderously, looking ready to jump onto the roof at any moment. I engaged reverse gear and slowly pulled back, the family hanging off every side like Christmas decorations.

At a safe distance we stopped for a serious talk. The listening silence was electric, their attention riveted to every word I said.

'Calma ragazzi! Attenzione!' growled the Papas. Mammas slapped young sons into order. Not another peep came from up top other than stern reprimands until we got back to camp when a celebration fit for the winning Cup Final team broke into full swing.

*major domo – a head steward or butler
* *Santo Cielo! Eccheccazzo!* – *Good heavens! What the hell!*
* *Calma ragazzi! Attenzione!* – *Calm down guys! Watch out!*

There are no foreign lands. It is the traveller only who is foreign.
Robert Louis Stevenson

Firing Up The Landy

Rory Young

When I was 18 years old and a guide at Fothergill Island I got very drunk one night. As I stumbled home to my hut, I vaguely remembered that I needed to check if I had enough fuel in my Land Rover as I had to get going early the next morning. It was an old British Army model with a fuel tank under the seat and a fuel gauge that didn't work. It always said E for enough. I pulled off the seat, opened the fuel cap, looked in and couldn't see anything because it was dark. So I lit a match...

Sue Maas

The fumes instantly burst into flame and instantly I was sober. Somehow (due to adrenaline) I ripped the fire extinguisher with its steel bracket out of the passenger foot well, then pointed it into the fuel tank and blasted. Amazingly it worked. Afterwards I sat on the floor in relief and heard laughter. I looked back to see two other guides doubled over in hysterics, just as I was thinking 'thank God no one saw me'.

A Wager at Sheddies Time

Greer Noble

Those were colourful, vibrant, exciting days! The Rhodesian bush war was in full swing and so was our hotel on the shores of Lake Kariba. Live hard play hard... Why is it that in times of war one really *lives* each day... as if it were your last? Perhaps because in many ways it could be... and for some it was... we'd be playing darts one night... and the next we'd hear that one of the boys had lost an eye, a limb or... his life. So not knowing if you'd ever meet again one tended to be a little reckless... and did things one would not normally ever dream of doing!

'Land on the what?' It was more a consideration than a question. Ian,* the young helicopter pilot had heard right the first time but could never resist taking the mick especially with the brown jobs!

'Yea, we bet you a crate of beer... don't we guys?' the soldier challenged, winking at all his buddies. Always the brown jobs against the blue jobs - army versus air force... great rivals.

Well into the night, well oiled, bets came as easy as the shedding of uniforms at our hotel's traditional *sheddies time* when all and sundry tumbled into the warm water of the swimming pool in various stages of undress after pub closing time. This ritual would also often take place during full moon from a cabin cruiser in the middle of the lake – there were no crocs in deep water in those days and hippos grazed on land at night.

The dare accepted, the wager was on... settled. It would be the next day. Even inebriated, wagers were honoured! They had to be for the consequences were almost as foreboding as a court-marshal... which would surely follow if ever found out!

Every so often air force helicopters had been known to land on our beach... pre-arranged clandestine landings at first light and we would be whipped down the Zambezi, below the dam wall, for a joy-ride. Elevated over the great river watching crocs peel off the sandbanks into the warm flowing water, while lazy hippo merely ignored this great big hovering bird with a disgruntled snort, elephants shrieked at the intrusion and buffalo stampeded – it only took one to panic to set them all off. And the kaleidoscope of colours that time of day was indescribable. What a thrill!

Sometimes an uninitiated air force private would be 'dropped' out of a helicopter into the top swimming pool of the hotel, to the applause of guests and fellow air force personal lazing around the pool... until one day an over-zealous private jumped out prematurely and landed in the shallow end injuring his coccyx – a very painful stunt which landed him in hospital, poor guy and put paid to any further stunts of that nature.

And now, for the first time, a daring (in more ways than one) helicopter landing on the small skiing jetty which was positioned some distance from the shore to lessen the skier's chances of getting the dreaded bilharzia.*

Our hotel was strongly patronised by the forces and the air force lads, having started their day at 04h00 would, barring emergencies, start drifting in from 11h00, transported from the nearby air force base some kilometres away, to work on their tans! Only this particular morning there was a certain buzz in the air, a tangible feeling of excitement between the few guests, air force and a number of the soldiers who'd managed, all in uniform, to slip down from their barracks in the Kariba heights, for the great wager.

All armed with beer in hand they gathered around the top terrace overlooking the lake... and the skiing jetty. It wasn't long before the unmistakable sound (hence its name) of a chopper could be heard. It grew louder and louder and soon there was Ian hovering over the skiing jetty. Everyone held their breath. The long blades of the military helicopter whipped up the lake around the jetty as if a tropical storm had hit it. The water now choppy made the jetty bob and sway like a drunken trooper. Anchored by a thick, heavy metal chain embedded into an enormous concrete block to withstand our tropical storms, it wasn't going anywhere. This made landing on that postage-stamp (in relation to the size of the helicopter), even more difficult than first anticipated... but what really made it incredibly tricky were the parallel looped hand-rails of the old-fashioned type swimming-pool ladder affixed to the one side of the wooden jetty.

Tension mounted while everyone on the top terrace held their breath. Considering all the spectators, including ourselves, our waiters and our coxswains in the small harbour below, there wasn't a sound. As if in mid-air everyone had stopped what they were doing. Gradually and masterfully, Ian brought the great bird down and momentarily its wheels touched the jetty. As if a great burden had been lifted, there were raucous shouts and screams and hoots and whistles as everyone clapped in unison.

But then disaster struck... as the helicopter lifted off, one of its wheels snagged on the one looped handlebar of the ladder. This sent shivers down everyone's spine and a huge *whoa* echoed from his shoreline compatriots as the massive blades worked overtime, straining against the weight as it literally lifted the entire jetty out of the water. Only well and truly anchored, there was no give. An impossible tug of war ensued.

Touching down once more Ian tried to extricate the wheel from the ladder... but to no avail. Again there was a futile tug of war... but each time the jetty won. The silence from the land-lubbers was deafening, akin to a symphony quieted by the baton of their maestro. A dread came over them, a sinking feeling, a prickly sensation as the blood drained from their very veins... as this seemingly hopeless procedure was repeated time and time again, the brave pilot desperately trying to unhook his helicopter, its engine whining objection, the rotors labouring in the agony of it all.

The tension was now electrifying as thirty odd pairs of eyes were glued, unblinking, to the impossible spectacle before them. Each time the big machine came down and tried to unhook itself from the loop there was a wave of *whoooo* and *Oh God* emanating from the small crowd.

Another set of eyes suddenly popped out of the lake between the jetty and the harbour, the little piggy eyes of Howard, the resident hippo. He'd come for his morning cabbage snack thrown to him by my father from the end of the pier. Now confused with all the commotion, he too watched. Twitching his ears he blew water from his large nostrils showing his annoyance at this giant bird attacking his jetty!

I was more worried about Ian than the helicopter. What would happen to him if he had to ditch the chopper... his career, his entire future was on line... if he aborted this crazy wager? I noticed some of his fellow pilots sweating and I didn't think it was due to the heat of the day. As my focus returned to the jetty it was, for the umpteenth time on an upward spiral and yet again the wheel was hooked but suddenly, with some sort of strange manoeuvre the loop of the ladder glanced off the tyre, the tyre rolled free, released the helicopter unexpectedly. With a sudden jolt, it catapulted up into the air. There was a frenzied round of applause as Ian took it up, up and away with everyone madly waving.

Howard went unnoticed as he submerged and swam away, no doubt disappointed there was no cabbage that day but probably pleased that the big bird did not get his jetty.

A hero's welcome awaited Ian that evening and true to their word, the brown jobs presented him with a crate of beer... only to be flattened by the blue jobs in record time.

Spirits were high as celebrations continued until sheddies time when everyone piled into the pool as usual. Suddenly two stainless steel waiters' trays were clanged together to attract everyone's attention. It was one of the officers.

'Party over... emergency call up... back to base... pronto!' he shouted. *'On the double... transport awaits.'*

I was always amazed that when this happened no one ever complained, no matter how much they were enjoying themselves. Such character, our boys!!

A mad scramble ensued as glistening wet bodies in water-logged briefs, frantically trying to locate their uniforms with nothing to see by but the light of the underwater pool light. Eventually giving up they belted it to the hotel car-park but seeing no transport had arrived became suspicious that it might just be a hoax. Madeleine, our receptionist and I, having hidden their uniforms were a dead giveaway – doubled over with laughter, we had been unable to contain ourselves. Needless to say we were both unceremoniously tossed, fully clothed, into the pool.

Kariba will always have a very special place in my heart.

*Ian Harvey – Flight Lieutenant, No 7 Squadron, Rhodesian Air Force, became the first pilot to fly 2,000 hours in an Allouette III helicopter.
* bilharzia – a parasite that lives in snails that feed off water hyacinth on the water's edge, it requires a human host to complete its cycle.

The difficult we do immediately; the impossible takes a little longer
Air Force Motto

Never Say Never

Mike Ballantine

Many Kenyans make light of their ranking by Transparency International on its Corruption Perception Index. But to be ranked 143 out of 180 countries listed is certainly nothing to be proud of – even though 15 other African countries, including Nigeria, Zimbabwe and Uganda, have even worse scores.

Lawyers in Kenya, more commonly known as advocates or the Italian equivalent avocats, joke about the gravity of the rankings by saying that there/s no bribery and corruption in Africa. "Here it's called business!"

One such 'business' was frequently practiced by knowledgeable experienced travellers when crossing southern borders into Mozambique. During high season lengthy immigration and customs queues and inspections were (and still are) the norm, with up to eight hour delays not uncommon. This not inconsiderable inconvenience was avoided by 'employing', for a few dollars, a runner vouched for by a third party insurance agent we first encountered at the border post. Within 15 to 20 minutes he returned with our correctly stamped passports and a customs gate pass. Everyone scores – it's 'business' as usual.

Conspiratorial Catch

Greer Noble

My father and his old cronies, usually about five of them, used to love their deep-sea fishing trips to the Indian Ocean. Their fishing grounds were in and around Mozambique's Bazaruto archipelago. They'd hire a huge old trawler, a real tub of a boat that had seen better days, from a notorious local resident and share the cost.

He related this story after one of his more adventurous trips.

After an exceedingly revelrous night they all stumbled out of bed calling my father all sorts of unprintable names after he had woken them with his traditional 4am cup of steamy, sweet, black coffee. With packed breakfasts and lunches from Santa Carolina's Paradise Island Hotel (later shelled during the civil war), and with enough beer to start them off again, they all found themselves aboard within the hour.

During the course of the morning a westerly wind came in off the mainland and the sea became choppy. That's all that was needed for the tub to start rolling from side to side. Too much for one of the old chaps, he said '*cheerio*' to his breakfast overboard and, unfortunately for him, his false teeth joined the jettison. Although it wasn't funny for Jimmy, the rest of the gang laughed until their bellies ached. Then someone had a 'light-bulb' moment and surreptitiously conspired with the rest.

When the next fish was hooked Joe, who also had false teeth, would quickly remove them and pop them in the fish's mouth. They could barely contain themselves. It didn't take long. Eric, my father, hooked a yellow fin and being very good eating fish, it was gaffed and brought aboard. Unnoticed by Jimmy, Joe shoved his teeth into the fish's mouth. Then my father made a big thing about removing the hook, calling for Joe to pass him the pliers, when he suddenly exclaimed, '*Good God!*'

Everyone turned expectantly, poker faced. Jimmy was solemn, still extremely upset about the loss of his teeth.

162

'This is quite extraordinary,' my father embellished, pushing Joe's teeth further down the fish's gullet. A couple of the others were now at his side, making a big thing of peering into the yellow fin's mouth.

'Come quickly, Jimmy, old buddy, you're not going to believe this!' remarked Brian, enthusiastically.

'What?' Jimmy said flatly, in no mood for their foolery.

'You have to see this for yourself,' exclaimed another.

Jimmy trundled over, still feeling a bit green around the gills. They all stood aside to let him through. He peered in and on seeing the false-teeth his whole face lit up.

'*Wait, let me help you,*' offered my father, gently removing them with the pliers and handing them to Jimmy.

Jimmy took them as if they were some precious gems, scrutinised them, then said, '*No, these aren't mine,*' and tossed them overboard.

Now it was Joe's turn to be furious. '*What you do something like that for?*' he chastised Jimmy.

But it was too late. That was it.

Like a bunch of teenage schoolboys everyone else cracked up laughing, tears streaming down their faces.

After a few more beers and promises from the others to pay for two new sets of teeth, even Joe and Jimmy started to see the funny side of it.

'*Do not tell fish stories where the people know you. Particularly, don't tell them where they know the fish.*' **Mark Twain**

Malawi Shashliks

Kevin Graham

Back in the late 80s and early 90s, at the height of the Mozambican civil war, a couple of times a year a group of young bachelor friends and I used to travel by road in an old pick-up from Zimbabwe through the Tete corridor in Mozambique to Salima, on the shores of Lake Malawi, for choir practice – a serious week-long binge of the highest order. With two in the front and as many as three or four of us in the back, the imbibing of scotch and water used to start before sun up.

Sometimes we travelled with the ZNA* military convoy and other times, like this trip, we took our chances. The greater the consumption dictated the level of risk so the thought of a minor clash with the RENAMO* rebels on that terrible stretch of road to Tete was shrugged off with another gulp of the amber medicine.

Half way to the border and driving into another fine African sunset, the double vision and mind telescope of the passengers was truly well set in. Piss-poor planners that we were, the first thing to run out was water which necessitated stopping to fill our bottles from cow-dung filled rain puddles - how we never got dysentery is a testament to the excellence of the Scotch, a cheap but then-readily available brand by the name of Cluny.

We arrived at and cleared the Zimbabwean side of the border at Nyamapanda on Christmas day. Then on the Mozambican side, pulling up at its post, a ramshackle, scabrous, seen-better-days, no electricity, hovel, our nominated driver, the soberest, went in with all our passports to clear customs. I took the opportunity, shoeless and shirtless, to climb a two metre high anthill in front of the border post door. No sooner had I sat cross-legged on the top of this pile than gravity took over. I tumbled down, much to the hilarity of all spectators who, by now, had grown in numbers, as all old Africa-hands know, can swell from zero to hundreds from nowhere, in minutes - literally.

In halting English, the deadpan response from the senior official

165

there was, '*Too much Clismas!*' followed by a huge round of communal laughter.

Many hours later and several hundred miles into the trip, we were somewhat refreshed by an alcohol-fuelled slumber and on the road to the lake. Northeast of Mwanza, on the Mozambique-Malawi border, young African lads started rushing up to the roadside as we drove by their huts, brandishing what looked like rural kebabs. Intrigued, we decided to pull over to see what was actually being offered for sale.

To those of us with a more delicate constitution, despite having long since been fortified with Scotland's finest, what confronted us was, in turn, revolting, then sickening, then humorous. They were skewered rats. Through our rudimentary understanding of chi Nyanja, the local dialect, and their pidgin Engreesh, we were told that they were Nyasa delicacies, much sort after by local travellers as a roadside snack, all for 5 Kwacha each (about 2 or 3 US Cents). We decided to counter their offerings with one 'so generous' they would find it hard to refuse.

Each youngster jostled with the next, thrusting four or five of these shashliks into our faces, flaunting a veritable plague of rats which, by their appearance, had only died that morning. It was time to respond.

I offered the closest hawker, with the wettest looking tidbits, 5 Kwacha - not for me to ingest but rather, for he to. As an incentive, I offered a further 5 Kwacha if he ate the whole thing.

Haltingly, hesitatingly, in fits and starts, inch by inch, with much encouragement from us, he brought the head of the rodent (I swear its whiskers were still twitching) to his lips. Then in one petrified grimace, he took a huge bite, two or three crunchy chews, turned a ghostly grey and violently vomited the hideous projectile at least half way across the road. Already falling around in fits of merriment, one of us, with deadpan visage, then monotoned, '*Maybe it would have tasted better with salt*'. Bladders partially emptied and ears touched behind heads, such was the crescendo of laughter. One up to the mzungus*.

*ZNA –   Zimbabwe National Army
*RENAMO – Resistência Nacional Moçambicana (Mozambican National Resistance) political party
*mzungu – white person

Africa is not a country, but it is a continent like none other. It has that which is elegantly vast or awfully little. **L. Douglas Wilder**

Oscar's Combat Jacket

Greer Noble

Our neighbour on Africa's east coast had a very sweet boxer dog called Oscar, only with a decidedly nervous disposition. This was quickly detected by the mischievous vervet monkeys that live in the coastal forest and when they came to steal the bananas and paw-paws, they would taunt Oscar. Trying to bravely protect his territory he would, in turn, bark at them, only one day they attacked him. He was so badly mauled he had to be rushed to the vet to have stitches – too numerous to count. To combat this wicked primate behaviour his mistress had a special imitation leopard-skin jacket made for Oscar which seemed to do the trick, a leopard being a monkey's worst nightmare. This he wore with pride and it helped to reinstate his bruised ego. They never attacked him again.

What counts is not necessarily the size of the dog in the fight; it's the size of the fight in the dog – **Dwight D. Eisenhower**

Lake Nakuru Mishap

Joe Khamisi

Anything can happen on safari. That's why some tour operators advise holiday-makers and adventure-seekers to be prepared for the worst scenarios. I've never roughed it in the bush but have spent many nights in tented camps. My preference is and will always be a contemporary dwelling; a lodge - possibly a tree hotel with a balcony overlooking a salt pit, deep in a national park, where I can watch wildlife from a safe sanctuary and drink my gin and tonic in peace.

Some years ago, when I had some time to spare, I took off with my wife in our Toyota Prado to look for just such a place. We were looking for a destination that was easily accessible from Nairobi, had a brand name, and could provide the kind of comfort levels we are used to. We chose Lake Nakuru Lodge, once a favourite drinking hole of the colonial farmers, in the Nakuru National Park.

Leaving the hustle and bustle of the Kenyan capital city behind, we headed for the spectacular escarpment, part of the Great Rift Valley, and entered the park, known for its teeming pink flamingos. As we passed through the gates, a feeling of serenity and placidity engulfed us. It was a therapeutic feeling. Everything went well during our first game drive. It was after we decided to venture close to the banks of the lake the following day that everything we expected to go right went awfully wrong.

After visiting the buffalo cliff which gave us a spectacular view of most of the lake as far as we could see, we decided to drive as close as possible to the water birds to a suitable spot where we could get down on our knees and feel the algae-filled lake waters. It appears our boundless determination was misplaced.

After determining that the banks were as solid as a rock, I eased my vehicle as near as possible to the shoreline, That turned out to be a big mistake. As soon as the wheels made contact with the shoreline, the vehicle came to a sudden halt. The more I revved the more the vehicle dug in. Four-wheel drive did not help. When we tried to step out of the car, we found the wheels had disappeared into the mud.

We were in really deep trouble.

It was getting late in the evening. In the near distance we could see herds of buffalo and other animals making their way to the lake. We panicked. It was at that time that two tourist vans miraculously appeared. They had seen us and had noticed we needed help. The only ropes they had that could have pulled us out were ordinary sisal ones which had seen many a pull. Every time they tried to pull us out, the ropes broke. After several attempts, our helpers gave up and decided the time had come to take their guests back to their lodge. However, the drivers promised to alert the game wardens who, after an hour, came to our rescue in a long-wheelbase open safari van. They too failed to bail us out of our muddy pit. We all agreed that since it was getting dark, we would leave the vehicle on the banks of the river and try again the following day.

The wardens drove us, tired, hungry and thirsty, back to the lodge where we rushed to the bar for two stiff gin and tonics. It was then that I realised how foolish I had been to do what I did.

The next morning it took the wardens less than five minutes after they had connected the tow cables to drag out the car. The under-carriage was covered with a thick layer of dry mud, some of which had to be whacked-out to allow the wheels to rotate smoothly.

Although I have returned to the park several times since then, I now avoid the river banks.

The Other Side of Paradise

Greer Noble

Living in paradise has its downside but one of the more blissful aspects of living in the Seychelles archipelago is upon waking. Drawn to the balcony I open the double doors, breaking the seal of the comforting coolness of my mosquito-free, air-conditioned bedroom. The contrast is tangible as I'm immediately enveloped by the warm blanket of the tropics, the quietness intermittently broken by the sweet tune of birds as the first hint of light filters through the haze of dawn.

My eyes drink in the splendour before me, the mystery of the mist shrouded Silhouette Island in the distance surreal, the expansive sea, mysterious and as silky as a rippling sari, exquisite colours, shimmering silver and gold. From high in the mountain, the warm water beckons below as it caresses the fine, white, powdery sand. Palm fronds as still and calm as the ocean itself, sparkle in the early sunlight. How very blessed I was to live in this paradise.

After a particularly revelrous night and the heavy slumber that follows, I had overslept and would have to forgo my glorious morning dip and rush down to Port Victoria instead, to give instruction to the booking office at the Pirates Arms Hotel. Our new arrivals, a deep-sea fishing party, had chartered Mako, a particularly handsome motor yacht complete with marlin out-riggers and harpoon deck. The crew had to be summoned, rods, reels and other fishing equipment sorted as well as provisions for the next few days, purchased. Time was of the essence so I dashed into the bathroom and that's when horror struck.

My face had been mutilated. How had this happened? What was it? A terrible disease? I'd never seen anything like it. All down the one corner of my mouth, in a perfect line, were what could only be describe as mini volcanoes; hard, red, circular welts. Oh God, scarred for life! Once I got over the initial shock I showered and went through the daily ritual of preparedness, jumped into the car and was soon over the mountain, parked and walking into the Pirate Arms.

171

The friendly Creole girls, instead of their usual warm greetings just stared at me as if they'd seen a ghost... then burst out laughing.

Self-conscious, I immediately tried to shield my face. '*Yes, isn't it awful*', I exclaimed. '*What is it?*'

'*You've been kissed by a cockroach,*' they chorused, as if I'd won the clown of the year award!

They got in everywhere... that I knew only too well... even between the sheets at night! At first I would wake, giggling, dreaming I was being tickled as they'd run up and down my body. Needless to say I became quite paranoid. But not in my wildest nightmare did I imagine they would *attack* me... actually *feast* on me! Clearly even paradise has its price.

I was on the war path. My duties done, my first port of call was the chemist. In Mahe anything was possible, no prescriptions required... well not in those days. '*I need some poison,*' I told the pharmacist, '*The most lethal.*'
'*Why, you want poison husband?*' the white jacketed Chinaman wanted to know.

That evening I spread newspaper all over the patio, sprinkled the pink poison with gloved hands, added icing-sugar to the mix as instructed, then lay on my stomach on the bamboo couch... and waited. Within an hour it was like a horror movie. They came in their thousands. I was witnessing a tsunami of cockroaches as they feasted on the lethal concoction. I watched, fascinated, mesmerised. They would roll over kicking then explode as the poison took effect. It was shocking, disgusting. Then as if that wasn't bad enough more came and they started eating each other!

I shuddered at the thought of them eating my face, their mean little heads rotating in that circular movement as their tiny jaws masticated. Strangely there was no pain, only a numbness which meant they must anaesthetise the area first. Remarkable! I'd heard of cockroach eggs found in Egyptian tombs, hatching after thousands of years when exposed to friction and light. What hope was there of ever getting rid of them?!

Back to normal my face, amazingly, soon healed and while I never got over how infested the island was with those large, healthy, shiny hermaphrodites – revenge, nonetheless, was sweet!

A cockroach can live 9 days without its head. It only dies because it cannot eat. The earliest cockroach-like fossils are from the carboniferous period 320 million years ago. No wonder an urban legend claims they're immortal.

– Wiki

Heartbreak Tip

Rory Young

A friend and safari guide who will remain unnamed had spent many months lonely and guiding only elderly married clients.

One day a beautiful, young, single Spanish woman turned up. He was immediately infatuated with her and begged me to make sure that he was allocated as her guide. They clearly got along and my friend was obviously in love and dreaming that maybe this could be something special. I was very pleased for him as he is a really good chap and, wearing his heart on his sleeve, tended to get jolted quite frequently.

One night he didn't return to his hut. I thought to myself how happy he must be. Next morning I saw him sitting dejectedly in silence, waiting for his clients to wake up. Surprised I asked him why he looked so sorry for himself. He told me what had happened. The He told me what had happened. The young lady in question had asked him to join her for a private dinner. One thing had led to another and she had invited him back to her room. They spent a very special night together.

In the morning she leaned over, kissed him, thanked him for a great time and handed him $200. Although it wasn't what he had in mind, his client certainly felt he went the extra mile.

174

Skewered by an Elephant

Rob Fynn

With packed breakfasts we left Fothergill by boat for Croc Creek, my favourite gateway for game walks into the Matusadona. With me were a family from the Swiss embassy in Lusaka, a reverend and his wife from a small Sussex church in England and my trainee guide, John, who was recovering the shock of a landmine blast in the bush war. Not far into the walk we came across one of the biggest herds of breeding elephant I'd ever seen in the Matuse, more than a hundred strong.

'We're going to have to move out of their line of scent guys and smartly,' I urged my group.

The breeze was pushing in from the lake behind us. We needed to get downwind. Breeding herds are probably the most dangerous animals to encounter on foot. Their protective instincts are ferociously developed. The slightest whiff of man can turn a peaceful gathering into an angry, killing rampage. I aimed for a small plateau of open ground a few metres above the Kanjedza spring, with a great view back down the river and nicely downwind. We headed into the jesse* thicket parallel to the river, hightailing it for the foothills. Thirty sweaty minutes of adrenalin pumped walking, crouching and dodging thorns, buffalo and whatever else lurked in the dense vegetation, brought us to the plateau.

Worth every drop of blood-drawn thorn-scratches, a panoramic view opened below us. The great herd stretched towards the lake with buffalo, eland, waterbuck and even rhino dotted amongst them. Marabou storks and vultures wheeled, indicating a kill. All agreed to spend the rest of the morning soaking it all in.

Not five minutes after we'd settled down I heard a sharp crack behind us, a branch breaking further up the hill, downwind. Nobody else paid much attention, but I knew instantly it was an elephant, almost certainly an auntie, a defending cow posted on the outskirts of large breeding herds. The wise thing to do would be to withdraw, move further up the hill, find a higher vantage point and put

175

ourselves downwind of this elephant.

I didn't do a thing. The festive season had come to an end and I was too tired from the long and continuous stint of guiding. Idiotically, irresponsibly, I continued to sit there without saying a word, hoping the problem would quietly disappear.

Minutes later the peaceful group of four cow elephants we'd been watching, calves at foot, drinking from the spring just below us, looked up the hill in unison, straight at us. I knew they hadn't seen, heard or smelt us. Auntie behind had given our position away in that low frequency communication they are known for, inaudible to the human ear, but penetrating kilometres through the bush to other elephant.

'Okay guys, it's only us. Don't get in a tiz now.' Our cover broken, I was gently letting the herd know where we were, hoping to avoid any sudden surprises. As often as not, they will move away on hearing human voices. On the other hand... a mini charge broke out up the short slope towards us. Shaking and lifting their heads and trunks as they came over the ridge, ears out, they were testing the ground – typical fear-inducing elephant tactics, effective, but not too serious.

My group huddled behind me as we backed off; trusting as ever that the guide had this one under control. I shouted back at the herd, a good deterrent in close up contact, my rifle at the ready. They stopped, then swayed on their knees and waved their trunks in an attitude I knew was a focused consultation.

We stood our ground, my shouts growing in volume and profusion. They would either charge now, when I would reluctantly have to shoot the leader, or they'd run away. Thankfully, they turned and ran off along the ridge.

Wiping my brow and turning to reassure my group that all was under control, I was greeted by a terrifying sight – a big, well tusked, determined cow elephant in full charge, head and trunk tucked in, coming down the mountain straight for us, leaving a swathe of flattened trees and grass behind her. She was coming in for the kill.

176

My group panicked, understandably, and scattered in every direction, every person on red alert escape mode. I had to get to the place where the elephant would break out of the jesse before she picked on somebody. Dodging fleeing bodies, screaming like a banshee, I got ready to shoot.

She broke out of the bush, all feet forward, and then skidded to a halt. Have we a stand-off? The last thing I wanted was to shoot our valiant leviathan. In the pandemonium, my rifle up and pointing at her head, we collided; knocking me back and causing an accidental pull of the trigger.

The round harmlessly grooved her forehead. Our world stopped for a millisecond following the deafening report. I was standing next to a huge enraged elephant with an empty rifle - big hunting rifles require each round to be individually loaded. To do just that I leaped behind a nearby mopane tree, finding my trainee, John, shoulder to shoulder behind the same tree. John ran off but she knew who the troublemaker was. In my frantic attempt to reload, the cartridge breached. Eject. Reload. Walking backwards, watching the elephant closing, I stumble over a rock, fell onto my back, dropping my gun.

In an instant, the gigantic, roaring, slobbering, rough-haired mammoth was on top of me. Her strong scent, so peculiar to elephant, filled my whole being. How uniquely extraordinary is our mind in these desperate critical moments. Life's journey flashed past in an instantaneous fast-track movie. I even had time to think how tough it was going to be for my wife, Sands, to carry on alone and bring up the children.

'*Go on! You ghastly beast, you!*' the minister barked, bravely standing a few metres away, reacted in typical British manner, in an attempt to shoo the elephant away. I wished he'd move further off. In his anxiety, he'd pull the trigger on his cine camera now and then – I still have his short bursts of film showing the elephant rounding the tree, me backing off, then falling out of the picture when the elephant seems to leap on top of me. I remember calling loudly on God and my guardian angel for help.

I switched into high-level survival mode, trying to escape through her back legs, anything to get out of the turbulent front-end action. She was doing her best to kneel on me, tusk me, throw me anyway she wanted. My shell-shocked, poorly concealed group reckoned afterwards the hand to trunk tussle went on for about two minutes. Two incidents remain clear in my mind. The first when her tusk ran along my shoulder blades while I was scrabbling on all fours, and scooped me up through my shirt collar. Hanging three metres up on its tusk, a huge angry elephant eye glaring in my face, all I can recall is how good the view was.

My collar finally gave, dropping me to the ground again; I desperately tried to get out through those hind legs. Her dragging back tactics were gaining ground, clearly leading towards a terminating squash any moment.

I next remember a tight squeezing around my waist. I couldn't breathe. She had me in her trunk from where I expected to be imminently flying through the treetops or pulped against a mopane trunk. Then I found myself with both hands on her tusks and tried to wrench my way out of her grip. An impossible feat – elephants pick up 300kg logs with their trunks. The fact was that I had reached the point where I simply had nothing left in me – adrenalin all used up.

I'm not sure what happened next but I flew into a spiky bush, thorns in my mouth and face, arms pinned back, waiting for the *coup de grace.*

I waited... and I waited... and I waited. But nothing happened. Slowly and painfully I extricated myself. There was no more Mrs Elephant. She'd gone! Unheard of, normally squashing their victim into strawberry jam. Had my angel worked a miracle? My being here is surely proof of that.

* jesse (English – bushwillow) – spiky deciduous straggling shrub

It's interesting to note that elephant possess very human qualities, not only being able to memorise and recognise their own as well as humans and objects but also to feel emotions such as love, anger and remorse... so what's to say they don't also harbour grudges. – **GN**

That Could Have Been Me!

Eve How

During the bush war in Rhodesia in about 1970 my father and his contemporaries were operating in an army unit called PATU, nicknamed Dads' Army. The unit was for older men who wanted to serve their country but were too old for national service. On this particular occasion a small unit of about six or seven of them was sent into Mana Pools area to look for evidence of terrorist activities.

Mana Pools in those days was teaming with wild life of every description imaginable in the African bush; lion, elephant, leopard, buffalo roamed free. So not only did they have to watch their backs for terrorists but also for carnivores hunting for dinner.

The men patrolled with vigilance, rifles at the ready at all times never knowing at any moment what they would encounter. Their tail-end Charlie on this occasion was Toby, a good pal of my dad's. The terrain was open grassy bushveld dotted with the odd mopane or acacia tree and the guys had spread out quite a lot.

Suddenly someone said, *'Stop! We're missing Toby.'* He was indeed missing, nowhere in sight. They immediately turned about and followed their footsteps back calling *'Toby'* in muted tones. After a couple of kilometres they heard a muffled voice coming from the direction of a large mopane tree.

'Toby! What the hell are you doing up there? And your rifle... why did you leave it at the bottom of the tree?'

Toby eyed them without a smile and pointed at several piles of dung lying close by. *'That could have been me!'*

With that the men burst into raptures of laughter.

'Seriously guys, it's not funny,' he admonished, *'I was tailing you when I suddenly got the feeling I was being watched. I turned and*

looked behind me and saw a whole pride of lion padding after me. I was about to become dinner! Now will you get me out of this tree, I don't even know how I got up here in the first place!'

When treed by lion you may as well enjoy the view! – **GN**

Malevolent Cave Dweller

Lloyd Wilmot

Ever since childhood I have enjoyed exploring caves, particularly if I could find paintings, pottery or any form of artifact. The late Peter Smith had found a rather old carved buffalo in a cave at Savuti and this encouraged me to explore every nook and cranny of Savuti's Gubatsaa hills. One cave on the so-called Bushmen Paintings Hill looked promising because it had a porcupine burrow in the bat guano that littered the floor. Peering closely I saw the burrow simply went under a rock overhang. As I did, a bat flew out which meant a possible cavern beyond. Next morning, assisted by Modalla, one of my staff, I spent almost the whole day digging out rocks and guano to get beneath the overhang. I could hear the porcupines inside trying to hide.

Early next morning we were back and I noticed porcupine tracks from where they emerged to go and forage. As we penetrated deeper the guano dust was blinding and very irritating to my nasal passages and throat. Finally, I had opened a tunnel just wide enough for my body and by pushing the last guano ahead of me I got my head into a small cavern. The dust was so thick I could barely see. As I pulled myself through, the dust swirled and almost choked me. I thought I saw a dark snake curled up in a hollow against the rock-face but dismissed this as a trick of my imagination. Pushing past I crawled to the back of the cavern to escape the dust and breathe cleaner undisturbed air. There were no porcupines. To save battery power I switched off the torch and sat in the dark to wait for the dust to settle.

After ten minutes or so I switched on the light and looked around. The ceiling was only about a metre and a half high and the cavern about three metres long. Then I spotted it - a large black mamba in that hollow near the entrance. I realised then that the porcupines had dug the hollow trying to escape my digging the previous day. Sometime during the night the mamba had entered. With my renewed digging in the morning it had simply slipped into the best refuge it could find. I had no stick to defend myself and could not risk trying to kill it with a few stones within the cave. With a pounding heart I decided the only hope lay in trying to get past it while it was still afraid.

Approaching very carefully on my elbows and knees I held the torch ahead of me and with my free hand I pushed up some guano. Manoeuvring further I made a tight turn and began probing with my feet to find the exit. The mamba lay staring at me impassively in the torchlight from less than two feet away. When they strike they first usually show a black mouth. If it had opened its mouth I was going to give it a mouthful of guano and hope for the best.

I hardly dared to breathe as I moved past the snake and found the exit. Wiggling in reverse, using by elbows to push myself down the tunnel I could at last part company with the unwanted guest. Once I felt safe I used both hands to push myself through, yelling to Modalla to get away. The urgency in my voice and my hasty exit must have convinced him of trouble because when I emerged he was bounding down the rocks with great agility.

I have visited the cave since then but never found the courage to penetrate the burrow again. There could be some sort of artefact in there but someone else can find it.

Olive-grey snake, it's Africa's fastest, most venomous. Its repetitive strike injects neuro-cardio toxin with each strike, fatal within 20 min. **Nat Geo**

The Rat Theory

Greer Noble

Interestingly, the similarity between Mahe in the Seychelles and Marrakesh in Morocco are that buildings may not exceed the height of a palm tree... and rats... but that's where the similarities end. Morocco is Muslim, Seychelles is Catholic, Morocco is desert, Seychelles is tropical...

I met a sailor when living in the Seychelles and he had a theory as to whom or what would take over the world.

'First it was communists,' he began, *'everyone was worried that the Russians would take over the world. Now everyone worries about Muslims or the Chinese taking over the world. Well let me tell you they're all wrong. It's rats...'* he elaborated, *'rats are going to take over the world. I've seen new ships take every precaution to ward off rats, but you'll never stop them!'*

My first reaction to the Seychelles, before our plane even touched down, was, *'Oh my God, I could die here'* so spectacularly dazzling was the vista... the last thing on my mind were... rats. My first reaction to Morocco, while also euphoric, was bewilderment. Seychelles is a place you never want to leave, Morocco is a place you can't wait to leave... yet feel somehow compelled to return... despite the rats! It's undeniably fascinating.

Simply wandering around the medina with its fibrous network of dimly lit souks is alone enough to jolt the senses; the babouches*, kaftans, jewellery, silk and carpet vendors, while they can be as irritating and persistent as flies after fish, they're also intriguing. A venomous viper draped around my neck, its one-eyed owner grinning gaping rotting teeth, inspires little confidence. The daunting sight of dozens of leopard pelts, *'Enough of the same size, madam, to make very nice full length coat,'* enthused the vender, makes my blood boil! (I did report this, twice, to a wildlife icon but sadly he never responded) and I have to admit, here, rats did come to mind. While you might not necessarily *see* them, you can *feel* them, *sense* them.

The transformation at night into a maze of food stalls covering the entire square was surreal. Dishes were varied, catering to every taste, all suspect, some tasty and some had one gagging. Belly dancers, snake charmers, pick-pockets, beggars... they were all there. A mixed crowd of ethnic diners, sharp expats and wide-eyed tourists delighted at having stumbled across the Marrakech they'd always heard so much about. And yes, it wasn't hard to imagine how the infestation of rats would descend nightly on the aftermath. For the same reason I couldn't stop thinking *'fire'*. While it would be devastating, wiping out that unbelievably intricate, ancient and alluring labyrinth of stalls and souks and century old trading, it would nevertheless, be cleansing, decimating infestations of rats.

So when the night manager at our down-town hotel found us a guide willing to take us into the desert, we were delighted. It would be a long drive, some seven to eight hours, depending on stops along the way. So suitably clad with traditional djellabas* we set out, via Quarzazate, on our journey to the Sahara, leaving behind the heat, hustle and bustle and... the rodents of Marrakesh... or so we thought.

The road wound higher and higher, up into the Atlas Mountains. It was when we reached the pass, which has snow virtually all year round that the car spun out of control, doing several 360 degree spins. With sleet on the tarmac we came terrifyingly close, several times, to the sheer drop below while our guide grappled frantically with the wheel. To use a cliché, it was a close shave.

On our descent into the Draa Valley we made several stops to have mint tea, buy souvenirs and, of course, the traditional indigo-blue Berber headgear - a skilfully bound cloth into a turban, protection against the desert dust. Atop a steep cliff we were afforded the opportunity to look out over the rugged terrain; canyons and weird rock formation which looked more like a moonscape.

We at last arrived at Zagora, a small town in south-eastern Morocco, close to the Algerian border. Known as the Gateway to the Desert, aptly indicated by that famous sign, '*52 days to Timbuctu*'* – by camel-back of course.

Late in the afternoon we quickly mounted our waiting camels and

185

headed off into the desert. While not entirely new to this (I had ridden camels before in Baalbek, Lebanon's Beqaa Valley some years previously), I'd never ridden these ships of the desert for any length of time. Well let me tell you that the seventeen kilometre trek we did became more arduous by the minute. Nothing like horseback riding, it wasn't the movement that I found uncomfortable but the width of the beast. It felt as if I was doing the splits which made me sorely tempted to ride side-saddle but in fear of falling off my rather high mount and disrupting our caravan's rhythm, I suffered in silence instead. I need not describe how relieved I was when we arrived at our camp.

The Berber tent was a patchwork affair of blankets stitched together, much cruder than what I had expected. We sat on the carpets covering the sand to enjoy the Moroccan feast we were promised. Traditionally served, the lid of the clay tagine was lifted with aplomb, only to reveal the humble chicken and couscous. Incredibly, the chicken was so tough it was rubbery and had the floor been concrete it would have bounced. So after an awkward ride and a disastrous dinner our guide bid us good night and we settled down on the austere floor of threadbare blanket bedding.

Only it was too cold to sleep. Fully clothed, in our boots, trousers, thick jerseys and djellabas I was sandwiched between my husband and my son for warmth. It was the coldest night of our lives.

I had eventually dozed off at about four in the morning when a huge jerboa, a hopping desert rat with icy feet, trod across my face. Well that was it! I was beginning to believe that sailor had a very valid point – rats *were* taking over the world! I've never had a Muslim or a Chinaman land on my face while sleeping, heaven forbid!!! Nor have I longed for dawn to arrive so badly in my life either.

But when we stepped outside at first light the sight that met our eyes was indescribable. It had all been worth it! To experience the Sahara at sunrise must be one of the most awesome sights on earth, the feeling of freedom unequalled... rats and all!

*babouches – leather slippers
*djellabas –   hooded robe

If I don't put my hand in the gutter, the rats won't bite me.
Moroccan Proverb

Passing the Flinch Test in Samburu

Brian Jackman

The Maasai Mara may be Kenya's top tourist destination but its soul lies in the north, where the green highlands fall away into an arid wilderness the size of Britain and the proud Samburu people, a desert tribe of warrior nomads, still follow their herds across the surrounding rangelands.

Samburu is elephant country, hence the distinguished presence of Iain Douglas-Hamilton, the world authority on elephant behaviour, and the headquarters of Save the Elephants, the organisation he founded in 1993.

Just a few miles upstream from Iain's office is Elephant Watch Camp, created by Oria, his Kenyan-born Italian wife. Shaded by giant river acacias on the banks of the Ewaso Nyiro, it's a perfect fusion of luxury bush living and Bedouin bohemia, and in a reserve over-endowed with big noisy lodges it is by far the nicest place to stay.

Today it is Saba, Oria's eldest daughter, who runs Elephant Watch Camp and it is hard to think of anyone more suited to the task. When she was just six weeks old her mother decided she should meet her first wild elephant, a matriarch called Virgo, one of the 400 animals her father was studying in Tanzania's Lake Manyara National Park.

'Although far too young to remember it I was told that when Virgo saw me she reached out her trunk and took a good long sniff to get my scent,' she says. *'Then she brought her own calf forward as if to introduce it to my mother.'*

One year later Saba's sister Dudu was born and the pair of them ran wild in Manyara, learning bush-lore from the Tanzanian rangers and bathing close to the elephants in the Ndala River.

'Everything in our lives from the very beginning was about elephants,' says Saba. *'All my toys were elephants, all my books and my earliest memories, especially the scary ones like the time when, at*

the age of maybe three or four, I was charged by a big bull called Casimir.'

After University she worked with Save the Rhino Trust in Namibia before eventually joining Save the Elephants as her father's chief executive in 1997, and it was then, while working for STE, that she was talent-spotted by the BBC Natural History Unit and embarked on a career as a wildlife filmmaker.

In 2006 she married Frank Pope, a former *Times* correspondent and marine archaeologist, and the couple now live at Elephant Watch Camp with their three girls: Selkie, aged seven, and the twins, Luna and Mayian.

On my first night in camp I was awoken in the small hours by the cracking of branches. An elephant was feeding just outside my tent, the first of many I would encounter during my stay.

Nowhere else in the world, I discovered, can you be on first name terms with so many wild elephants. In the course of her father's research it was necessary to get to know Samburu's elephants as individuals, since when 900 have been named and separated into families, and early next day we drive out to meet them.

The morning sun falls like a blessing across the Samburu floodplains, pouring away towards the sacred mountain of Ololokwe in the blue distance beyond, and I ask Saba if she has any favourites.

'I'm very fond of Yeager,' she says. *'He's the bull who came into camp and woke you up last night. It's an incredible privilege to have a wild African elephant feeling so secure in our presence.'*

'There is an etiquette to approaching elephants,' says Saba. *'You never encroach on their space. Instead you let them make the decisions and allow them to feel confident enough to ignore you. It's something I acquired from my father, learning how to read the nuances of animal behaviour and then reacting appropriately.'*

I hope she is right because standing right in the path of our vehicle is a large bull elephant. *'That's Edison,'* she says, and it is all too apparent that Edison is in musth, the season when, stoked up with testosterone and eager to mate, elephant bulls can be unpredictable.

And I've seen what they can do.

In the Visitor Centre at Save the Elephants' headquarters is the trashed Land-Cruiser in which two researchers nearly lost their lives. It happened in 2002 when they witnessed a battle between two bull elephants known as Abe Lincoln and Rommel. When Lincoln gained the upper hand, Rommel took out his frustration on the vehicle and flipped it over with his tusks.

Now, as Saba switches off the ignition, Edison strides towards us, extending the tip of his trunk until it is hovering only inches from my forearm. Slowly he follows the outline of my body until I can feel his warm breath on the side of my face. Then, inexplicably, he brushes past and stands behind us with tusks and trunk laid out full length on our canvas roof.

Time stops, and in the silence I can hear wood doves calling all around us. Then he is gone, a dark shadow drifting away under the trees. *'Well done,'* said Saba afterwards. *'You passed the flinch test with flying colours.'*

It was an unforgettable meeting involving total trust between all three individuals involved - two humans and one elephant - and only if you stay at Elephant Watch Camp are such close encounters possible.

Africa changes you forever, like nowhere else on earth. Once you have been there, you will never be the same. But how do you begin to describe its magic to someone who has never felt it? How can you explain the fascination of this vast, dusty continent, whose oldest roads are elephant paths? Could it be because Africa is the place of all our beginnings, the cradle of mankind, where our species first stood upright on the savannahs of long ago? Maybe that was what led Karen Blixen to say in Out of Africa, *'Here I am, where I belong'* – **BJ**

Themba Chivuli's Goats

Colin (KK) Brown

Sue Maas

It had been clear to Lucas Ndwandwe and the other Tribal Elders from the very outset, that the District Commissioner had not fully comprehended all the implications and complications that surrounded the legal matter concerning Themba Chivuli's goats.

When the D.C. had first instructed the Elders that they must deliberate and reach a verdict (upon the matter of the goats) in the Traditional Court, they had graciously accepted his file of evidence.

They had studied it briefly, then set it aside and quietly made enquiries of their own. And it had soon become apparent to them that in this particular case, confrontation with the secular authorities was to be expected: if not, indeed, inevitable.

As always in these tribal matters, the judgment of the Traditional Court would be submitted to the District Commissioner, who would review it before either accepting the verdict, or overriding it and resubmitting the case through more formal legal channels.

With quiet resignation, Lucas Ndwandwe had sat with the other Elders while the DC, speaking very slowly in the Shona dialect - as if the Elders might experience some difficulty in grasping the significance of the details - had methodically listed the facts...

1. Chunu Mudzi had reported the theft of nine goats from the dam where they were being tended by Mudzi's nephew, Siphas Jongwe.

2. The young herd boy had told his uncle that the goats had been driven away by Themba Chivuli and two of his brothers, who had also administered a beating upon the unfortunate Siphas Jongwe when the youth had attempted to protect the goats. There could be no separate prosecution for the assault upon Siphas Jongwe - the District Commissioner informed the Tribal Elders - because the extent of the beating and the degree of injuries sustained therefrom could not accurately be established. This - the DC further explained - was due to a subsequent beating suffered by Siphas Jongwe at the hands of his uncle for having failed to protect the goats: in the first place.

3. Seven of the goats - still bearing the brand mark of Chunu Mudzi - had been discovered at Themba Chivuli's hunting camp in the thick bushveld at the base of the Mavuradonna Mountains where Themba Chivuli's own nephew, Lovemore Ndindi, was guarding them.

4. The skins of the other two goats (also bearing the brand mark of Chunu Mudzi) were found at Themba Chivuli's kraal, where they had been treated with coarse salt, and were drying in the sun.

5. Themba Chivuli had made no attempt to establish that he had either bought the goats from, or been given them by Chunu Mudzi: or any other person. This was so during the initial investigation by the young District Assistant (when Themba

Chivuli and the DA had sat eating curried goat in Themba Chivuli's kraal) and during all subsequent interrogations.

'The facts ...' the District Commissioner had concluded *'... are plain and simple. You must consider them and make your*

recommendations in terms of the Tribal Authority vested in you by the Government of Rhodesia, in order that a verdict may be pronounced and sentence confirmed by the relevant competent court, in due course.'

After two days of deliberations, and further inquiries and discussions, Lucas Ndwandwe and the Elders had made an appointment to relay their verdict to the District Commissioner and after pleasantries demanded by custom and good manners, Lucas Ndwandwe had delivered the findings of the Tribal Court.

'Themba Chivuli was not guilty of theft, but he should return the remaining seven goats to Chunu Mudzi.'

As Lucas Ndwandwe had predicted, the DC's reaction had been somewhat less than favourable. The white man's normally placid features had contorted, glowing suddenly much redder than was demanded even by recent exposure to the scorching African sun.

'The verdict ...' – the DC had declared angrily – '...was both 'inconsistent and contradictory'...' The DC had then once again laboriously listed all the facts of the case, and demanded that the Elders reconsider their verdict before *'...arriving at a decision that would not make a mockery of the Tribal Courts: which authority had been bestowed upon them by Government of Rhodesia....'*

Lucas Ndwandwe and the other Elders had retired with quiet dignity and arranged to meet at Lucas Ndwandwe's kraal the following afternoon.

There, they had taken a further five days to complete their renewed deliberations and investigations: although this extended period had not been entirely necessary to consider the case in question. After a very short discussion amongst themselves, it was decided that before any further deliberations would commence, four days should first be set aside, mutely to express the degree of their **own** dissatisfaction concerning the high-handed attitude of the District Commissioner.

A goat was slaughtered, and beer was brewed. Much local business was conducted and satisfactorily concluded. In addition, details were finalised concerning the forthcoming marriage between

Lucas Ndwandwe's granddaughter and the youngest son of fellow Elder, Thomas Chikweta. Yes, the extra time had been put to good use, and the duly extended Government *Daily Retainer Allowance* would certainly go some way towards relieving their general financial discomfort.

In the shade of a thorn tree outside the District Commissioner's offices in Mount Darwin the following week, they sat smoking their pipes in silent contentment before the meeting at which they would convey their revised decision.

Lucas Ndwandwe slowly surveyed each of the wise old faces of the Elders around him, and he felt a growing contentment as he contemplated the ultimate justice of their amended verdict in the case of Themba Chivuli's goats.

The smoke from his own clay pipe was restful. The gently smoldering bowl contained a mixture of Drum tobacco purchased from the general store in Mount Darwin's dusty main street, with a few pinches of the sweetly pungent *dagga** leaves that had been cultivated at his kraal under the careful, but illegal, supervision of his senior wife, Tandile.

Lucas Ndwandwe took another sip from the communal gourd of corn beer, and passed it on. The combination of alcohol and *dagga* had washed away his initial unease about the reception that their revised verdict would elicit from the District Commissioner. In his heart, Lucas Ndwandwe felt content that the final judgment reached by the Elders was the most equitable that had been available to them considering the constraints by which they had been bound.

Certainly, the nine goats in question had borne the brand of Chunu Mudzi. This fact had never been in question. Neither had it been contested that the missing goats had been discovered upon Themba Chivuli's land and in the care of Themba Chivuli's nephew. Nor, indeed, that the nephew was acting directly upon Themba Chivuli's instructions.

Further, it was common cause that Themba Chivuli had neither bought the goats from his accuser, nor offered him any compensation for their loss (even though two of them had been slaughtered at Themba Chivuli's kraal in order to placate the restless spirits).

Themba Chivuli had simply answered all questions with quietly dignified conviction. *'The goats are mine.'*

Yes. Lucas Ndwandwe knew that the District Commissioner would again be angry when he heard the revised verdict and the new sentencing recommendations of the Elders, but there were no longer any inconsistencies or contradictions with which the District Commissioner need concern himself.

Because, it had now been decided by the Elders that Themba Chivuli was not guilty of theft and that he should **keep** the remaining seven goats. Because the Elders had made their own enquiries, and they knew what the District Commissioner did not know.

They knew that Chunu Mudzi had violated the third wife of Themba Chivuli, and she was a plumply pretty young woman, and seven live goats were, after all, not too high a price to pay for such treachery. Not with a couple of extra sun-drying skins thrown in, as well, even: and the remainder of a goat curry in the cast iron pot outside Themba Chivuli's cooking hut.

But the District Commissioner would not have understood such niceties, so there was no point in confusing him with them.

(With apologies to Jim Latham)

*Dagga – Marijuana

Corn can't expect justice from a court composed of chicken.
African Proverb

The Rainy Season

Vered Ehsani

In my mind, September and October in Kenya are associated with the purple bloom of the Jacaranda tree, the delicate film of ant wings and our wedding anniversary. These three elements have no connection with each other, apart from the fact that they occur at the same time of year. A heavy night rain summons swarms of flying ants from their nests in the ground. They swirl like a pixelated cloud around the top of the street lamps (at least, the lamps that are actually working). In the morning, lacy silver wings and purple Jacaranda petals carpet the ground.

It's not quite as poetic inside the house where ants have squirmed their way in, attracted by any source of light, even a computer screen. They knock themselves against the light, the window, the computer and our faces. They cling to the mosquito nets and collect in corners where they shed their wings and crawl off to another corner to die. I think I'll focus on the Jacaranda petals.

Promises, Promises

Gary Hannan

Carlos and Victor were crooners. Most Friday nights you could hear their lilting harmonies soaring over the rumble of regulars congregated on the large open patio area that was part of the Triangle country club in Zimbabwe.

Fraternal twins, Carlos and Victor's only similarity was a heavy Portuguese accent and an insatiable appetite for sweet Madeira wine. They would meander from table to table, and then finding an acknowledging nod, Carlos would drop to one knee, most times in front of a pretty wife or girlfriend and, with Victor standing behind him, would break into song... Julio Iglesias step aside... these boys could bring a tear to a glass eye!

It was at the end of one such encore performance that Carlos, still on his knee, focused on my father Jim's face and popped the question... *'Jeeemy... me and Victor heard you are going camping at Gonarezhou – we want to come too... peeeeze Jeeemy, we will make chicken peri peri?'*

'Well Carlos,' my father replied, *'You guys would have to sit on the back of the Land Rover with our helpers, Silas and Gary. Be at our house at 6 am... with your katunda.*'*

Six am arrived to find them standing beside the vehicle, all ready to go. As we all climbed in, a loud undignified squawk from beneath some of the luggage announced we had yet one more travel companion.

'Oh don't worry Jeeemy, it is just a chicken we brought to make the peri peri with,' smiled Carlos.

'Get that bloody jongwe* out now or neither of you will be going on this trip,' my mother Lovona berated him.

'Sorry Lovoooorna, no problem, we will leave it behind, with the gardener'.

The drive to Gonarezhou game reserve was uneventful right up until the time we entered that precarious area known as half-shaft hill. Aptly named for all the vehicles it had damaged, the road, deeply potholed, was strewn with rocks. Any overladen vehicle had to crawl along at a snail's pace to make it.

Up to now, we had seen plenty of game, but no elephant - then suddenly there they were, all around us. Carlos and Victor were terrified, huddled together and stared anxiously at the great grey beasts while we crawled along in second gear. For the most part, the elephants ignored us and then one curious juvenile bull approached our vehicle, ears flapping. He trumpeted and that was all it took for chaos to ensue. Attempting to squeeze my skinny frame through the rear window I got stuck – half in and half out. Carlos and Victor were both screaming and fighting with each other trying to dislodge me and get out themselves. Silas on the back was yelling at the elephant, my mother in front was shouting at my poor father to speed up and dad was yelling at all of us not to panic. Perhaps amused at the mayhem he had created, the young bull casually turned around and ambled off.

Shaken but euphoric at having survived such an attack we pulled into the camp site overlooking Clarendon Cliffs. Beginning to offload, I noticed Carlos looking around for the rondavels* he had been told existed there.

'Carlos,' dad told him, 'with the exception of the ablution block which only holds one toilet, there are no other closed buildings here. We sleep in the open.'

Decidedly uncomfortable, Carlos and Victor placed their sleeping bags so that somebody else would be sleeping on either side of them – as bait.

Later that afternoon, while searching for firewood, my father pointed out many hyena spoor around the camp, no doubt attracted to the frequent smell of food being cooked there. I could tell by now that our guests were regretting their decision to have embarked on such a trip, but a couple of bottles of Madeira later they loosened up a little and broke into song while we braaied* our steaks and Silas made sadsa*.

Sitting around the fire after dinner and with a wink in my direction, my father told stories of man-eating lions, rabid jackals, scorpions in sleeping bags and of course a hyena that had mistakenly ripped a

199

sleeping man's face off because of the smell of meat that lingered on his lips after such a dinner like the one we had just enjoyed. Carlos and Victor sat silent throughout. We could only guess at the scenes that were playing out in their tortured imaginations.

Around midnight, we all got into our sleeping bags and nodded off to sleep... or so we thought.

Early morning, I awoke about the same time as my dad and, still drowsy, made our way to the ablution block. It was locked... from the inside... so we waited patiently for a couple of minutes and then knocked on the door. There was a groan and a shuffling sound that came from beneath the door and the latch was released to reveal both Carlos and Victor. They had moved to the enclosed safety of the toilet to spend the night, their sleeping bags laid out on either side of the long-drop*!

Embarrassed, all Carlos could say was *'Pleeeese Jeeemy, don't tell anyone ... pleeeeese, people won't want to hear us sing, they will laugh at us.'*

My father promised and has never spoken of this story to anyone else, but I on the other hand, never made that promise.

Back in Triangle, Carlos and Victor continued to sing on Friday nights, wine still flowed and women still pretended to swoon... but it was now them that paid for the round of drinks after performing at our table!

*katunda – baggage in local lingo
*jongwe – chicken in local lingo
*rondavel – round room usually under thatch
*braaied – barbecued
*sadsa – maize meal made into a stiff porridge (Africa's staple diet)
*long-drop -bush toilet (wooden box with hole over a deep pit)

Their vocal vibrations in the night, as haunting as a hunter's moon, their amber eyes stalk the subconscious... hold my hand and come with me... I will take you to my lazy, playful lions – **GN**

Townhouse Leopard

Kim Lepper

'**O**ur' young leopard lived in a dentist's townhouse in Harare, Zimbabwe's capital, and I was a nearby resident. One day the cub charged me - for a third time. I thought the little blighter had learned his lesson but he came at me and snaffled a juicy ankle! I stupidly tried to pull my leg away but realised with alarm that he would not just unseat me but drag me with him! I clung on for grim death hollering for help.

The poor dentist was aghast. '*What will people think with you screaming 'HELP, HELP Ken, it's HURTING me'* – *they will think I am hurting you.*'

So not just a deeply punctured ankle, but a wounded pride too.

Later, at supper in the Monomatapa hotel, the wound started to leak. Sensing warm drops trickling down to my foot, I blurted, '*Oh bugger, that leopard bite has opened up again.*'

Four American tourists looked distinctly uneasy hearing this so we invited them back to the dentist's townhouse to meet the cub. I think they thought that leopards were fairly commonplace pets in Zimbabwe!

Evil Eyes

Greer Noble

Seventeen kilometres of dongas, a couple of African villages, hardly a track let alone a road; wild, wild terrain and at last we arrived on the river bank, on the Zambian side of the lower Zambezi.

Night was almost upon us so we set up camp under tall tamarind trees in anticipation of the intense heat that we knew would come with the first rays of sun the next day. This required levelling the Land Rover for sleeping comfort in our rooftop tent and necessary for the gas fridge to function, pulling out a couple of folding chairs and a table from behind our bench seat and making a fire.

The moon shone eerily above the gorge across the river on the Zimbabwean side, a hyena's manic whoop echoed, reverberating across the water. This was the Africa I knew, the Africa I loved.

Suitably sprayed with mosquito repellent we settled down around our fire to enjoy a drink and absorb the scents and sounds of the night around us, soothed by lapping waters as the river flowed gently eastwards on its long winding course to the Indian Ocean. Soon a build-up of cloud obscured the moon. Everything went quiet. A streak of lightning prompted me to start preparing dinner – a storm was brewing.

The Land Rover parked on the only level spot, some twenty paces from our fire, required three or four trips back and forth, carrying food, cooking utensils and other supplies. And while built-in drawers at the back of the vehicle made access to everything relatively easy, the light within was dim. But familiar with the layout it didn't hinder me; I'd know where everything was even blindfolded.

On my approach I kept stepping over a heap of cow dung close to the back of the vehicle. There was dung everywhere. Cows from the villages meant flies during daylight. Pity, I thought with a resigned sigh. As if the intense heat wasn't enough. The dung began to niggle me so on my last approach I decided to shove it out of my path. Only something stopped me. Call it instinct, a sixth sense or by virtue of my many years spent in the wilds but something cautioned me. I bent down to take a closer look... and the blood drained from my veins. The glazed evil eyes of the biggest, thickest puff-adder I had ever seen surveyed me menacingly from its coiled camouflage.

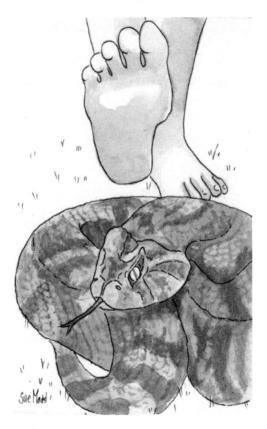

I quietly backed off not letting it out of my sight. '*Snake*', I announced as calmly as I could but loud enough for my husband to hear. '*Bring the spade*,' was my urgent command. I would use it to sweep it well away, down the slope to the river.

My husband came running. Horrified, with one swift chop of the spade, he'd decapitated it. I can't say I was altogether sorry. Watching it by the light of the fire where we'd placed it, it seemed to live on as it writhed and twisted for some time – even evil in the throes of death.

To this day I shudder to think of what could have happened had I kicked it or worse still, had our young son been awake and trodden on it; we would never have made it in time to get an antidote, Lusaka being several hours away and the border post with Kariba closed for the night. God knows how many times I must have stepped over it on that dark night. I've watched them strike at close quarters, in captivity, being fed poor little day old chicks, walking all over them, totally oblivious of the fate that awaited them. They might look sluggish but they sure make up for it with their lightning strike.

It is the bright day that brings forth the adder and that craves wary walking
William Shakespeare

A Wee Too Many

Sue Maas

Our gardener Gideon Mutetwa was a very flowery character (excuse the pun) who was extremely fond of visiting the shabeen* in Nyamunga, a small village in Zimbabwe, on his squeaky bike which he rode with a limp as polio had crippled one leg.

On this particular evening he dressed for the occasion in his best creation - a pair of leather shoes painted baby blue with enamel paint, olive green shirt and longs and a glorious impala skin waistcoat he'd made himself, topped with a very smart straw hat, also painted blue.

Our imagination ran riot and we nearly wet ourselves picturing him when, still dressed in his glad rags and still very much in a state of inebriation, he told us the next morning about his 'horrific' return journey from the shabeen.

He had stopped for a wee in a dip along the power lines when, after relieving himself, he noticed that the tree close by seemed to be moving. To his horror a huge elephant rounded the tree and Gideon took off with the tusker in hot pursuit. Thankfully it gave up after only a short distance.

*shabeen - local beer hall

At night it is better to be charged by an elephant than stalked by a lion **GN**

Remedy for a Lion Attack

Rob Fynn

While we were away on a trip, my mother Maasie, at the age of 62 years, insisted on coming to the rescue and holding the fort on Fothergill, our island safari camp on the then Rhodesia's Lake Kariba. She relied entirely on gut instinct, carrying on in all spheres *'As we always do, darling.'* The best of British.

It was the hot season. On a balmy night one of our guests had pulled his bed on to the veranda of his chalet to enjoy the cool of the evening and sleep under the stars. Unbeknown to him or the staff, there was a sickly lion roaming the camp that night. He woke up to find the lion tugging at his arm. His cries woke his wife who screamed so loudly the lion let go, gave a good roar and loped off into the dark to find less cantankerous prey.

'Don't worry, it was only a lion attack. Hot tea and cakes are being served in the dining room and the bar's open. Do come up.'

Maasie walked through the camp, reassuring all. Her remedy for most things was brandy which she insisted the unfortunate victim of the lion mauling should have in copious quantity and in which she joined him.

The lake was rough, as it often was in the early hours of the morning. The anabatic wind blew into the valley from the highveld as it cooled through the night. The boat trip to Kariba and hospital had to be delayed. When our guest finally got there the medical staff waited for four hours for him to sober up before they could administer the anaesthetic and operate.

John Stevens, the Matusadona warden, came down the next day in a helicopter that was fortunately doing some game capture work in the park. He found the lioness lying up a few hundred metres from the lodge and shot it from the air with a single bullet in the back of the head. In the discectomy, he found an emaciated liver that would have seriously curtailed her hunting ability.

Who is brave enough to tell the lion that his breath smells?
Berber Proverb

A Salutary Reminder

Lloyd Wilmot

In February 1971 three South Africans arrived at Crocodile Camp in a small car, hoping to explore the Moremi Game Reserve. They were crestfallen to learn that only a 4 x 4 vehicle could get through. I suggested they hire a Land Rover in Maun and I would be their guide for three days. This they did and we set off the next morning. In those days one could camp anywhere and that afternoon I decided on a quiet backwater near the Bodumotau area. Going along the edge of the swamp I succeeded in parking the Land Rover close to a large tree where we could camp.

It was hot and the water inviting despite the risk of crocodiles. Keeping to the shallows we all had a dip and I noticed the heavy croc drag marks that confirmed their presence.

That night I gathered the dirty dishes after supper and asked for a torch to go wash them in the river. The woman gave me a small pencil torch. The light was adequate and I followed the hippo path through the long grass past the Land Rover. Still grasping the torch in my fingers as I held the plates with both hands, I reached the water and shone around. Nothing. No red eyes. Then I shone at my feet to wade in. There, right at my feet, half hidden in the grass lay the head of a large crocodile with his jaws on the mud.

It was a heck of a shock that gave me an instant jolt of adrenalin. Dropping the dishes on its head I leapt backwards and bolted to the Land Rover a couple of yards away. There was a loud splash as the croc did an abrupt turn back into the river. I could not understand why it had not seized me. I was so close and about to take a step forward.

The clients shouted from the camp, asking what the commotion was. I told them then got a spotlight clipped onto the Land Rover battery. There, in the water not far off, not one but two large crocs stared back with interest. The clients couldn't believe it and shuddered when they realised it was the same waist-deep water we had been swimming in that afternoon. It was a salutary lesson. Perhaps it is true that we have guardian angels.

Experience is the name everyone gives to their mistakes – **Oscar Wilde**

Donkey Cart Furore

Ken Tilbury

It was June 1968 and my daughter Nicky had been born three months prematurely. She was struggling to survive in the incubator Rhodesia's (now Zimbabwe's) Triangle Hospital had quickly bought especially for her. Liz, my wife, was also in a bad way.

Because of her weak condition it was urgent to get a sample of her blood to the blood bank in Bulawayo to get blood mixed to match hers exactly. Nobody in the Lowveld at that time had a plane, so the only way to get this done was for me to drive to Bulawayo and back as fast as possible.

I was at work 17 miles away from the hospital and was not aware of what was happening until I was sent for. My car was old and unreliable and we were on petrol rationing but when I arrived there my brother-in-law, Clive Style, was waiting there for me with his car and petrol coupons for the trip.

It was a long trip – Bulawayo was 290 miles from Triangle – and I needed someone to come with me. Phil, a friend of mine, was stationed at Triangle police station so I asked him to accompany me. He was ready ten minutes later and we set off at 10 am after re-assuring my wife.

From Triangle we drove on dirt roads towards Fort Victoria then took a short cut to the strip road from Fort Victoria towards Bulawayo, where the piece in between the strip had been tarred to a width of nine feet. It was like a roller coaster with numerous twists and turns and narrow low level bridges.

Speeding over a rise and round a bend, the road suddenly dropped down towards yet another small low level river crossing. As the causeway came into sight I slammed on brakes and skidded to a stop in a cloud of dust and flying gravel. The road was blocked. There, right in the middle of the causeway were two donkey carts. They had collided head-on with each other. Their traces were tangled together and they were unable to move either forward or back. The owners of the carts were having a heated exchange in the dry river bed while the four donkeys stood quietly waiting.

After failed attempts to get them to move their donkey carts, Phil and I managed to untangle the traces and move the two teams off the bridge and onto the side of the road. The two owners who, unable to resolve their differences, were now sitting on the rocks in the river bed, throwing abuse at each other, taking not one bit of notice of what we were doing. It was quite clear that they had both been binging.

By the time we got going again we had lost thirty minutes and time was precious. Leaving them to their own devices, we got to Bulawayo an hour and a half later.

After waiting three hours for the blood to be mixed to the required sub-group, we were handed a cooler box containing the blood and set off back for Triangle at 4 pm. We assumed that it was in glass bottles in the cooler box and had to be held to stop it tipping over and the bottles breaking. Needing both sets of eyes on the road ahead, whoever was passenger, Phil or myself, sat in front with one arm over the seat holding onto the precious cooler box.

Back at the causeway, where the road had earlier been blocked by the donkey carts, we were surprised to find the carts still there. They had been moved to the shade of a tree and the two men, who had obviously resolved their differences, were asleep under another tree with a number of empty Chibuku* cartons lying on the ground near them. It was dusk and already quite cold with the sun having set. Clearly they would not be getting home that night.

With the road blockage and the longer than expected delay in Bulawayo I was worried about Liz's condition and so we were travelling fast. We had to be extra vigilant as we sped along, keeping an eye out for cattle known to stand on the warm tar road at night in the winter. As it was, on two occasions we had to screech to a stop while cattle moved slowly and reluctantly off the road.

We finally arrived back at the hospital at 8 pm. Handing the cold box to the nurse I rushed to the ward to see my wife. She was very weak but stable and pleased to see me back safely. The doctor came into the ward with the cooler box and took out the blood. It was in plastic bags and would have been quite safe without being held so carefully all the way!

Transfusion was started immediately and I watched in wonder as the colour came back into my wife's face.

*Chibuku – millet beer, a local brew.

A donkey always says thank you with a kick – **Kenyan Proverb**

Evening Bath on the Lugenda

Larry Norton

L ast year six of us kayaked down the Lugenda river, which traverses the Niassa Game Reserve in northern Mozambique. We found ourselves camped on a swampy island, midstream. It was day three of an eleven day trip and a bath had become necessary. The sun slipped behind the tall riverine forest. Conscious of crocs, I found a spot where a very small channel elbowed a large fallen tree. Easing my foot into a small gap between big logs it felt deeper than expected so I stood on the limb, washing with scooped mugs of water. Following me, Mike Scott, an old mate and hardened campaigner had fewer reservations and less imagination and plunged into the same gap. Covered in soap, he repeated this, immersed completely in surprisingly deep water.

Back at the cooking fire, in clean dry clothes and smelling like roses, we nursed our whisky ration. Night had fallen quickly. Banter ensued with a comparative discussion of washing spots. We insisted that we had chosen the best spot, virtually a Jacuzzi!! For emphasis Mike casually shone his torch towards the fallen tree, twenty metres away.

Well-spaced red eyes stared back. A massive, evil looking croc had emerged from exactly the spot where we had bathed. It seemed very possible that the beast may have been lurking in the undercut of the fallen tree throughout the ablutions. Fearless, it swam lazily towards the light. Horror, dread and paroxysms of the screaming willies!!! Double whisky ration... A few times that night I woke to visions of that massive gnarled head slowly moving upstream.

One cannot resist the lure of Africa – **Rudyard Kipling**

'Insects' of Another Kind

Greer Noble

It was in the late 50s, in what was then still Rhodesia, that I saw my first unexplained phenomena. I've always been a night owl and love to lie at the window, curtains open, and watch the stars. It was on one such night that a huge 'sun' rolled past, blocking the entire window. Extremely excited, I leapt out of bed and ran through to my parents in the lounge. By the time we returned to my bedroom it had vanished. Disappointed, I felt they somehow didn't believe me so you can imagine my delight when an article appeared in the morning paper to say others had seen it too.

Many sightings continued to be reported all over the country every year. Then in 1994 the most remarkable of all... a UFO seen by multiple witnesses flying over the countryside which, two days later, actually *landed*! There it was, in amongst some trees in broad daylight during break-time at Ariel School in Ruwa, just outside Harare. Alien beings then alighted! This was witnessed by 62 school children aged between 6 and 12 years.

A UFO researcher, Cynthia Hind, interviewed the children. It was so remarkable it caught the attention of Harvard child psychiatrist,

Dr John E Mack. He too came and interviewed the children, separately and collectively.

They all drew and described similar things – a round silver ship with red lights and lots of little hovering ships. Creatures with slanting insect-like eyes disembarked then stood staring at them, making them feel uneasy. Dr Mack confirmed that in his opinion, they were not making any of it up. One girl even experienced certain telepathic communication. The alien entity looked at her and *telepathically* conveyed to her that we had become too '*tech-knowledged*' (interesting in itself as she was too young to even know what that meant) and that they were also concerned about deforestation and damage to the atmosphere.

None of the children had ever been exposed to mainstream media. In fact they knew little or nothing of UFOs, yet all descriptions and sketches were uncannily similar.

Fourteen years later a follow up study was done with some of the same students. Now adults, they were all still adamant about what they saw.

These sketches were selected from drawings done by the 62 children who witnessed the incident – **John E. Mack Institute**

'We're not dealing with mental projections or hallucinations on the part of the witness but with a real physical phenomenon.' – Dr. Richard Haines – Chief of Space Human Factors Office, Pilot & Astronaut Research Centre – **NASA**

Naughty Lions of the Okavango

Rachel Lang

In every bush-loving family there is *the* story. That legendary tale that gets told again and again around the campfire to new friends on full moon nights, when buffalo-shaped bushes shift in the wind, casting shadows that look like stalking lions...

This is *our* family's story, set on a night just as I have described, in the beautiful Moremi Game Reserve in Botswana at a campsite called Third Bridge. As its name suggests, the camp is accessed by a bridge – a rickety wooden pole crossing surrounded by reeds that filter the water, making it pure and perfect for drinking – an essential stop for filling up water tanks. The water collects in a crystal clear pool with a white sandy bottom, which is wonderful to swim in... just beware of crocodiles.

I was about eight years old on this particular bush holiday. One night, exactly like the one I've already described, dad had been telling us a spine-tingling tale of the man-eating lions of Tsavo during the construction of the Kenyan-Uganda Railway in 1898 when the resident Third Bridge pride of lions began roaring, my favourite sound in the world. As its intensity increased so our circle of five camping chairs got smaller and smaller. I even remember taking off my gumboots so that they didn't melt in the hot coals.

It was common knowledge that these lions walked across the bridge almost nightly, silent at times, grunting and growling at times, but that night mum had a funny feeling and we were sent to bed earlier than usual. Lying in our rooftop tents, one for our parents and one for us kids, we listened to the lions.

'Dad, do you think they've reached the bridge yet?' my brother quietly asked him through the canvas.

Suddenly there was a thud and our Land Rover bumped sideways. My brother Caiden, taking the role of protector over his sisters, whispered, *'It's OK Rach and Beth, that's just dad rolling over.'*

219

I tried to go back to sleep but something was wrong, perhaps it was because the bush had become silent. But I must have drifted off to sleep eventually because I suddenly woke with a torch shining in my eyes and my dad's voice, unusually tense, *'Caiden, Rachel, Bethany, are you all here? Answer me ... Caiden? Are you OK Beth, Rach? You are all here?'*

'Stop shining the light in our eyes dad!' we groaned.

'Yes, we are all fine,' I said, *'What's going on?'*

I could hear my parents talking and my mum's voice was full of panic. What I couldn't see from my little cosy tent was blood smeared all over the side of our Land Rover, which was also a bit dented.

A little later, dad stuck his head in, *'Come into our tent guys'* We wriggled our way through sleeping bags and blankets and huddled, the five of us, in one tent, peering out through the mosquito net windows over our moon-drenched campsite..

Then I saw something, a hyena? It was chewing on our rope swing. But as my eyes became more accustomed to the night, I saw it was a lion. Shadows began to emerge from all corners of our camp – there were nine of them in total, nine lionesses in our little camp. I started to cry out in nervous exhilaration but was quickly told to *'ssshhhh'*.

'Dad, do you think the lions could climb up the ladder and tear open our tent?' asked my little sister Beth. *'No love... well, they could but they won't, we are safe up here.'*

But all I remember thinking was, *'All that stands between me and the lions is a thin layer of mosquito net!'*

For an hour we watched the lionesses playfully pulling our camp to pieces, tugging the washing off our line, chewing on our rope swing and eventually exasperating my dad enough to make him throw his takkies* at them, trying, in vain, to prevent further damage to our camp. I squeezed mum's hand as a large lioness strolled right underneath us. It was an incredible night, almost a dream. When the big cats finally tired of our camp and moved on it was with takkies and torn up clothes hanging out of their mouths.

The next morning, we surveyed the crime scene. As well as the blood on the Land Rover, there were drag marks into the bushes and it was clear that an animal – probably an impala or lechwe – had been killed against the vehicle.

I then understood why my parents had been so frantic about us. They had heard the thump against the vehicle, shone a torch, seen the blood and thought it had been one of us kids who had fallen and been killed. What an horrific, nightmarish thought for any parent! From that night on, for the rest of the trip and many subsequent trips, while we were still kids, mum would stay up at night keeping watch through the tent window.

*takkies – tennis shoes

Civilization is a limitless multiplication of unnecessary necessities.
Mark Twain

Hell's Angel

Greer Noble

It was a perfect morning when our dear friend, Bob, opened his eyes. Birds sang sweetly and there was not a cloud in the sky. He rose quietly not wanting to wake Betty. Both in their seventies he still marvelled at how handsome she looked in her sleep.

He stepped out of the caravan into the sweet, fresh African air. The dew sparkled in the first rays of the sun which filtered through the tall trees but he knew only too well that within an hour the heat of the day would be upon them. In October Moçambique was probably at its hottest. Although it was dark when they'd decided to call it a day and pulled over for the night, the forest enclave had served them well, hiding them from prying eyes or uninvited passers-by.

Bob got into his track suit, slipped on his sandals and headed for the driver's side of his vehicle. He climbed in, careful not to slam the door and turned the key in the ignition. The engine purred into submission and he glided out of their hideout back onto the tarmac of the night before. It was always good to get an early start, especially in that heat. He would give Betty another hour then pull over somewhere to make tea and a light breakfast. Only ten minutes down the road however nature called. He cursed himself for not having relieved himself earlier and brought the vehicle and caravan to a gentle halt alongside a cashew plantation dotted with coconut palms.

Betty stirred, rubbed her eyes and seeing that Bob wasn't there presumed he'd gone out for his early morning constitutional. She decided to do the same. Slipping her flimsy pink robe over her matching nightgown Bob had given her for their anniversary, she inched into her favourite slippers and climbed out treading the soft, damp undergrowth until she found a suitable bush to crouch behind.

Bob watched in fascination as his deluge of urine washed away a series of perfectly moulded mud tunnels made by a colony of contentious ants. Full of holiday spirit he sprinted back to the car as if he was thirty again and gently pulled off whistling as he went.

Betty's contribution to the insect world was not nearly as destructive, simply adding to the already damp foliage. Looking forward to that first cup of tea she was sure Bob was already brewing she made her way back to where she thought she'd come only to find nothing there. Frowning, she walked up to the tarmac and looked up and down the road. Still nothing. Damn Bob, he'd done this once before, playing silly buggers. But this wasn't funny. How could he leave her high and dry in the middle of nowhere and in her diaphanous *nightwear*.

Bob whistled away, not a care in the world, window down enjoying the feel of the warm tropical air on his face. He glanced at the time and thought he'd give it another twenty minutes or so before he started to look for a suitably shady breakfast tree.

With very little traffic he virtually had the road to himself – a truck carrying logs and a small van wired together having seen better days, carrying goats and locals. And now a motorbike. What was it doing, hooting and creeping up his rear, lights flashing? Damn these Hell's Angel types. Irritated, Bob pulled over. Best let the damn thing pass, impatient asshole.

Alberto, or Al as his friends called him, was proud of his new acquisition even though the Harley was pre-used. He'd taken delivery in the port city of Beira and was on his way to Vilanculos, a small coastal village to the south, to meet up with his pals. Having grown up in Africa he was used to dodging elephant, buffalo, snakes, the odd buck or deer and even the occasional lion crossing the road but never a wild woman in a pink negligee. No way would his friends believe this!

Hell's Angel began to overtake.

'*By God,*' Bob uttered aloud, '*it's a Harley too!*' Its chrome glinted in the sun, almost blinding him as it sped past, its driver waving excitedly. What the hell does he want, Bob frowned? It was then that Bob noticed this apparition on the back, clinging to the biker for dear life, white hair and pink veils flying. If he hadn't known better he would have thought it was Betty. Then a double-take. Bob's mouth dropped open… '*What the… it IS Betty! How the dickens?*'

Of course Bob never lived that down... nor did Betty... bless their hearts! A tremendous fun couple, if ever there was, both of whom I remember with great fondness.

Cautioned by a fellow bushwhacker in Moçambique, '*If you don't want to be fined, remove your sunglasses when driving.*' He'd met a traveller who'd received a spot fine for not having a prescription for his sunglasses! – **GN**

Red Rag to a Bull

Lloyd Wilmot

It was July (2006, I think) and I was on safari in the Santa area, which lies off the south eastern corner of Chief's Island in Moremi Game Reserve, with four good friends from Namibia - the Kleins. Jurgen and his son Jannie loved fishing so one late afternoon we drove to the clump of trees we call Grant's Corner and parked the vehicle at the water's edge. Jurgen and Jannie promptly occupied the two best spots for fishing so despite the cold water I kicked off my shoes and walked down the river (generally shallow) to a spot where it emptied into a deep, dark pool covered in water lilies. Dorothy and her daughter-in-law, Ruth, remained in the vehicle using their binoculars to spot birds.

There were elephants on both sides of the river, feeding and crossing over towards Chief's Island from time to time. On my way down I had to pause in the current till a large bull had crossed ahead of me. About two hundred yards further, I reached the sandbank where the water poured into the rather sinister looking croc water pool which promised good fishing. On my left an elephant breeding herd of cows and calves continued feeding out of sight in the forest. After landing two fish, I saw a young male elephant about 12 years old, emerge from the bush and head straight toward me through the water. He had obviously not seen me with the setting sun in his eyes so I called out to him. He stopped, spread his ears and looked hard. I moved and clapped my hands to reveal myself thinking this would deter him to seek another crossing. Instead, he advanced towards me and trumpeted loudly. I thought it wise to retreat downstream into the dark pool to allow him to pass.

Standing in water over my knees, I was annoyed to see him reach my sandbank a few yards away, trumpet again and make threatening head movements. He swung his trunk and splashed water at me. Grasping my fishing rod in my left hand, I bent and splashed him back. He trumpeted again. I hurriedly took off my shirt to throw at him as he advanced and I retreated to waist-deep water. Throwing the furled shirt directly in his face I saw it open, stick briefly then drop into the water. Instead of scaring him as I had hoped, he charged through the water. All I had left in defence was my rod so I hit him hard across the face, breaking the rod. He bore down on me like a locomotive and as I went back in the water I put both feet against his forehead and pushed hard to jack-knife myself away.

Swimming away under the dark water a short distance, I grasped some water-lily stems and heard him thrashing about trying to find me. My heart was pounding as I realised the young idiot wanted to kill me. Unable to hold my breath any longer I surfaced under some water-lilies, drew air and submerged to swim further away from him. Surfacing once more, I saw him leaving the pool so I swam to the other side only to see 3 or 4 cows come charging out of the forest to see what the commotion was about. Keeping very low in the water I was relieved to see them turn and head for a crossing below the pool. Then I heard the vehicle start and come racing over.

My friends found me wet, shaking with cold and excitement. The women said they had watched everything through their binoculars and had called to the men that I was being threatened by an elephant. Intent on fishing both ignored the women saying '*Oh, Lloyd knows how to look after himself.*' Only when they shouted that it was killing me did they put down the rods and jump into the vehicle. It was too dark to retrieve anything so we came back the next morning. After a few dives, I located my shirt and broken rod.

Courage in Small Packages

Greer Noble

W hat could possibly go wrong in paradise? We'd dropped out for several months, living in the wilds of the Matusadona National Park, a delightful camp at the mouth of the Ume River... our base. Just the three of us. Apart from an ablution block with a few showers and toilets and a small ferry that came once a fortnight with modest (pre-ordered) supplies (if you were lucky), there was nothing there... which is part of the magic. The first time we ordered a bottle of brandy (whisky being hard to come by), one miniature arrived! Holding up the miniature I told the captain that my husband was a big man, not a little man, which caused much laughter.

Initially we worried that we'd get bored but as it turned out, anything but. Apart from being too hot - it was October, generally known as suicide month, temperatures reaching 46 degrees in the shade – we were too busy fishing, eating, drinking and simply soaking up the magnificent environment, the birdlife, the abundance of game and the glorious sunsets and sunrises, not forgetting the heavenly night skies.

It was the second night that I woke to a tearing, cracking sound. I stood up outside our rooftop tent, the better to see, and there, in the moonlight, was the culprit - a big bull elephant desecrating our *only* bit of shade, plundering the branches of the wild fig tree. I was incensed and before I thought of what consequences there could be I shouted, *'Bugger off, that's our tree!'* There was dead silence. My boldness dissolved. What had I done? And here my husband and eight year old son were fast asleep, not that they could have done anything. I froze and stood there, waiting, my heart in my mouth as I truly have the greatest respect for these magnificent giants. To my great relief he slowly moved off. Victory was mine and I felt quite pleased with myself having saved 'our' tree!

The days slipped by, fishing up all the little coves in our inflatable Zodiac, for our dinner. It was one such day that we went to our favourite spot along a little inlet where my son and I would sit in the

227

water on the sandbank, keeping a keen look out for crocodiles, digging for beautiful black mussels before the 'cat burglars' (black storks), got them, while my husband fished from the shoreline for bream.

We tired of this after a while and, having filled our bucket with mussels, we went on a little exploration. This being wild country my husband gave a cautionary reminder... besides buffalo, there were lion around.

We followed the inlet further inland until we came to a deep pool with reeds and beautiful, huge smooth boulders. My son grew very excited as he'd discovered something quite remarkable which he wanted to show me. Like the proverbial monkey he was far more nimble and sure-footed than me so I proceeded gingerly until I reached the spot in question. There was a perfect hole as if someone had drilled into the rock but then splayed it out as if moulded on a potter's wheel. I manoeuvred around to get a better look but at that point the rock was slippery from water seeping out of the rock hole and that's when I slipped.

As if in slow motion, as I skidded down I spotted two crocs on the opposite bank slither in. My dread was indescribable. I frantically tried to scramble out, all the while hearing the little gulping sounds made by baby crocs obviously in the nearby reeds. Where was mama and where were the two crocs that I'd frightened or maybe excited?

There was no calling my husband, he being too far off and out of earshot.

My little son held out his hand. I didn't know what to do as I knew the chances were that by accepting his help I could be endangering his life too by inadvertently pulling him in with me as I was undoubtedly twice his weight. But there was no other way out.

'*Come on mummy,*' he urged encouragingly.

Very carefully, I took his little hand and felt his strength as he began to pull me out. To my amazement it was working... until he too began to slide on that slippery surface. Determined, he steadied himself then strengthened his grip on my hand and pulled. I was out! Miraculously! To this day I don't know where he got the strength.

What a story we had to tell dad! On the way back as my husband came into view, we burst out laughing. There he was sitting fishing, half asleep, his floppy hat pulled down over his eyes, completely oblivious that he was being eyeballed by a big buffalo on a mound just above him. Seeing us approach it merely snorted and ambled off.

Footnote

I knew that adrenalin, triggered by fear and sudden danger, gives us amazing strength, stimulating muscles by electrical impulses, enabling us to lift extraordinary weights, only I never before appreciated by just how much – **GN**

Fancy Footwork

Lloyd Wilmot

In 2004 I spent a month in the south of Gabon at Iguela Lagoon. I had been invited as a consultant on elephant but was soon assisting and advising on the new Iguela Lodge that was being developed. Across the lagoon lay the newly proclaimed Petit Loango Game Reserve, a former hunting area extending to the Atlantic Ocean. There were large sounders of forest hogs as well as plentiful forest buffalo and forest elephant. These elephant loved to emerge from the jungle in the late afternoon to enjoy the cool onshore breezes off the Atlantic.

One assignment was to team up with Ahab an American biologist and Mireille Meersman the lodge manageress, to put up a fly-camp near the beach. A group was due soon and planned to use this fly-camp for explorations into the jungle which bordered very close to the sea. Three other people accompanied us with Phillipe, the Gabonese guide toting a shotgun. He took them on foot towards some forest elephant headed for the beach while we busied ourselves setting up the fly-camp. We watched Phillipe's group disappear after the elephant and knew their plan was to walk back along the beach before sunset.

Towards evening we finished our work and I, always wanting to explore, suggested we go into the jungle nearby. We drove about 500 metres along the shore before getting out on foot. After penetrating the facade of dense trees and vegetation we entered what looked like a green cathedral. As our eyes adjusted to the dark interior we could see small clearings where light poked through the towering jungle canopy. After walking further and roughly parallel to the beach, we emerged in an open space. As we did, there was a stampede on our right, headed in our direction.

I shouted to the others to run, not knowing whether it was elephant or buffalo. They gapped it and I ran to the nearest cover, a fairly thick tree that had been broken by elephants. Its crown of branches had toppled at a 45 degree angle and it was covered in fiery jungle ants.

The next moment a breeding herd of forest elephant burst out of the jungle and the lead cow spotted me before I could hide behind the tree trunk.

She screamed as she kicked sand and leaves over me and the rest of the herd stopped. She then backed off a short distance and stood trying to figure me out.

Sue Maas

With no gun, I stood under the fallen branches and used my little Sony underwater camera to pop off two flashes hoping to scare her. Without warning she came on like an express train and I barely had time to spring clear as she hit the fallen crown and fell to her knees. Jungle ants were showered over me but there was no time to deal with their stings. I dodged her probing trunk by going behind the tree and standing near her back legs. She seemed to growl with anger then got to her feet and charged again. This time I dodged with fancy footwork going round the tree in the opposite direction, just out of her reach. Withdrawing, she then went round again and once more I evaded her but only just.

One of the other females then came up and I knew I was in trouble. But the cow was so pumped up with aggression that she turned on her companion and in that momentary confusion I bolted for another tree. Reaching it I climbed frantically till I was high and well clear. Only then could I pluck the fiery ants off my body. Calling out to my companions I saw that they were low and exposed on another tree. I shouted to them to get clear, climb higher. I then yelled at the breeding herd to try to make them move away. They did and stood about 70 metres away with a large bull. With falling light I had to somehow get to Phillipe and the Land Rover to come back and rescue Ahab and Mireille. Climbing back down was the last thing I wanted to do, but had to.

Keeping a wary eye on the elephants I descended quietly then stood behind the tree to see if there was any reaction. Though they looked in my direction, they made no move and I slunk away as quietly as I could, before running for the beach. Phillipe's party had passed and a few breathless minutes later I reached them.

Having explained what had happened we climbed into the Land Rover and using low ratio I forced it through the jungle as far as I could. Phillipe then followed me carrying his shotgun loaded with heavy slugs as we quietly threaded our way back to the others. Calling softly we got their attention and led them away back to the Land Rover.

Mireille was highly excited and chain-smoking. The beers we broke open were most welcome. It turned out that the onshore sea breezes had carried the scent of Phillipe's party on their return along the beach. This had reached the breeding herd which stampeded into the jungle for cover. We happened to be in the wrong spot at the wrong time.

When you have really exhausted an experience you always reverence and love it – **Albert Camus**

Casa dos Leões
Africa's Lost Eden

Greer Noble

Gorongosa National Park was only a few hours' drive from where we lived in Umtali, a small town on the Rhodesia and Mozambique border. Maybe my fondness of Gorongosa stems from the frequency of our visits, but I still think it's one of my most favourite wildlife sanctuaries in Africa - at least the way I remember it. It's also where, if not for my father's extensive bush experience and knowledge, I could have become lion fodder on more than one occasion. At the time the park was reputed to support the densest wildlife population in all of Africa, and was especially renowned for its extraordinary number of lions. No wonder that it was once known as Africa's Lost Eden.

Apart from the characters we'd come to know over frequent visits to the park, there was not much need to go game viewing as the game came, we'd joke, to view us. We had warthogs all over the camp begging like dogs and the Chacma baboon and Vervet monkey were never far off, making a nuisance of themselves, their sharp eyes not missing a beat. From dung beetles to elephants, from bushbuck to buffalo, from bats to birds and even snakes! Simply game viewing from our chalet was to be entertained for hours, their antics, especially warthog, were too funny to see.

And safer it would seem…

On one of our late afternoon game drives I spotted a little wagtail with a broken leg, hopping about in the sand next to a clump of vegetable ivory palms. I was determined to rescue it. My father had to physically stop me climbing out of the vehicle. Furious, I accused him of being mean and cold hearted but soon had to eat my words. Only metres away obscured by the low-lying palm fronds, was a full-maned lion courting his lioness!

Then there was the time we stopped right next to a lioness. I leant out of the vehicle and stretched down to stroke her. My father moved faster than she did or I would, at the very least, have lost my hand or arm. I could feel myself being mesmerised even though I knew she was dangerous. She looked so loving I could not resist.

Then there was Scarface, one the biggest lions I've ever seen. Incredibly old, he'd become somewhat of a legend in the park, served hand and foot by the wardens. After all the fights he'd been in during his lifetime he had only a few teeth remaining. He was kept alive by offerings, usually in the form of a dead donkey, part of which was dragged along and placed at his feet every few days, with the occasional wild hare or cane rat in between for snacks. As it was he was living on borrowed time. Sooner or later he would become hyena dinner! We never had trouble finding the old man as he waited at the spot he knew his next meal would be delivered. On his haunches, he licked his great paws, looking down his scarred nose at any human in total disdain.

Daisy was another favourite. Away from the hippopotamus congested rivers, it's not uncommon to come across the odd isolated pool during the dry season. One such pool was occupied by a lone hippo who we named Daisy, despite the fact that father insisted 'she' was an old bull that had been kicked out by younger males in the pod. We felt sorry for 'her' all alone like that. Her pool was clearly too shallow, her body unable to submerge completely. The little mound above the waterline was black from the sun and she'd been there so long that a blanket of green sludge covered the area of water surrounding her which was probably just as well; at least it prevented the water from evaporating completely. But to be able to drink her average 250 litres of water a day she obviously headed for the river at night. Only we were intrigued. We'd not as yet seen her leave her little hideout.

One evening our patience paid off when, as the sun sank behind the ivory palms, she started to emerge. We all had a jolly good chuckle when we saw that Daisy was completely pink from the hump down and father was right – while they're difficult to sex due to their retracted testes, the very size of the animal convinced us that she had to be an old bull! Re-christened Sir Pigalot, we watched him trot off self-consciously as fast as his stumpy little piggy legs would allow!

But the highlight of these periodic stays and what really intrigued me as a child was the Lion House or Casa dos Leões. Built on floodplains in the early days as a camp for tourists, it was abandoned due to heavy flooding of the Mussicadzi River during the rainy seasons.

So it was, on the off chance of seeing some lions there that my older brother Jon and I set off early one morning on a game drive in that direction. The approach was easy as it was winter and the ground firm and dry. Lions are known to have a fondness for derelict buildings and Gorongosa's felines had long since claimed Casa dos Leões for themselves, hence the name. As always, we took bets as to whether they'd be in residence or not!

We were rewarded with two bored looking sentries on the roof. We sat watching them for some time to see what they might do but under a cloudy sky they were content with their cool elevated posts.

Eventually Jon jumped out of the Jeep to go and do what boys do. I nervously kept watch and was just beginning to wonder what I'd do if one of the lions were to climb down when a huge full-maned lion suddenly strolled out of the interior of the building.

235

Without thinking I jumped into the driver's seat and not really knowing much about driving as I was only about eleven at the time, turned the key in the ignition and jerkily shot off, my foot flat on the accelerator, weaving around in first gear, adrenalin shooting though my veins. Feeling particularly vulnerable in an open Jeep, I nervously looked back hoping to see Jon and saw instead that the lion was watching in utter amazement at this spectacle as were the two on top of the building. Then out of nowhere Jon leaped in and shouted at me to move over.

The relief was so overwhelming that I started giggling – which of course set Jon off too. Despite the eleven year age gap we were kindred spirits. We were wild and this was our playground. It was always good to relate our day's adventures in the evenings over sundowners.

Another unusual aspect of the camp was the continental restaurant and wonderful aura. Run by colonial Portuguese, the food, of course, too was Portuguese and scrumptious. The complimentary peri-peri chicken livers with big chunks of home-made Portuguese bread for dunking into the delicious rich gravy, to compliment the famous Manica beer; Peri-peri chickens to send your taste buds to a dizzy height and the same can be said for the prawns, oysters and other seafood, the port of Beira being in relatively close proximity.

Those were truly wonderful days where living came first and money took a back seat!

Footnote

In 2004 the government of Moçambique and the US-based philanthropist, Greg Carr signed a 20-year agreement to restore Gorongosa, its game count down by at least 95%, to its former glory and rebuild the park's infrastructure, its wildlife populations and spur local economic development, opening an important new chapter in the park's history. I was thrilled to have returned around about that time... that story you will find somewhere else in this book! – **GN**

Lubba Worms

Mike Ballantine

Many fishermen on their way to Kariba Lake buy small bags of earthworms from enterprising youngsters selling them on the side of the road before even reaching Karoi. Knowing that much of the shoreline is devoid of this precious bait we did likewise. But after a few days' fishing at Tashinga, a campsite in Matusadona National Park, we ran out of worms and resorted, less successfully, to various other tidbits.

Almost daily I dug here and there for them until I found a very small clew of worms near the ablution block. To ensure a regular catch of fresh fish I closely guarded my source. But that, too, became depleted. Then one day, while knee-deep in mud, on the banks of a nearby inlet digging for mussels, I felt what I at first thought was a root, only to unearth a giant earthworm. About a centimetre thick, it was some 40 centimetres in length – and almost double that if you stretched it! This could only be the legendary rubber-worm which locals hold in awe as I was soon to find out when a burly black man appeared on the scene.

Feeling like a thief I handed him a bottle of my prized beer which he promptly opened with his teeth, extraordinarily white and evidently very strong. With a broad grin he picked up the king-sized worm and, having difficulty differentiating between an 'r' and an 'l', he announced, '*lubba worm*', then enthusiastically proceeded to help me dig out a few more. I'd at last found the ideal bait.

Since then, given the opportunity, I've often boasted about my catch of six bream, about a kilogram each, on one earthworm! A story worth repeating as long as the worm's size is not revealed!

Friendship is honey - but don't eat it all – **African Proverb**

Fish Eagle Over Kariba

Colin (KK) Brown

Who fears the turning of the final page?
Not I!
For in that new Kariba dawn
Rising boldly crimson 'gainst life's fleeing, skulking, dying sky
As early ripples kiss lake's waters, smooth and warm
There'll be another Eagle, flying high
And, with pristine feathers tautly stretched 'gainst lofting winds
He'll join the rest - with childlike zest - to soar and swoop and glide
and cry
'Kaieee! Kaieee!'
And - far below - grey land-bound folks may faintly hear his distant
joy
And some may even pause, and turn
And wave a fond goodbye

Herpes

Greer Noble

Anyone who knows Kariba would have been to or at least heard of Spurwing, a dear little island across the lake and adjacent to the spectacular Matusadona National Park and mountain range.

On one of our many explorations on that magnificent lake, we'd tired of fishing, not having had a nibble in hours, and the day was too hot for game viewing so we decided to pay Spurwing a visit and enjoy whatever refreshments the lodge there had to offer. We edged towards the jetty and my daughter Carla jumped out to secure our small cabin cruiser to an iron mooring ring.

We suddenly became aware that we were being watched... intently. There, on the jetty stood one fearless, very expectant and rather forward goliath heron, all one and a half metres of him! He'd been busy trying to swallow a rather large rubber sandal which he now disdainfully discarded, clearly in hope of a better prospect. But when he saw the three of us disembark empty handed, he literally pranced off in disgust to another jetty from where, in the distance, a small fishing boat could be seen approaching. Haughty, he stood there pretending to ignore us but all the while, be it surreptitiously, he kept a beady yellow eye on us, until the new arrivals drew nearer, and at which time he lost complete interest in us.

Quite a remarkable specimen, we agreed that his audacity matched his size. He could have almost been regal if it wasn't for his knobbly-kneed, bandy black legs. Captivated nonetheless, we started arguing as to whether *he* was in fact a *she* when, trying to be nonchalant, he self-consciously started preening himself. My husband was soon outvoted when my daughter and I decided on a *he*, his characteristics being decidedly male, i.e. vain, arrogant and unshaven, with bits of tangled hair around his bald, greenish looking head.

Once at the bar, some distance away and out of sight of the jetty, curiosity got the better of me. I had to find out more about this huge, rather comical bird.

'Ah, you mean Herpes,' responded the manageress.

'Herpes?' I smiled quizzically, thinking I might have misheard.

'Yes,' she explained, *'he's called Herpes because he won't go away.'* Encouraged by our laughter, she continued. *'He waits all day for fishermen to come in with their catch and they've learnt to throw him a fish or he can get quite belligerent.'*

That explained everything. A clever bird at that, standing on the jetty waiting to be served, instead of foraging for hours in the dark murky water in the hopes that a fish might swim by, a game of hit and miss as he tries to jab it with his long, black, opened mandibles.

'*Highly territorial,*' she continued, an avid, be it amateur ornithologist herself, '*and heaven help another goliath or any other kleptoparasitism who comes anywhere near his beat!*'

'*Typical candidates being fish eagles and storks?* my husband offered.

'*Oh yes,*' she confirmed, '*they frequently pirate fish.*'

As we glided out of the harbour a few hours later, we all waved farewell to Herpes. With his long neck extended, he gave a loud '*kroo*' sound with a brief flap of the wings as if in reciprocation. We often talk about Herpes and later learnt that he'd abandoned Spurwing for the opposition, another nearby island lodge called Fothergill, frequented by more fishermen.

That was one spoilt, lazy, demanding and fickle feathered gentleman!

I never saw a wild thing sorry for itself. A small bird will drop frozen dead from a bough without ever having felt sorry for itself – **D. H. Lawrence**

Crocodiles' Inherent Fear

Rachel Lang

As an aspiring conservationist, I recognise the importance of appreciating all forms of life – the cute and the beautiful, the ugly and the ferocious. But, quite frankly, I have always found it most difficult to love crocodiles.

When I was a child I had a recurring nightmare in which I watched hopelessly as my dad got dragged into our dam and was devoured by an enormous croc. My fixation with J.M. Barry's *Peter Pan* may have added to my fear, especially when watching the theatre production with the larger-than-life tick-tocking croc biting off Captain Hook's hand.

Would it have been different if I could fly like Peter Pan? Recently, I had the unique experience of doing just that and it made me wonder whether crocodiles have nightmares too.

The icy air on my face made my eyes water as we walked to the airfield. The bush was still waking up and I tried hard to stifle a yawn. We casually made our way down a dust path surrounded by long yellow grass. Unbeknown to us, a pride of six lions was sleeping just a few metres away. With each step my excitement grew – I was about to fly with John Coppinger in his microlight over Zambia's beautiful South Luangwa National Park. John and Carol Coppinger own Remote Africa Safaris, fittingly named for this little piece of paradise. Knowing about John's vast flying experience, I could relax and enjoy every minute. I was in safe hands. As we took off, a hippo munched nonchalantly in the middle of the runway. *Only in Africa,* I thought. Once in the air, I was overcome with awe, my heart beating with the urgency of trying to take it all in. Surely this must be the most beautiful place in Africa!

I remember laughing at how funny the giraffes looked from above, with their legs splayed out awkwardly as they cantered in slow motion. We flew close enough to see a baby African fish-eagle in its nest – a complete novelty – as well as a giant eagle-owl, staring up at us, reflecting my own wide-eyed wonderment.

243

But I couldn't help noticing that none of the animals were particularly perturbed by us, except for the crocodiles! While the hippos lazed like immovable shiny boulders, their scaly neighbours took off like darts, every one of them shooting straight off the riverbanks and swimming wildly to the centre of the river as if their very lives depended on it. *'Why was this?'* I wondered. The Luangwa river is notorious for its monstrous crocodiles, but in the short moment that we flew over them, they were so helplessly vulnerable!

One explanation for this bizarre behaviour (inspired by the theories of John himself) is that perhaps the microlight reminds the crocs of the birds that tormented them as juveniles? Yes, birds – eagles, herons, marabou storks and ground-hornbills. Imagine for a moment that you are a new born crocodile, only 30 cm long, opening your eyes to the world for the first time.

After her eggs have hatched, a female crocodile carries her young, squeaking, in her mouth, to the water's edge and releases them to the reedy unknown where only one, maybe two, of the 50-plus hatchlings will survive. The rest will be eaten by by monitor lizards, otters, the odd hyena lurking at the water's edge and, you've guessed it – birds.

Although staring into the eyes and fake toothy smile of a croc is still pretty unnerving, I often look back at the microlight trip and smile to myself, knowing that crocs have a vulnerable side too. I spent the whole of breakfast that day trying to hide my joyful grin, not only because I'd been delighted to witness the soft side of crocs, but also because the entire experience from beginning to end had been truly dream-like.

We are all in a race for dear life: that is to say, we are fugitives from death.
Theodore Reik

Harbour Howard

Greer Noble

Among the phenomena in wildlife, Howard, an adult hippo, was definitely one! One day he (for all we knew 'he' could have been a 'she') turned up in the little harbour below our hotel, known then as Venture Cruises, and made it his home. This was a bit disconcerting at first as I taught water skiing to guests and, weather permitting, tended to ski myself most days. So as long as Howard kept to the harbour area it wouldn't be too bad, I tried to convince myself.

We'd built a skiing jetty anchored some distance from the lake shore to avoid getting bilharzia, a parasite that lived in snails around the water's edge which needed a human host to complete its nasty, invasive cycle by penetrating the skin and multiplying in the bloodstream. The snail, in turn, thrived off water hyacinth, a prolific grower and itself a menace and alien to the lake, clogging inlets suffocating fish and other water creatures. While easily curable, bilharzia could be deadly if undetected and untreated. The actual treatment itself was thought to be damaging to the liver and kidneys.

Howard, it turned, out had a beautiful nature. My father threw him a cabbage or two every day from the end of the long pier which protected the boats in our harbour. This became a ritual and eventually somewhat of an attraction for our guests.

A young Hollander, who'd just landed himself the job as our new barman, one day dived off the pier and enthusiastically swam out to Howard, mistaking his friendliness as if he were the family pet. Thank heavens our coxswains working on the fishing boats in the harbour quickly alerted my father who came tearing down, shouting at Gerhard to get out of the water at once. Bewildered and hurt he did so, only later understanding the immense danger in which he'd put himself.

This amiable relationship with Howard and my father continued for some years but every time I skied, not knowing where Howard might be, I made quite sure I took off and landed right back on the skiing jetty. Needless to say I became quite expert at it but had to put off

246

those wanting skiing lessons as we could no longer guarantee their safety. While Howard was relatively tame, he was still an unpredictable wild animal that needed to be respected.

For some time Howard had been hanging out with our ducks, the harbour being their home too. As they were domestic ducks they had to be securely housed every night to protect them against predators such as leguaan, Africa's large amphibious monitor lizard, and civets, small lithe-bodied nocturnal cats whose musky scent is, interestingly, used in perfumery.

One day, on inspecting a new retaining wall that was being built above the harbour to reclaim land, thereby extending the area between the top swimming pool and the lake, my father witnessed the most remarkable sight.

He'd been keeping half an eye on a martial eagle circling high above the harbour area. Distinguishable from other eagles by its massive two metre wingspan, it suddenly stooped sharply and lunged to where the ducks were paddling. Amazingly, with one bite, Howard snapped it in half.

Sue Maas

My father stood dumbfounded. Amused at and admiring Howard's tremendous loyalty demonstrated by his gallant action in protecting his friends, he was also saddened at the demise of this magnificent and incredibly powerful bird. The largest of the African eagles and capable of knocking over an adult man, it was extremely vulnerable, having suffered great losses at the hands of farmers shooting and or poisoning them, believing them to be a threat to their livestock. Other threats were power-line collisions, the steep sides of farm reservoirs, causing them to drown, and the systematic destruction of their habitat – yet another example of how progress is the nemesis of nature.

All the same Howard was a hero and the hotel mascot. In time he became a legend... until one day... when a notorious character arrived on the scene. Showing off in his new power boat to the thrill of his admiring followers, he suddenly spotted Howard who'd surfaced to see what the commotion was about. Before the coxswains could stop this menacing cowboy, he proceeded to play cat and mouse with poor old Howard, trying to run him down every time the old chap surfaced, encouraged by the raucous cheering of his drunken fans. The water in the harbour churned as if hit by a hurricane, the jetty tossed this way and that, straining at its mooring, all the boats rocked, colliding into each other and the ducks took off towards the shoreline in fright, scurrying into the reeds for cover. Howard was nowhere to be seen.

That night there was one of those torrential downpours when the heavens open their floodgates. The next morning we had reports from Mopani Bay Campsite, further along the lake on the far side of Cutty Sark, our neighbouring hotel. According to their night watchman a *penga* (crazy) lone hippo had chomped several of their canoes in half. It was Howard, of that we were certain.

Had he been hit by the cowboy's attack, had he been injured, cut by the boat's propeller and taken it out on those canoes or was he just afraid and angry? We will never know but sadly he never returned... and nor did the cowboy! He was the only person ever to be banned from our hotel. Times like that, I really do prefer animals to humans.

Action is the real measure of intelligence – **Napoleon Hill**

Bewitched

Bart Wolffe

The boy's skin was wet. A matt of unkempt hair covered his ears, clung to his neck. Sweat beaded his sunburnt nose and the noise and movement in the undergrowth at the river's edge betrayed his presence to the snakes and water monitors that slid away and crashed through the spiked reeds into the Marodzi River.*

He brushed aside the tangled branches of river growth, to allow himself passage, stumbling momentarily on a water-polished rock, black and smooth, but swiftly regained his footing, found himself panting with excitement and thirst in the heat of the African day.

It was the holidays and boarding school was very far away. At least another three weeks before he went back, a victim to incarceration among the bullies and the books. Now, at least, nature unfolded its pages for him to discover the adventure before him. Weaver birds darted from their nests that overhung the spilling waterfall, flitting through the surrounding greenery about his head. The sounds of the currents sang and played, coursing forward downriver. It was a magnet that drew him to the old road bridge which stood astride the flow, broken in parts, but still solid enough among the rocks.

Here, the village girls came to pound their washing on the smooth stone. Here, they bathed, young breasts exposed at one with the wild and the caressing touch of the sun. This world was lost to the machinery of time, moved with the seasons, a brown dream of river and earth between the overhanging banks that held the Marodzi to its liquid path.

They giggled and pointed at the white boy who looked on. Something caused him not to hide. He represented no threat, felt no fear. He was the snake boy, the one who had a strange way of plucking the emerald green coils from the branches like fruit. It was as if he belonged to this world of free creatures and creation's children.

This river had a particular smell, a taste, a familiarity for him. It spoke and revealed itself; the small fish that swirled and circled in its pools, the fresh-water crabs scuttling from an upturned stone, the myriad birds along its way, the unexpected revelations as some startled animal crashed out of sight at the interruption of the visitor who explored the muddy spirit world moving on and on, through trembled reeds, past islands in its journey, carved through steep banks that exposed the roots of trees.

Even when he lay in his bed at night, the Marodzi would call him in his dreams.

'Come back soon. I am waiting for you like a mother for her child.'

And tomorrow's sunrise woke the river with light and colour, ready to feast his senses with the new day's welcome once more. His childhood soon passed but the memory of this river would always run hidden like secret bilharzia in the blood beneath his skin.

That boy is me.

* Marodzi River – in the old Rhodesia – now Zimbabwe

The Dough Boys

Sue Maas

Sue Maas

Fresh bread was made daily in Kariba and like most people we loved to be at the bakery just as it was coming out of the ovens onto the cooling racks before being distributed.

The bakery was on top of the mountain in the village overlooking the lake and because of this the bush came almost to the door. Due to the heat in Kariba the bakers would load the rack with the fresh bread and place it close to the exit door, presumably to cool in the breeze.

Soon the resident troop of baboons cottoned onto this practice, albeit short-lived, and realised that these delicious loaves were there for the taking. They could be seen leaping into the trees close by with arms full of bread, then sit and eat it right in front of the irate bakers! No amount of shouting and banging of pots and pans would put them off.

251

Mixed Emotions

Tamsin Williams

Some of my travel companions thought I was mad but spending long nights just sitting at the floodlit waterholes at the rest camps in Etosha National Park in Namibia was my idea of a good night out.

This particular night was especially thrilling. - a pride of young lions stopped for a drink at the waterhole and were soon on their way again but thinking of them being so close while I slept in my tent was so exciting!

It was quiet for a long time after the lions left, just a couple of water birds poking about in the shallow water. Then the silence was shattered by the sound of panting. Something big was out there, huffing and puffing and grunting like an old steam engine. I couldn't imagine what it could be and those of us there looked at one another without speaking - what was it?

Out of the surrounding bush burst the same lions - and in their midst a young rhino. The lions were trying to jump onto the rhino and bite it. But each time they tried to gain a hold on his body the rhino would find the strength to lunge at them. Only they were determined to down their prey and continued circling and jumping. This truly was a battle of strengths.

My emotions were in turmoil. Part of me wanted to witness a real live lion kill, I am not ashamed to say. The other part of me was screaming *'Stop, stop, let him go! He's an endangered species!'* (Quite what difference that made, I'm still not sure). The battle raged on for what felt like an eternity and then something in the lions' behaviour changed. Their body language suggested they were nervous and their attacks on the rhino stopped.

Out of the darkness crashed a larger rhino - mum! She charged the lions, her horn dangerously close to gouging those slower to respond.

The lions scarpered and mum went over to her son, greeting him with concern. He was panting and had a few cuts but was fine otherwise. They sniffed noses. A German woman sat next to me turned to me and said: '*I'm crying!*' I knew how she felt.

Exhausted by the emotions of what I'd witnessed, I decided to go to my tent and made my way up the dark path to the camping area alone. Mulling over what I'd seen, I suddenly stopped dead in my tracks, my heart thumping in my chest as I heard a long, low growl. Oh Christ. The lions didn't get the rhino so they'd jumped the fence to find an easier meal. I stood stock-still, I didn't dare breathe and didn't dare move. What should I do? If I ran, they'd charge at me. Never have I felt so exposed and vulnerable. No one was around, no one knew I was here, no one could help me. I heard another growl.....then another.....and I dared to move a tiny bit to try and see where the lions were. I looked to my right only to see I was standing next to a yellow tent. As another growl echoed in the night I began to laugh with sheer relief - the lions weren't after me, the growling was coming from the tent's occupant, fast asleep and snoring like a lion!

A charging black rhinoceros is nothing to mess with. When it is headed straight toward you, it is the ultimate exercise in sphincter control.
Boyd Norton

Why?

Greer Noble

We introduced our son Michael to the wilds when he was two years old. Our Land Rover with its two roof-top tents became his jungle-gym, the bush his playground. He would carve up anthills (rather scary as we later discovered they are the favourite abode of the most aggressive and venomous African snake, the black mamba), climb trees, fish, dig for worms and collect insects. He was a delight on these trips and enjoyed them as much as we did, if not more so. But like some little boys he was fearless which was a bit unnerving.

On one occasion, at one of the seven natural wonders of the world, Victoria Falls, he disappeared at the crocodile farm – not a good place to lose your child. We'd been looking into a pen when he suddenly vanished. My blood ran cold. To my horror I discovered the next pen had a gap in the fence - one of the upright railway sleepers which served to fence these enclosures had fallen inward, making an ideal slot for a little two year old to slip through. And sure enough, there he was, standing no further that a metre from their prized croc, a nineteen footer, with its mouth wide open, sunning itself.

My husband, mustering his sternest voice, hissed, *'Stay right where you are, don't move!'*

'Why?' came the indignant response, *'he's sleeping.'*

Before I could blink my husband leaped over the fence, lifted our son by his collar, ran back and handed him to me over the fence.

Later, one of the staff there demonstrated what a 'sleeping' croc was capable of doing. In another enclosure we all stood on a bridge looking down on much younger basking crocs. The handler took a long broom-stick and lightly tapped a 'sleeping' croc, with jaws wide open, on the snout. With lightning speed, too quick for the eye, the croc had snapped the broom-stick in two as if it were a dry twig. Our son's eyes widened in disbelief and we hoped that he was suitably impressed.

Then not long after that hair-raising incident, we were pushed to set up camp in the Savuti area late one afternoon, it being our cardinal rule to do so while there was still daylight. We preferred to camp away from the designated camp sites – that was before the authorities became such sticklers about it – and where there were no elephant paths. That was another lesson we learnt the hard way – never camp between water pans and avoid camping on game paths. That's the theory but in practice it's not always possible. This was one of those times. Light was fading fast as it does that time of the evening, and there were paths crisscrossing everywhere. All we could do was choose a lesser used one and hope for the best.

We had camping down to a fine art. Our Land Rover had a self-designed interior, modelled after a miniature I made out of cardboard and matchsticks. There were inside drawers for all our groceries, cutlery and crockery; built-in water-tanks; extra fuel tank; gas fridge; table and chairs that slid out easily; roof-top tents; and a hatch over the front seats for game viewing and emergencies.

Within a few minutes we'd deploy our tents, slide out the table and chairs from behind our bench seat and make a fire... and when in designated camps as opposed to the wild bush, often be the envy of other campers slaving away, setting up their camps.

This time we hadn't even started our camp fire when I happened to look up. An unusually large elephant plodded towards us... with our son running to meet it. I froze. They come so quietly and so suddenly... and that we were clearly in its path was bad enough but to see our two year-old run up to it was terrifying.

Again his father called loudly, in the sternest of voices, *'Michael! Come back here... AT ONCE!'*

Again came the interminable *'Why?'* The cheek of it, hands on hips, totally fearless.

'Because it's very dangerous and can hurt you!' his father firmly reasoned.

With that this little mite turned around, faced us and, punching the air with his little fist said, *'No it won't, I'll bouf him!'*

Maybe elephants instinctively know that a child is no threat because thankfully, it suddenly veered off and took another path.

'See!' remonstrated our son believing that by his mere action he'd scared it off.

The question is, are we happy to suppose that our grandchildren may never be able to see an elephant except in a picture book? **David Attenborough**

Saved by a Bedroll?

Lloyd Wilmot

I was camped at Makutchom-wa-bokhuto on a tributary of the Santantadibe river in the Okavango area of Botswana a few years ago. A crowd of us including my children and some of their high school friends were among the party. With game-viewing, fishing and swimming everyone had a great time. The kids seemed to have endless energy so when I bid an early *goodnight* after supper I was called a *fader* and a *party-pooper*. I didn't mind. With a good book, a headlamp to read by and a comfortable bedroll in my small tent I was soon settled. Outside, the chatting and laughing around the fire went on about thirty yards away. After a couple of chapters I dozed off.

Sometime well into the night I was suddenly woken by two loud slaps against my tent. I sprang up in bed thinking the kids were playing a prank. Sitting in the dark I listened carefully but could hear nothing. Then my tent moved. Fumbling in the dark I found my headlamp and switched on. Something was pressing against the tent above my pillow. I thought perhaps a feeding elephant had accidentally stepped back but there was no sound. Quietly unzipping my tent I stepped outside and peered round the back. There, staring back at me was an emaciated leopard holding my bedroll in his claws trying to pull it through the unyielding tent.

In the light I could see a major bite wound on his right upper leg. The poor devil had obviously been in a fight and was starving to death. He must have heard me snoring and tried to seize me through the canvas.

Tip-toeing away I went to wake one of the guests to come see. On my return he was gone but there were tracks and other evidence of his struggle. The following morning the vervet monkeys spotted him and we drove out for a better look. He sprang from his hiding place with a heavy limp and his appalling condition moved us all to pity

Without a firearm we had to let nature take its course. Everyone was warned to be alert but he was never seen again.

Souls will be forever bound by the love of Srimati Maya Devi. Limited duration bodies are shadows of our eternally shape-shifting selves – **Vedas**

A Close Shave

Rob Fynn

One morning, on the last lap of our game walk around the island,* strolling down the airstrip, smelling breakfast cooking, we spotted a breeding herd of elephant in the scrub mopane, next to the shoreline plain. We hadn't seen any previously, so diverted to have a closer look.

Approaching to within 50m along a game trail, a gentle breeze coming from the herd, we positioned ourselves nicely downwind. My clients lined up to take photos, the lake in the back ground, a herd of impala warming in the early morning light. A perfect picture. I cautioned everyone to be particularly quiet, recognising the pointy-tusked matriarch as one for having a short fuse.

One of the party coughed, that awful tickle rising in his throat just when he knew he shouldn't let it out. Without the slightest hesitation, the feeding matriarch, not having heard or seen us up to that point, lowered her head and charged straight for the sound, her herd of two cows and three youngsters close behind her. I yelled for everybody to run back up the path, bringing up the rear myself. A portly couple were not making sufficient speed. I could hear the elephants crashing through the trees, closing the gap. Another couple decided they'd be better off running away from our slow moving group. Things were getting chaotic.

Glancing over my shoulder, trying to chivvy the portly couple along, I saw the matriarch break through onto our path – twenty metres behind me. In full charge, head down, clearly intent on skewering somebody. We were not going to get away. I stopped, turned and fired.

She fell crumpling onto the ground at my feet, my boot caught under her head. As we moved away, the rest of the herd gathered round her, trying to resuscitate their leader. Giving us a chance to regroup and retreat.

Mortified at having to take down such a gallant stalwart, who did her job of protecting her herd so well, and had lost her life because of our clumsiness, I was sombrely unresponsive to the excited chatter and questioning of my clients as we made our way home. Somehow, breakfast had lost its flavour.

*island – Lake Kariba where the Fynn's had their bush camp island named Fothergill

A king who always cares for the elephants like his own sons is always victorious and will enjoy the friendship of the celestial world after death
Kautiliya, scholar of Buddhism in India

Shakawe to Savuti

Greer Noble

S ometimes we do crazy things in life... this is one of them.

'Of course you should go, that's what Land Rovers are for,' encouraged Eileen and Jan Drotsky of Drotsky Cabins in the Okavango delta of Botswana.

They were right of course, only we had hoped their three German guests with two late-model 4x4s would join us. Perhaps put off by our almost vintage series 2 Land Rover they changed their minds at the last minute opting to head for Kasane via Maun on the well-trodden road instead.

After allowing for contingencies Mike, my husband, estimated it could take as much as four days to do some 275 kms to Savuti camp and needed some way to get help were we to break down. Jan said he'd radio Lloyd Wilmot, Eileen's brother who had Lloyd's Camp at Savuti, the plan being that if we hadn't arrived by the fourth day, he could at least fly over our intended route in his small plane to look for us. Eileen and Jan had been so good to us, what amazing hosts.

Early next morning we said our goodbyes and, on a nearby ferry, just big enough for a car, we crossed the Okavango, at that point about 100 to 150 metres wide. Heading south-east along but not in sight of the river we quickly covered some 80 to 90 kilometres without incident until we ran out of road when we reached the first village where all the villagers crowded around our vehicle as if they'd never seen one before.

There being no discernible road to the next village, a young man offered to show us the way and sat on the bonnet. Stretching out his leg like a ballerina, he proceeded to point with his toe, using it to indicate the direction he wanted us to take. This took a bit of getting used to and if the vehicle didn't respond instantly, his leg went quite wild as if doing some weird mid-air ritual. Needless to say the three of us – we had our young son with us – were doubled up with laughter, so much so, we nearly wet ourselves.

261

At the second village we were shown a track which was quite distinctive even though the elephant grass was taller than our vehicle. Many miles on, now on our own again, we came to a third village, only this village was totally deserted. It was as if everyone had just vanished leaving their maze crushers and various other paraphernalia used in a typical African kraal. It was quite eerie. I remembered a friend, when flying commercial aircraft over Africa, telling me he had often spotted deserted villages and I wondered if this was one of them. He thought they may have been wiped out by some killer disease.

Very soon after that the track became waterlogged; a real swampy area, too deep to take any chances. We skirted this and after jacking a rear wheel out of a mud-hole with nothing but a plastic bag full of cans to support the jack, there being no foliage or rocks in the area, eventually made it to the other side.

Then we were at a loss as to which way to go next. It was still early on in the day so by compass we headed off in the general direction until we reached a wooded area. That was more of a challenge as the trees were confusing. I sat on the roof and tried to guide Mike, doing the same ballerina antics with my toe as our previous guide had done. But, when the one driving is hard of hearing... and the one on top is short sighted... OK, you get the picture. I had a stick and was supposed to bang on the door if I saw a problem.

The problem came – this place was fraught with hurdles – on a downward slope. I beat the door so hard the stick snapped but Mike still didn't hear... and we sailed into one of the worst black cotton mud dips ever. It literally sucks you in. Light was fading so we had to work fast. We were also in a thicket of tangled thorn bushes and Mike had to literally hack his way out through a partially open door with a panga, broad-bladed knife. In fact he had to clear around the entire vehicle as we couldn't get out our side either.

'*The Lord works in mysterious ways,*' I couldn't resist. Mike was not partial to gardening. Normally he would have responded with some wise crack but what with being scratched, the hacking, the heat and now the mosquitos, wave after wave of them, saps you of everything, including your sense of humour. Then to top it all, I hear a little voice behind.

'Daddy, daddy, look! A pretty snake!'

'Snake! Where's the snake my boy?' asks his father nervously, his rapid eye movement taking in everything around him. But it had vanished... which was worse. It made the task a little more onerous.

At last, mission accomplished highlift-jack in place, resting on branches cut from around the vehicle – we were ready to roll. Rather than drop the jack and reverse gently, Mike decided it would be better to 'gun it' off the jack. In theory it sounded feasible... but in reality... well it came out as planned but... straight back into another quagmire behind us.

'That's it, we are going to have to spend the night here,' there was a tone to Mike's voice that intimated, *'Don't even think about challenging me'.*

We weren't even on the level and nor could we open our rooftop tents. But I could see that Mike's 'gardening' had exhausted him and, in any event it was getting too dark to do anything. I made our son comfortable on a mattress in the back while we sat up much of the night sipping neat Scotch as we couldn't even get to our food or our little gas cooker to at least make coffee or soup. It was also stiflingly hot but we had to keep the windows shut to ward off the mosquitos – they were possibly the meanest and hungriest we'd ever come across. Needless to say it was one of the worst nights of our lives... and certainly one of the most uncomfortable. At first light, with perseverance, we eventually escaped our entanglement and headed off once again, our spirits lifted.

'See that tree over there,' Mike pointed to a tree that stood out from the rest. I nodded. *'Keep directing me towards it and that should put us on the right track.'*

I enthusiastically sat on top again, doing my single-legged ballet act but oh dear, the next thing I looked and, being short-sighted, all the trees seemed to have merged. I could not distinguish one from the other but didn't have the heart to tell Mike so just continued to point my big toe in the direction I thought looked right.

Eventually we came out into a clearing and saw car tracks!

Hurray, some fellow humanoids! However, on closer inspection we discovered they were our own tyre marks. Then close by, we came across the site we'd used a bag of cans for freeing ourselves from the mud-hole.

'You realise we've come full circle, don't you?' Mike exclaimed.

'Oh no!' I groaned. I couldn't believe it. We'd wasted almost an entire day!

This time we tried a different route and found ourselves in a mopane forest.

'I'm going to have a look around... just stay near the vehicle and if I'm not back in ten minutes start hooting so I can find my way back.'

I wasn't happy. And it wasn't wildlife I was worried about – that was another weird thing, since we'd left Shakawe we had not spotted a single wild animal. My son and I waited. Every minute seemed like an hour as I watched them ticking by. Even if we had cellular phones, and we didn't, there wouldn't have been a signal out there in the middle of nowhere anyway.

At last the ten minutes up... I was about to start honking the horn when Mike appeared. What a relief.

'I think I know the way.' There had been higher ground and he was able to see quite far. *'Still no road but if we keep going in this direction we should be OK.'*

Again I sat on top armed with stick. Mercifully the going got smoother. Then quite suddenly we came out onto a plain and actually drove right *over* a track. This time I really banged and shouted. Mike had seen it too. It seemed to be the track we were looking for and we followed it for miles and miles. We even saw a beacon but there should have been a track off to the left which we could not find despite backtracking on several occasions.

There was nothing for it but to continue on the track we were on until eventually and completely unexpectedly, we found ourselves on a well maintained gravel airstrip... not a soul in sight.

'Where on earth are we?' Neither of us had a clue. We crossed the

strip and came out onto an amazing wide gravel road. It was surreal – so much so that for a moment I thought I was dreaming.

We followed this intriguing road for a relatively short distance when it veered left. There, low and behold, was a tiered commercial game-viewing vehicle packed with tourists – the first humans we'd seen in days. Strategically parked on the side of the road, they were gazing at a well patronised water-hole, teeming with game.

Mike stopped and spoke to the driver. *'Please tell us... where is this?'* Any other time we would have felt foolish, but we were beyond foolish.

Never mind the teeming game, everyone's eyes were now on us. We hadn't bathed, shaved, changed our clothes or combed our hair in days and must have looked like we'd been pulled though the bush backwards... while they were in designer safari gear and had, no doubt, just stepped out of their luxury, en-suite, designer tents.

'This is Kwai, sir. We are from Kwai River Lodge and these are our guests from America.'

We couldn't believe it... we were actually at Kwai! By the looks on their faces I don't think the Americans could believe it either because they'd completely lost interest in the game!

'How far to Savuti?' Mike wanted to know. The only full jerry can of petrol we had left we'd earlier funnelled into our tank. Having had no option but to drive much of the way in low-range gear, our petrol gauge was on red.

'About 100 kilometres, sir.'

I'll never forget the looks on their faces and felt sure the conversation at dinner that night was going to be about a different kind of 'wildlife'!

Light was fading fast and after some 70 kilometres I started to watch the fuel gauge.

'Is the needle still moving?' Mike kept asking.

'Yes, it's still moving.'

It finally became static just before we limped into Savuti camp with perhaps half a cup of petrol to spare.

After well-deserved showers, a hot meal and a wonderful sleep, the next morning we went across to Lloyd Wilmot to let him know we'd arrived. He very kindly sold us sufficient petrol to get us to Kasane... to where we headed a few days later.

How lucky we were! For us it was an adventure that taught us a lot more about survival... and ourselves.

There is nothing more thrilling to me than an impromptu safari into unchartered territories of the African wilderness – **GN**

The Thunder Box

Sue Maas

When we began building Tiger Bay high up on the banks of the Umi River which flows into Lake Kariba, Zimbabwe was still known as Rhodesia. It was wild country and we and our partners had to rough it under the open skies with an enormous tarpaulin as shelter until we had built the first chalets. With six of us sharing the shelter, we positioned one couple at either end with our two small children in the middle.

Top of the list were ablution facilities so a respectable enclosure was built out of walls of crisscrossed saplings and thatching grass. It was then divided into two sections, the one commonly known as a long-drop, we fondly named the thunder box. It sported a comfortable wooden toilet seat and an umbrella which was a godsend in the midday sun when one needed to contemplate the niceties of life. Of assistance in these matters was a large pile of magazines, a tin of chlorine (the air freshener), and toilet rolls on a stick. Later we added a handsome silver toilet roll cover in the form of an empty 1kg jam tin to protect the paper when it rained.

Our shower cubicle comprised a 20 litre bucket attached to an ingenious pulley system that swung up and out from a 44 gallon drum of water placed over a fire, the authentic 'Rhodesian Boiler'. The bucket had a shower rose with a tap attached to it so when it was anchored in place by tying the rope to a hook the bucket provided a warm shower at just the right temperature - very sophisticated for the wild African bush!

Later when the camp was completed our beautiful ablution block was demolished and my other half, in his normal practical way, decided the thunder box should be suitably remembered by planting a grove of pawpaw trees over it! I wonder if they're still there?

The first dust-dispersing drop, that earthy-scent, a pitter-patter crescendo spurred by God's electric lash, then a massive flash ignites the night sky as great rumblings unleash torrents of pure sweet water – aah, Africa! – **GN**

Fearless Muzungus

Bob Shacochis

On a sun-broiled morning in central Mozambique, we headed thirty kilometres into the bush, our destination a shrinking stretch of soupy pool, one of the last remaining catchments in the drought-withered river where the hippos had hunkered down during the wasting days of a dry season that refused to end. Afterward we would be choppering to other sites – remote wonders, unique to the area. The limestone gorge perhaps, where the Rift Valley arrived at its southern terminus? The lacy cascade of waterfalls off the westward escarpment? The cathedral-size grottos housing countless clouds of whispering bats?

Because of the heat, and I guess for the breezy fun of it, Segren, the young pilot from South Africa, unhinged the front doors off the R44, a Bell-manufactured helicopter aviators call a little bird, and the four of us ascended skyward from the small grass airstrip at Chitengo, the headquarters of Gorongosa National Park, once considered among Africa's premier game reserves until it was destroyed by decades of an unimaginably brutal war and savage lawlessness and its bountiful population of animals slaughtered, eaten and reduced to a wistful memory.

From the co-pilot seat, the veld ironed out into a haze of coastal plains spread east toward the Indian Ocean through my unrestricted view. I adjusted the mike on my headset and joined the conversational squawk behind me, Greg Carr and Vasco Galante stuffed into the rear seats, already sweaty between doors that couldn't be removed.

Greg and Vasco, it was becoming clear to me, were fearless; a matching set of *muzungus*, white men, with a true affinity for the bush. Like Greg Carr, the American philanthropist who had committed his time, wealth and energy to the restoration of Gorongosa, Galante too was a successful entrepreneur who slammed the brakes on the life he was living, made a U-turn and went to Africa.

Many of their sentences began, '*During the rainy season,*' and I would be directed toward something in the landscape that was not as it should be this deep into December – the evaporated Lake Urema, shrunk from two hundred square kilometres to ten; a wilting Gorongosa massif and its deplenished watershed; the burning flood plains of the savannah.

At Greg's instruction, Segren navigated toward the platinum thread of the Urema River emptying from the traumatized lake into the dusty jungle. The helicopter dipped down into the river's high-banked channel and roared along its downstream course at tree-top level, my companions remarking upon the bed's sorry condition – black patches of dampness embroidered with a fringe of hoof prints, scum puddles churned by expiring catfish and, increasingly, weed-clogged runs.

Some years ago, when CBS came to Mozambique to produce a feature on Carr and Gorongosa, the hottest conservation story in Africa, as they filmed the river from the air scores of Nile crocodiles flipped one after another off the banks into its robust current.

Maybe there were some crocs down there now but we couldn't see them. It was Africa's flamboyant birds who now owned the desiccated river. Egyptian geese, grotesque marabou storks showcasing the ass-bald head and plucked neck of carrion eaters, graceful herons and lanky crowned cranes, majestic fish eagles.

Then we were hovering over the upstream edge of the pool, a squiggle of crocodiles visible in the khaki water, and Greg pointed to a grassy bar about three hundred metres back where he wanted to put down. On the ground, Segren said he would stay behind and keep the engine running.

This was my first time in Africa but even before Vasco's warning, I realized we were in elephant country, their rampant footprints shin-deep in the hardening cake of fertile soil, an ankle-twisting hazard. I had also registered Vasco's sudden intensity of manner, the heightened alertness, his head rotating as he scrutinized our surroundings. *'Okay,'* he said, trying to sound light-hearted, *'this is a place where elephants come. If you see an elephant coming from the north, you go south. Turn and go.'*

Although more people are killed by hippos than any other wild animal in Africa, the remaining elephants of Gorongosa were unforgiving. For generations they had been engaged in a kill-or-be-killed war with humans, once prolific herds decimated by rebel soldiers harvesting ivory to finance their insurgency or gathering a windfall of meat for their cadres or just being gunned down for the wicked hell of it. By the end of Mozambique's civil war in 1992, only three hundred of an elephant population ten times larger were left alive, and those three hundred, according to National Geographic cameraman who had been filming in the park for a year, were *'skittish and aggressive.'* If you were on foot, as we were, walking into an elephant's range of smell or sight could be justifiably categorized as suicidal. But as we approached the pool, crocodiles and land-foraging hippo were a more immediate and tangible concern.

Greg and Vasco climbed higher for a better vantage point to scout downriver and, I suspected, to be better positioned in case of a charge. In the wild the ancient primal verities still apply. Extreme caution and mild anxiety translate as ingrained virtues, rational responses toward the perilous unknown, yet once Greg and Vasco trained their binoculars on the water, I could feel the tension in the air undergo a euphoric meltdown. Hippos! Exactly where they should be according to their birth right, at peace in their own habitat... after being wiped out completely, 3500 of them, during the endless war.

The pilot, for a reason known only to him, had shut down the engine. Occupied by the marvel of the half-submerged pod, we simply noticed an improvement in the depth of the silence around us and made no mention of it. There we stood, spellbound and revering, allowed by the moment to believe in an endemic world so harmoniously, benevolently perfect, one forgets to remember that the most readily available dish on the menu might very well be us.

The glory of the hippo seems shaped by bizarre hallucinogenic juxtapositions–the utility of its rounded amphibious design packaged in the exaggerated ugliness only seen elsewhere in cartoons; its blob-like massiveness adorned with undersized squirrel ears and stubby legs, bullfrog eyes that are nevertheless beady, pinkish peg-toothed jaws like a steam-shovel. We were enthralled, flies on the wall of hippo heaven. Then we withdrew, back to the helicopter, which maybe had a problem. But dreamy and high with hippo love, we didn't much care.

We climbed in, Segren muttered something about weak batteries, we climbed out.

'I don't think I'd let my mom ride in this helicopter,' said Greg. He and I walked upriver and sat cross-legged across from baboons collecting on the far bank, remarking on what we could figure out about the tribe's hierarchy and habits, occasionally extrapolating our insights into opinions about the monkeyshines of the primates on Wall Street, the two of us content and carefree.

Then Vasco walked down the bank to tell us what we had already suspected – the helicopter wasn't going to get us out of here – and even then we greeted our predicament as a frivolous interruption to an otherwise magnificent day. But we were in no-man's land since no one knew of the fix we were in, let alone where, exactly, to come looking.

There was a boyish brightness in Greg's eyes when he suggested

272

we cross the river and hump all day through the forge-like heat of the primordial jungle into the happy zone of cell phone reception to text the cavalry.

'So what do you guys think?' Greg pondered. *'Wanna walk?'*

Vasco and I looked at one another and shrugged. We were not bound to see much indecisiveness from Carr, a man whose permanent optimism was exceeded only by his irrepressible, well-aimed and sometimes kooky enthusiasm (like plopping down on a restaurant floor to do push-ups).

I asked if either one of them had the foresight to bring along a sidearm...*'you know, just in case.'* Greg said no and Vasco showed me the miniature penknife he carried in his pocket. I was the only one with gear, a shoulder bag crammed with nothing useful except our water bottles. To lighten the load I removed a book, William Finnegan's chronicle of Mozambique's civil war and tried to give it to Segren who did not want it. But regardless of his schoolboy's distaste for reading, the book stayed.

For several kilometres we hiked upstream along a game trail flattened through the grass, the river bed still glazed with stagnant water beneath a lush carpet of weeds, an ideal habitat for lurking crocodiles as advertised by the warthog carcass we hurried past.

Further on Greg convinced himself conditions had become favourable for a clean and effortless crossing. *'Let's try it,'* he said and I watched in horror as he and Vasco took six steps out into what I assumed was quicksand, their legs disappearing in a steady downward suck. I responded in the manner most typical of 21st century Americans, grabbing my camera to record the flailing of their last astonished moments. It was a bog of liquefied silt. They bottomed out crotch deep and eventually extracted themselves from the goop, though in a matter of minutes Greg plunged into another bog. This time as he struggled free he noticed that wherever a plant with tiny yellow flowers grew the bed would support his weight and farther on we came to a place where the yellow flowering zigzagged across the channel. In an instant Greg race-walked toward the far shore as if he were trying to beat oncoming traffic. I had begun to learn Greg's momentum was an indomitable force, at times imprudent, and uninhibited by ambivalence. Certain now that what we were doing was crazy, I resigned myself to the crossing.

We scrambled up a natural drainage chute carved into the bank, found the seldom-used safari track we had hoped was there and followed it back downstream for three kilometres, a stretch where several days later Vasco and I would find elephants coming up off the river, and a hippo cow and calf napping in the bush not ten metres from where we now walked. Then the track turned away from the river into the windless, stifling heart of the jungle and we were soon inhaling intense fumes of the unforgettable leathery piss odour of wild Africa.

For the first kilometre the trees were stripped, smashed, toppled over, leaf-eating pachyderms passing through like a tornado and we became instant students of their mounded dung, studying the colour and relative dryness to determine the herd's proximity. '*Just keep talking*,' Greg said hopefully and whenever our conversation flagged, I would loudly announce to the jungle that we were, in fact, still talking.

We walked with relentless determination, which is how one walks when Greg Carr sets the pace and you intend to keep up with him, although after an hour it was evident that we lacked sufficient water to stay hydrated. Sweating profusely in jeans and leather boots, I envied my companions' bwana shorts and minimalist footwear – Jesus sandals for Vasco, preppy sockless boat shoes for Greg – the current muzungu styles for a jaunt through the goddamn jungle.

The second hour, Vasco and I began to drag our feet ever so slightly, the monotonous slog of the trek contradicting its urgency. Greg, on the other hand, was having a terrific time, supernaturally energized to be shipwrecked in the middle of nowhere, an opportunity flush with the thrill of rule-breaking, and by the third hour, as my need for two-minute breaks became more frequent, he would shuffle restlessly, unable to stand still as Vasco and I squatted in the shade, parched and mindless.

Our slow-down finally summoned Greg's inner antsy child and he suggested we stay put while he went on alone searching for the elusive cell phone signal. No way, Vasco and I protested. Our pride would not allow it and we stuck together for a couple more kilometres until, on the verge of heatstroke, it became painfully obvious that our pride wasn't quite the virtue we had imagined.

We shook hands, wished Greg god speed, and watched his blithe disappearance around a bend in the track, wondering what body parts he might be missing if we ever saw him again.

The late afternoon sun had begun to splinter into golden beams, planting shadows in the jungle and, unable to depend on the success of Greg's solo mission, we began walking again, our pace marginally faster than zombies. After a way Vasco snatched up a long stick.

'*What's that for?*' I asked a bit dubiously.

'*Just in case,*' he said. '*For animals.*'

Minutes passed in silence and I kept thinking I should pocket one of the occasional rocks I saw in the track. '*Vasco,*' I said, '*what kind of animals are you going to hit with that stick?*'

'*You never know,*' he said and we both laughed at this absurdity.

By four o'clock we arrived at a landmark that Vasco, for the past hour, had expected to see '*any minute now*' – an old concrete bridge spanning a dry wash.

'*This is it,*' said Vasco, removing his shirt and collapsing flat on his back.

I laid down as well, dazed and blistered and generally indifferent to what might happen next. We had walked sixteen kilometres from the near side of the river, plus another five or six trying to find a crossing. It was unlikely yet that Greg would be in cell phone range, seven kilometres further on, so we were puzzled when we heard a search plane overhead, flying out toward the hippo pool, unaware that our failure to return in the early afternoon had set off an alarm that had now reached the highest levels of the government, or that a large herd of elephants was nosing around the disabled helicopter

275

while Segren, engrossed in Finnegan's book, read the first eight chapters.

When Vasco asked what time it was I told him 4:30. They'll come for us by 5:00 he predicted and as night fell upon Gorongosa they did.

We found Greg blissed out, up to his sunburned neck in the cool blue water of Chitengo's new swimming pool, eating a fresh fruit cocktail, a full moon rising behind the happiest philanthropist on the face of the earth. The safari guides would call us *damn fools* for our reckless misadventure. Fair enough and we would have to live with the mischievous glow of that assessment, persuaded that our bad luck an outlandish privilege, a backhanded gift might never again play out with such serendipity, marching across Africa in league with just the sort of heaven-sent fool a better world could thrive on. A world, I would expect, where standing around waiting to be rescued is not an option.

In the wilderness I sense the miracle of life, and behind it our scientific accomplishments fade to trivia – **Charles Lindbergh**

Do Lions Go to Heaven?

Ginny Brock

Suddenly my senses were flooded with the warm scent of tall grasslands of the African bush, misty mountains in the distance and miles of fragrant gold savannah.

Drew was here; dropping in from the place he's in now. I was getting used to that whoosh of warm energy that signalled his arrival.

I waited. The air felt hazy to me. It seemed to be dusted with tiny flecks of glitter. The leaves of the red msasa trees fluttered on an invisible breeze. My senses told me that my son was sitting on the ground, leaning with his back against the mottled bark of a baobab. The tree's massive misshapen trunk blossomed into stunted branches that gave it a grotesque, prehistoric look. Drew's hair was tousled. He wore a pair of shorts and no shirt. His feet were bare.

He gave a little laugh. '*I like to be with the animals, lying here in the grass, waking up with them. They wake up gently - with snorts, sleepy growls and yawns. They're extra loving in the early mornings...*'

This would be Drew's heaven.

I got the image of a full grown male African lion. His muzzle was flecked with small scars but the thick black mane was ebony black and smooth. His coat was golden, untangled and I think it emanated a glow. His tufted tail flicked the air.

'He's special,' Drew said. 'I met his cub once on earth – remember the lion orphanage in the Cape?'

I nodded remembering Drew holding a ten week old cub. 'He watches his cub from here ...'

There was peace in this place far away from the whistle of rifle fire.

'Does your lion purr?' I asked him.

'He's purring now – can you hear him?'

I heard a deep rumbling coming from somewhere inside the animal. Then I saw him lift his giant paw and place it on Drew's knee.

'He says he wants me to be his cub. He'll teach me to run the way he can. He never got the chance to teach his cub to run and spring... He wants me to teach him to fly." Drew chuckled. "I told him I flew with the seagulls yesterday.... he says he ran with the Springbok last night.'

I saw the great lion draw himself up, shake his mane and breathe in deeply. Then I heard him say to Drew, 'I can fly with seagulls.'

Can lions fly in Heaven?

In the night of death, hope sees a star and listening love can hear the rustle of a wing – **Robert Ingersoll**

Fools Rush In..

... or more accurately, Idiots in the Bush.

Greer Noble

One evening, sitting around our camp fire after dinner, we heard a scratching noise coming from our garbage which, only a few metres away, had not yet been bagged.

Quietly approaching we shone the torch and there was a honey badger, licking cans we'd opened for our meal. It looked up, blinked and then carried on with its licking, reminding me of my grandmother's baking when we were allowed to scrape out the left-over chocolate icing from the bowl.

We stood and watched for some time, it on one side of our rubbish, we on the other, less than a metre separating us!

Its long dusty eyelashes kept blinking up at the torch while it used its really long talons like spoons to scrape out what it could. We thought it rather cute as it licked away, examining each tin in turn.

279

Eventually it turned and shuffled off into the night with its own personal swagger. Such attitude I noted with amusement and not even a foot high!

How foolish can one be! Had we known then what we later learnt, we'd never have ventured anywhere near this nocturnal scrounger. Reputedly it is one of the most aggressive, ferocious and fearless creatures that will immediately attack anything if remotely threatened, usually targeting the groin. Talk about fools rushing in…

There is something about safari life that makes you forget all your sorrows and feel as if you had drunk half a bottle of champagne, bubbling over with heartfelt gratitude for being alive – **Karen Blixen**

Big Cat Burglar

Rob Fynn

In the early hours of one morning, waking me, my wife, Sands, asked *'Why are the chickens making that noise?'*

'Probably an owl sitting on the roof,' I drowsily replied, willing her to go to sleep again.

Our vegetable garden and chicken run, heavily fenced in with three metre high wire netting to ward off the animal kingdom as we lived deep in the African bush, was close to our sleeping hut from where we could keep an eye on our farming effort. The dawn chorus from the chicken run was our most reliable alarm clock. Sands wasn't having any of it and nudged me again. I grumpily agreed to investigate.

The heat of October in the mud walls of our hut made it like an oven, so we slept naked. In this stark attire, we jumped off our bed and crept round the kitchen, armed with a torch which I planned to turn on at the last moment to surprise whatever was disturbing our little farmyard. Perhaps I'd reckoned our attire would do the rest? Switching on the torch as we rounded the kitchen corner, a great black-maned lion growled and leapt away, straight into our fence, boomeranged off, nearly falling on top of us and then bounded off into the dark.

'Oh, so that's what it was,' trying my best to sound real casual. I wouldn't have a wife on the island for much longer if this was going to be a regular occurrence.

'Rob, I want you to put a proper door on our hut… today!'
I didn't argue.

Surprise is the greatest gift which life can grant us – **Boris Pasternak**

Nxamaseri Nemesis

Lloyd Wilmot

In March 1971 I paddled some 300 kms from Shakawe to Maun in a borrowed 3.5 m fibreglass canoe. The first day was like sailing down the river on a Sunday afternoon... though I saw crocodiles and skirted some hippo, the Okavango current bore me down steadily till I pitched camp on Moonlight Island below Red Cliffs. The next morning dawned fresh and calm and I got going to reach Nxamaseri. Bee-eaters wheeled and dived and along a reed bed about 5 kms further I began photographing them as they perched on the reeds. By drifting quietly on the current they allowed me some close up shots. After that I paddled towards the main current.

I had only got about 30 metres when a sudden V-shaped wave broke from the reeds. I thought it was a hippo but glancing down I saw the ominous snout and eyes of a large croc below the surface. Using the paddle I struck the water and the blade of the paddle slid down to bounce along its knobbly back as it passed below me like a large mottled submarine. I spun round as it surfaced on my right, head and neck out of the water, its eyes bright with concentrated focus. I struck hard with the paddle. It didn't even connect. With a loud snap of the jaws the paddle was wrenched out of my hands.

I recall shouting in defence then instinct kicked in and I lunged over my camera case to grab my 30.06 rifle in the front of the canoe.

Stretched across my bedroll I grasped the rifle and loaded it in one smooth movement before swinging it round. The croc was right alongside facing away with the paddle in its jaws. Lying on my side I placed the barrel against the back of its head where the neck muscles begin and jerked the trigger.

The croc quivered and rolled over revealing first a large rear foot then the white expanse of its belly scales. It was huge, longer than my little canoe by at least a metre. Before it rolled over completely the arc of bright blood had begun falling back on itself before the head went down. Now the massive tail began to thrash from the secondary nervous system that saurians have. Water splashed over me as I instinctively reloaded then ducked to dodge the massive tail that threatened to sink the canoe.

The croc sank out of sight leaving ripples across the river. Without thinking I said a heartfelt prayer of thanks for timely deliverance. The canoe drifted and I gathered my thoughts as I looked over the current. Then my paddle popped to the surface. It had become dislodged when the croc hit the bottom. Using my rifle butt I turned the canoe and retrieved the paddle. Only then did I realise I had been paddling with a loaded rifle. Opening the breech I left it at my feet near at hand. If there was another emergency all I would have to do is close the bolt. My thoughts of the dangers ahead made me want to give up. But my concern about being called a coward was dispelled when I thought *'Hey, this only happens once.'* How wrong that assumption proved to be. But that is another story...

Africa touches me to the core of my being. The glory of Europe is its History, but the glory of Africa is its LIFE! **David Anderson**

Old Grumpy

Sue Maas

It took a very special couple to see the potential in an old fishing camp like Fothergill. Rob and Sandy Fynn were that couple. They named their safari camp after their predecessor, Rupert Fothergill of Operation Noah fame. Rupert was instrumental in saving the wildlife when the man-made lake was first filled - a task of mammoth proportion. At that stage Lake Kariba, in the then Rhodesia, was reputed to be the biggest manmade lake in the world.

It was some time after their safari lodge was established that my husband and I joined the Fothergill lodge staff. Still unused to the antics of the animals that frequented the island, we were one day asked to take some clients to meet the float plane that regularly ferried people across the lake. The plane landed at the back of the island so off we went, over a rise.

Suddenly we heard an elephant's enraged trumpet and we shot back up over the rise, the Land Rover in reverse with a bull elephant in hot pursuit.

Through the compound we flew. Thankfully the old bull eventually gave up and went back to his spot over the rise. Needless to say, when all was quiet, the rise was approached more cautiously. Fortunately the elephant had moved away and the clients could be dropped off at the plane which had probably disturbed the elephant in the first place.

'Why did you reverse?' Rob wanted to know. *'You should have stood your ground!'*

I believe Rob knew this grumpy old rogue, perhaps a game with them. But for those uninitiated like us, it wasn't likely to happen, especially as it was our first encounter with an irritated bull elephant.

The backbone of surprise is fusing speed with secrecy – **Von Clausewitz**

Sir Rosis of the River

Greer Noble

How do you explain to a 12 year old boy what's funny about a pontoon called Sir Rosis of the River?
'Why does everyone laugh when they see it?' he wanted to know.

My daughter, her husband and our two grandsons had made a pit-stop at a local safari camp on the banks of the Thamalakane river on the outskirts of Maun, Botswana's gateway town for supplies and fuel... and a night's rest after the long tedious haul from home before venturing off into the wilds of the Okavango delta. After that you are on your own.

As it turned out they didn't have to explain because sundowners around the pub revealed all. As the stars came out so did the stories and the inquisitive boy's eyes grew wider and wider as the night progressed.

Broad, wholesome, charitable views of men and things cannot be acquired by vegetating in one little corner of the earth all one's life – **Mark Twain**

Don't Bark at Locals

Adele Barton

M any years ago (vanity prevents me from saying how many) we lived in Nairobi, Kenya, for about 4 years. During this time we went on many holidays to various game parks and places of interest in our VW Kombi which my father had adapted especially for camping

One of our holiday jaunts was to go to Jinja on Lake Victoria's shoreline in Uganda to see the source of the Nile River. On this particular day dad had had a hard day's driving and was tired and we had been unable to find a suitable place to camp. So pulled off, as we frequently did, on the nearest flat piece of ground we could find as darkness was falling – it comes quickly on the equator – had supper and were into bed.

I don't think we had been asleep very long when we were awoken with a furious snarling and barking from Butch, our large, beautiful, mad boxer who went everywhere with us, his kennel being the bench seat in the cab.

Someone was shining a flashlight in the front window – while Butch was trying to savage the intruder through the glass. A frenzied cacophony made sure we were all awake. Dad eventually managed to calm the dog enough to find out who was disturbing our sleep. It turned out to be a local police constable who insisted we had to move on. After much pleading and complaining we discovered the reason for our eviction - we were parked on the fairway of the local golf course. We moved on.

I don't recall how many days it took to reach Lake Victoria but finally we set up camp close to the water's edge. On our first morning there we had let Butch out to have a run, while mum was busy brewing our early morning coffee and my brother and I were tossing stones into the water. Suddenly the dog spotted something moving in the water, nice and small, about a foot long, he could handle that and barked aggressively at it, telling it not to come any closer. It didn't listen and grew in size and was now three foot long, Butch's barking was a little less aggressive but still telling this creature to go away, then horror of horrors, it started to emerge from the water growing bigger with every step. The dog turned and fled to his family's protection as we witnessed a very large and very grumpy hippo emerging from the water.

Dad picked up dog, mum, coffee pot and all and literally threw us into the back of the van, slammed the door, leapt into the cab and started the engine, ready to beat a very hasty retreat. The hippo seeing that it had rid itself of us intruders, turned and ambled ponderously back into the water.

Lesson learned; don't bark at the locals.

Footnote
It is said that hippopotami are the most dangerous animals in Africa accountable for most human deaths, yet they are also known for their loyalty and compassion towards fellow creatures and humans. Are they any different from man? – **GN**

A Weight Off My Chest

Bruce Brislin

On a holiday with my parents, sister and cousin at the Wild Coast of South Africa over the festive season umpteen years ago, we had been warned about the large numbers of green mambas around the Mkambati area where we were staying..

Not long after we'd arrived my mum who'd hung some raincoats on a nail in a corner of a room in the primitive little hovel that the cottage had turned out to be, noticed that they had fallen down and called my cousin to hang them up again. There was a sudden yell from him and he flew out of the room leaving the raincoats in an untidy mess on the floor. A large green mamba was trying to extricate itself from within them. My dad dispatched it rather speedily and efficiently and from then on we were very careful.

We had brought basic foods with us but fishing was our main source of protein. My dad caught most of the fish at the Blowhole, a natural pond in the rocks, exposed to the sea through a narrow cleft and in which there was usually a catch big enough for a meal for all of us.

We three kids slept in the one room and my parents on the small outside veranda. In bed one night and covered only by a sheet I dozed off only to be awakened a little later by a weight on my chest. The Tilley lamp where my parents were sitting cast sufficient light through a window for me to see. I raised my head and, to my horror looked into the face of a large green snake that was coiled up on my chest.

In shock and frightened I flung it off and yelled blue murder. My parents dashed in with the lamp and after a brief search, spotted the snake which was also quickly dealt a death blow.

Two days later yet another mamba slithered across the veranda close behind me where I sat making a model boat. Again I yelled and it vanished into a shed full of clutter at the end of the veranda.

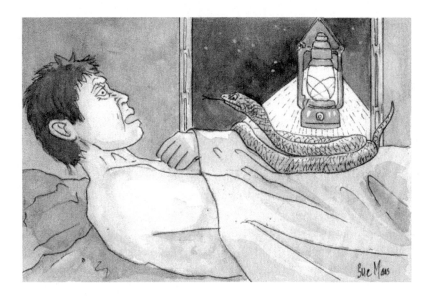

My parents eventually found it hiding up in a discarded length of drainpipe. They blocked each end with wads of smouldering waste, the one end with less waste to allow the mamba to squeeze through, which it did when the smoke took effect and dad killed it as well.

We even saw mambas on the beach. The apparent reason for their great abundance in the area was and still is the presence there of a prolific shrub called carissa macrocarpa commonly known as amatungulu or Natal plum. It has a reddish fruit about the size of a tree-tomato and is a favourite of some bird species. Green mambas being arboreal, lie up in the dense vegetation and when the birds come to pick at the fruit they are the easiest of prey.

A lazy man's farm is the breeding ground for snakes – **African Proverb**

Lechwe over Khwai

Lloyd Wilmot

Not far from the public campsite at Khwai is a deep pool much favoured by hippo. The Botswana Guides Association was allocated this site and we often booked it for a safari. It was here that I was camped with my friend Axel Bjerkoe one hot October. He had with him his son Bjorn and Dimitri, his son-in-law, plus two others. Axel had been on safari with me before but despite my best efforts and entreaties, I was unable to persuade him to adventure with me. Let's just say he was a cautious man.

One night after retiring to bed a storm was brewing - much thunder and lightning but no rain. Despite the elements I heard lions on the prowl and from their low calls I could tell they were headed in our direction. Putting on some shorts and shoes I unzipped my tent and went over to Bjorn and Axel. Knowing Axel would decline I invited Bjorn to dress quickly and come watch the lions go by. Bjorn eagerly agreed but Axel restrained him then flatly refused to allow him out of the tent. After trying to persuade them I gave up and asked Dimitri to accompany me. Trouble is Dimitri took forever to get dressed when all he had to do was put on trousers and shoes. By the time he emerged the lions were past the camp.

Switching on my Maglite from time to time to check for lion, we trotted along the access road and emerged at the open floodplain that lay along the river. Lighting upstream I saw the lions look back at us but they were already about a 100 yards away. I switched off the light for a few minutes and called to the lions repeatedly. Lighting once again I saw that one had turned back then another two followed suit. We moved to a clear patch with our backs to the water and sat down to await developments. The lions continued towards us through some low sage bushes and the next moment they flushed a young lechwe which came bounding in our direction with three lionesses in hot pursuit.

As the lechwe approached, it was blinded by the light and suddenly realised it was almost at the hippo pool. With a tight swerve it turned right in front of us then plunged through the river just above the deep pool. The lions nearly ended up in our laps as they followed the desperate lechwe which was now braving the crocs in a series of high leaps through the water. The lions, aware of crocs, stopped at the water's edge. As my beam swept the surface we spotted a large croc swimming after the lechwe at high speed. We watched with bated breath to see if the lechwe would make it. With a final jump it landed on solid ground and bounded away just ahead of the croc's jaws. The croc propelled itself well up the bank on the surge of water but defeated, it turned back.

The lions then turned their attention to us and cut us off from retreating to camp. One lioness came very close and I blinded her by shining directly into her eyes while readying my piece of wood to throw if she persisted. Dimitri was rather concerned but I told him to enjoy the experience.

After a few minutes he asked '*What do we do now?*'

I told him to do exactly as I say and on my word, we both stood up. The lioness backed off a bit and the other two watched intently. Advancing toward the nearest cat I rushed at it and stomped my feet hard. Blinded by the light, she lost her nerve and jumped aside with a growl. We were through and moved toward camp. I told Dimitri to move ahead of me while I played rear-guard to keep the lion at bay till we both reached the treeline. The lions lost interest and I led Dimitri back to his tent.

Axel wanted to know what had happened but I let Dimitri explain through the safety of his tent. After a final check that the lions had given up, I entered my tent and lay down. The storm was still rumbling away and the smell of raindrops on dry ground was in the air. I felt sorry for Bjorn that he had missed such an interesting experience and mentally blamed Axel for his timidity.

A young woman from USA was touring Africa and decided to go to one of those wildlife parks where you camp among the animals. She stayed awake all night, terrified of the hippos stomping around outside her tent, having been told they are one of the most dangerous animals in Africa. The next morning when she was able to get to a phone, she called her mom in the US and told her of her experience. Her mom said: '*But, didn't they warn you about the danger?* She replied: '*Mom, this is Africa. There is no 'they' here!*' – **Trish Jackson**

Jumbo Paparazzi

Greer Noble

W as it the surreal light in the sky that had all our hotel guests milling around like disturbed ants or was it the fact that my father was hosing down a wild visitor? Two phenomena at the same time was too much, even for Kariba. A great sense of euphoria filled everyone as day became night and then the sun seemed to bounce back, magically lighting up the entire lake, mesmerising the eyes with the warm ephemeral glow of the total solar eclipse. It reportedly occurs once every one to two years but is visible from less than half a percent of the earth's surface.... and there was my father and my little daughter, Carla, in one hand and a hosepipe in the other, spraying our latest guest, an adult elephant. The only person who wasn't that enthralled was my mother. It was eating her banana tree!

This majestic giant took no notice of all the guests now gathered around, emboldened by my father's and his grand-daughter's close proximity. It was like the paparazzi with cameras clicking both at the weird lighting in the sky and at the hosing scene, the elephant clearly enjoying his royal welcome as he later turned for his other side to be hosed.

If it had been anyone other than my father I would have been extremely anxious. I have an inbred respect for elephant and am acutely aware of their unpredictability but in his hands I felt at ease. An old hand in the bush he'd shot many a large tusker in his day and wasn't proud of it but he knew and understood them.

This was by no means his first run in with befriending an elephant either. When he and my mother ran Bumi Hills Hotel, high up on a plateau overlooking the lake, at the mouth of the Ume River, he had an elephant friend he named Churchill. Neither of the two hotel Land Rovers had brakes to speak of, both having seen their day, so down the hill my father would go, free-wheeling to the harbour or to the light plane landing strip and inevitably Churchill would give chase. It became a game with them and these two old men got to know each other well over the years. It's a bit nerve wracking when seven tons comes hurtling down behind you.

During his life-long association with these colossal mammals, my father could read them as well as they could read him. Maybe it was the tremendous love and respect he had for them that they felt.

What a magnificent and privileged life we all had.... never a dull moment and experiencing nature at its finest!

There's an old superstition... Once you drink the waters of the mighty Zambezi you will always return – **GN**

Police Road Block

Marilyn Garvin

Several years ago, prior to our last free and fair elections in Zimbabwe, numerous police road blocks were operational on all major roads. Between Harare and Mutare, for instance, a distance of only some 267 km or 166 miles, you could be stopped 8 or 9 times and checked for various things.

Once we were pulled over and thoroughly searched and when we asked the policeman what he was looking for, he said...

'We are looking for a hidden agenda.'

Needless to say he didn't find one!!

Laws control the lesser man... right conduct controls the greater one
Mark Twain

Mystery of Green Teeth

Ken Tilbury

F ollowing a track towards a small rise in the vista on the cattle ranch I worked at in Swaziland we reached a concrete reservoir with a drinking trough near it. The water level in the reservoir was very low and there was no water coming out of the pipe into it. Leaving the Land Rover we continued on foot following the pipeline running alongside a dry rocky stream. Pushing our way through some thick jesse bush I was amazed to see a huge hole in the rocks with a 30 foot high cliff on the opposite side.

Over the centuries water flowing down the stream must have dropped over the cliff and gradually worn a deep hole in the solid rock below. It was about 20 feet in diameter and the water level 15 feet below the rim where Mfanseni, my handyman and I stood. An exposed sandbank inside the hole was on the left side and the bones of animals that must have fallen in, lay bleached on the sand.

'The cattle herders say there is a very big crocodile living in this hole,' Mfanseni informed me.

'This hole is about 5 miles from the river. I don't think a crocodile would have walked all this way.'

'That is what they say.'

The end of the siphon pipe dangled about two feet above the level of water.

'We will have to pump water out for the cattle if we don't get rain in the next week,' I decided.

'Did you check the water in the rhino's hole?' Mike, my employer, asked that evening.

'Yes we did. I don't know how deep the water is but a sandbank has been exposed so there might just be enough to fill the reservoir.'

'How much is in the reservoir now?'

'There's probably enough to keep the cattle going for about a week.'

'Well if there's no rain we'll have to go down and pump some water out into the reservoir.' Mike pondered, stroking his moustache reflectively.

The rain did not come. The herdsman from South camp came to headquarters to report that the water was just about finished. I got Danger, the herdsman and another worker to load the pump and hoses as well as a ladder and length of rope and we went off to pump water out of the rhino's hole. The pump was tied to the rope and lowered onto the sandbank. The outlet pipe was coupled to the siphon pipe and then the ladder was also lowered into the hole.

'Okay Danger, climb down and get the pump started.'

'I can't go down there my baas. There is a very big crocodile in there. Look at all the bones of animals he has been eating.'

'That is nonsense Danger. There is no crocodile in there. Anyway I will sit here with my rifle and shoot it if it comes out of the water.'

Being a Shangaan and not wanting to show he was afraid in front of the Swazis, Danger reluctantly climbed down the ladder onto the sand bank. Looking around nervously then up at me he quickly

299

pushed the suction pipe into the water and started the pump. A few minutes passed with the pump clattering away when I saw the crocodile stealthily sliding out of the water onto the sand bank – its eyes fixed on Danger. It wasn't big but was covered in green algae and looked menacing. At first Danger didn't see it coming but when he did he looked up at me urgently.

'Baas. Shoot it quickly. It wants to eat me. Please.' He was sweating.

I took aim and shot the crocodile before it got within six feet of Danger. He immediately looked up at me with a huge smile.

'I was not afraid of the ingwena. I knew you would kill it.' Danger punched me playfully on the arm after climbing out of the hole. *'I could have killed it myself.'* They all laughed.

....

The nine foot crocodile was pulled out of the hole with the rope and put into the back of the Land Rover. When the reservoir was full the water level in the hole had dropped another foot. We took the pump out and went back to the workshop.

'I must confess, the herd boys have been telling me for years there was a croc in the rhino's hole but I didn't believe them,' Mike greeted us while leaning over the side of the Land Rover to examine the crocodile. *'It's a mystery how it got there and how long it has been in that hole. Even its teeth are green.'*

'Well I was amazed when it came out of the water. It must have been very hungry to want to eat old Danger,' I teased turning to Danger who stood looking sheepish. *'You should have seen his face when he thought he was a goner.'*

The crocodile was skinned; the skin cured then mounted on the wall in the store. The local witchdoctor who had heard about the killing, arrived to ask for the head of the crocodile and the feet. The ranch workers ate the meat claiming it would give them strength and virility.

'Crocodiles are easy. They try to kill and eat you. People are harder. Sometimes they pretend to be your friend first.' **Steve Irwin**

White Elephant

Rob Fynn

Sue Moss

'*Why don't you take White Elephant for a run?*' Dick Pitman suggested on hearing I had to visit Kariba. A young and adventurous British journalist who worked for his keep at our camp for half the day and wrote during the other half, so named the white short-based Land Rover he had recently bought.

After pushing it up and down the yard where it was kept at Kariba harbour for ten minutes, cursing its obstinacy and thinking it would have been quicker to walk, it finally spluttered into life, belching black smoke and vibrating like a wet dog shaking itself dry.

The police post was perched on the edge of the Kariba Gorge with a fierce climb to get up there. Determined not to have a repeat performance of starting it again, I parked in a suitable position for a quick getaway on the downhill side, leaving the engine running and handbrake on while I dashed in for my brief business with the charge office.

I hadn't been there two minutes when a constable appeared at the entrance enquiring whether I was the driver of the white Land Rover.

'Uuh...yuh, that's me' I replied hesitantly. Road tax out of order? Maybe it was stolen? *'Is it in the way?'* I asked innocently.

'Ahh no, it just went over!' he nonchalantly responded.

I dashed out to hear a kawomp... kadunk...clumpety clunk coming from over the edge of the Kariba Gorge precipice. I tore to the side to see White Elephant sixty metres below, neatly wrapped around a *mopane* tree with its front bumper and bonnet half way up the trunk, the engine breathing its last clunk ...clunk.

Feeling quite sick, I ran down the hill to Harry Maun, our friendly garage mechanic. I explained I'd wrecked Dick's landy and had clients waiting in the harbour for transfer to the island. Would he please retrieve, repair and send me the bill

After a morose journey over in the boat contemplating what I was going to say, Dick was waiting my return on the jetty.

'How did she go, Rob?' he enquired with his inimitable smile.

'Let's go have a whisky Dick,' I replied as casually as I could.

'What? But it's only lunchtime!'

He looked paler by the minute while I related the story. He needed more than one whisky, and took several days to recover, assisted by stress medication from Janet, our resident nurse.

He got his revenge. One afternoon, needing a break from camp, he borrowed an island Land Rover and my rifle. He parked it on an old termite mound; handbrake on – the usual flat battery – heard this bit before? – and was standing in front of it, surveying the scene through his binoculars when the hand brake slipped. It ran forward, pinning Dick under the front wheel. Unfortunately for me, he had my trusty old hunting rifle hanging on his shoulder and proceeded to dig himself out using its barrel.

Our first alert to this crisis was a slapperty slap as the Land-Rover arrived back in camp on a flat front wheel. Dick climbed out covered in dust, clothing torn, in no mood to answer questions. My twisted and broken rifle lay on the seat. Had he been attacked by a large and cantankerous bull? The story emerged later with another smile and another whisky. On him this time.

His latest book, *A Wild Life*, is filled with the humour we all enjoyed so much back there. Good friends to this day, he went on to launch The Zambezi Society, dedicated to the conservation of the Zambezi Valley.

Weak people revenge, strong people forgive, intelligent people ignore
Albert Einstein

Marvellous Bike Attack

Greer Noble

Sue Maas

His mother must have loved him very much to have given him a name like 'Marvellous'. Clearly, the ladies also thought Marvellous was... you guessed it, marvellous! So it was on this particular day, his day off, that Marvellous, in anticipation of a night at the shabeen* changed his waiter's uniform for his best, beautifully pressed pink jeans and matching shirt. With his prize possession, a silver bicycle bought and paid for over the year from overtime and hard earned tips, he headed for the Mahombecombe township, a small harbour village on Zimbabwe's Lake Kariba.

He took off in high spirits for the 10 kilometre ride as he'd done so many times before, not dreaming what fate had in store for him. It was fairly easy going from the Cutty Sark Hotel until he reached the incline up to the Total Service Station on top of the hill, along the main road. The last of the sun had dipped below the horizon so it was dusk when he dismounted to push his bike up that steep incline.

304

Whistling his favourite tune he didn't have a care in the world. Suddenly, out of the corner of his eye he detected a movement. His heart stopped and he began to tremble uncontrollably. A huge lioness stood before him, powerful, muscular, her yellow eyes mesmerising, focused intently on him.

Fear exuded his every pore. The only thing between them was his silver bike. There was only one thing to do. In a flash he hurled his precious bicycle at her and ran like he was in the lead of an Olympic sprinting event, just metres from the finish line.

It was the funniest thing to see this pink flash streaking across the forecourt of our service station straight into our café. Sweating profusely, he tried to catch his breath, blabbering, while he kept pointing in the direction from where he'd just come.

We all jumped into our car and headed in that direction. The lioness was nowhere to be seen, only one rather mangled silver bike.

It might have taken Marvellous a years to pay it off but it was worth every last cent as it had almost certainly saved his life.

*shabeen – beerhall

Every misfortune is a blessing – **African Proverb**

The Three Rhythm Boys

Greer Noble

Sue Maas

It was on our game ranch in the lowveld that we decided to dismantle an old derelict house on the hill. Miles from anywhere and short of nuts and bolts for our new home, our builder was about to remove the last bolt from the beam supporting the roof when loud creaking threatened imminent collapse. Rotten with age, the thatch was also weighted by soil white ants had carried up over time to build their colony. Only, as we were soon to discover, they were not the only inhabitants. We scurried out and none too soon as the roof suddenly caved in.

Before the dust had even settled we heard desperate deep, reverberating squawks, like something on its death-bed. It took a while to work through the rubble and there we found three of the ugliest, featherless chicks we'd ever seen. Puzzled as to what they were we somehow managed to rear them, a full time piccanin (young boy) catching grasshoppers for the greedy not so little chicks.

Soon realising what comedians they were, we named them after the joke of a devout Catholic lady who had triplets despite following her doctor's advice on various rhythm methods of birth control. Bumping into him a year later she introduced them, '*Meet the three rhythm boys, Leaky, Squeaky and Tweaky.*' Our three rhythm boys grew into the most handsome yellow-billed hornbills; free to go yet the bond was so strong (especially with the rear view mirror on the Land Rover!), they continued to fly from shoulder to shoulder every day, demanding food… and attention!

306

A Banana for a Baby

Adele Barton

Back in the early 1960s Nairobi wasn't the built up concrete jungle that it is today. It was, nevertheless, a jungle of the natural kind. We lived on the very outskirts of town in a rambling old colonial-styled house. It was common knowledge that if your neighbour drove passed your house and hooted it wasn't in greeting but to warn you that there was a lion on your front veranda or something similar!

My mum had recently come home from the local hospital with my brother, Glenn who was born two months prematurely and was a very unhappy, colicky, three week old baby. She had just managed to get him to sleep in his pram in the lounge. The heat was intense; it was humid and threatening to rain, so she left one of the windows open to catch any breeze that could cool things down a little. Mum was hoping that the ensuing storm would not wake him up. She went through to the kitchen to make a cup of tea and look through the accounts.

Sitting at the kitchen table she heard a noise coming from the lounge. She got up and went to have a look. There, standing in the room, holding the handle of the pram was a female baboon. What was this baboon going to do? Mum was scared stiff! What would happen if Glenn woke up and started to cry? Mum watched hopelessly as the baboon proceeded to shake and then push the pram. Thinking quickly Mum darted back into the kitchen and grabbed a banana out of the fruit bowl and went back into the lounge. By this time my brother had started to whimper. The baboon watched my mother as she tried to throw the banana out of the open window. It hit the frame! The baboon was now unsure whether it should leave the moaning baby for the banana. The banana won. She slowly sauntered over to get it, looking between the pram, my mum and the window. She then sat, on her butt in the open window, leg up on the frame, eating the banana, whilst keeping an eye on the baby!

My mum went back and got another banana. By this time the baboon had finished and was moving back towards the pram.

Mum took a deep breath, aimed carefully and threw the next banana through the window out onto the veranda. The baboon hesitated and then lopped out after it. Mum made a dash for the window and firmly closed it behind the hairy lady.

A few days later the unwelcome visitor came back but luckily my mum managed to close all the windows before she got in.

Mum, being true to her nature, didn't tell the parks about the incident as she didn't want them to destroy this troublesome 'mother wannabe' and my dad had burglar bars installed to prevent any further unwanted guests. It is a standing joke in our house how my mother had to trade a banana for my brother.

When we were monkeys, we were more human because we were at least not destroying the nature those days! — **Mehmet Murat ildan**

Dutch Courage

Greer Noble

Back in the day when the national parks weren't so particular about where you camped, we only used the public camps for pit-stops to have the luxury of toilets and running water, as we were completely self-sufficient and had only to top up our own water tanks. That is all there was there anyhow, certainly no shops, supplies or even petrol... thank goodness... still wild and totally unspoilt.

Arriving at Savuti camp, I had pulled out our table and chairs and sat enjoying what was probably one too many beers, already having had a couple in the Land Rover on our way in! I was waiting for my husband to join me for sundowners (he'd gone off to see if he could spot any game) when a bull elephant suddenly appeared from behind an old gnarled leadwood. He spotted me sitting there about the same time as I spotted him. We both started. He swung his mammoth hulk full-on and faced me. When I say all that was between us was the small table I'm not exaggerating. If he'd stretched out his trunk he could quite easily have touched me.

While I sobered up pretty quickly I must have still had enough in me to have the courage needed in such a situation. Normally I would have been shaking like the savannah in a brisk breeze, especially when this feisty gentleman shook his huge head at me, waving his enormous ears and pawing the soft sand with his ginormous foot to show me that he was the boss around here.

I'd never been this close to a wild elephant – on the ground – in its territory – and this vulnerable! It had the same effect were I to discover I was stark naked in the middle of a stadium surrounded by thousands of spectators... only worse! Thank God I was sitting, had I been standing I think my knees would have caved in.

Having spent a lifetime in and out the bush on safari, I have the greatest respect for them. I could *smell* his wildness, *see* the dust on his eyelashes and even remember admiring his tusks. Being resigned to my fate I thought, '*Well, if you're going to take me out, you're going to take me out and there's nothing I can do about it!*' A strange calm came over me.

309

I think as I didn't move he either got bored, didn't like the smell of alcohol or simply realised I wasn't a threat... or all three because he gave one more powerful head shake, sniffed me with his extended trunk eyeing me rather quizzically then turned and went on his way.

Wow, that was awesome. What a gentleman! I was just about to think what I was going to tell my husband when he appeared from behind the same leadwood. He'd actually followed the elephant... at a distance and, feeling totally helpless, had seen it all.

Savuti, a place where the game views *you*... not the other way around! Quite magical. I could so easily have been killed – amazing what a bit of Dutch courage can do!

If I have ever seen magic, it has been in Africa – **John Hemingway**

My Non-European'ness

Rory Young

I am an African of European decent. I was born in Zambia and am fifth generation African. I suppose I am what is sometimes called an Anglo-African.

Passing through the US immigration one day I handed my passport to the officer. He took it, looked at it, looked at me then looked hard at the passport again and then, clearly confused, asked, *'Are your parents missionaries?'* Quite obviously he could not comprehend that white people have been living in Africa for generations.

I answered, *'No.'* I did not see what my origins had to do with my status as a visitor to the US and felt this was rude on his part, so wasn't going to make it easy for him.

He paused then said it; *'How can you be from Zambia if you are European?'*

'I'm not European, I'm African,' I answered.

He looked annoyed, like I was being a smart-Alec. *'You're white. How can you be from Africa if you are white?'* he said.

'Well, let me put it this way,' I said. *'Are you an American Indian?'*

He stamped my passport, handed it to me and called out *'Next!'*

As I was walking up to the luggage carousel a black American man walked up next to me. *'I was behind you back there,'* he said. Then, *'Man, it's tough being a nigger ain't it?'*

I laughed till I was hurting.

The richest, happiest people I know are those who have nothing... or very little... and need nothing... they live in the wilds of Africa – **GN**

Good Intentions Dashed on Rocks

Mike Ballantine

Sue Mons

It was a Friday. We had camped at Nata, an ideal overnight stop at the junction of Botswana's roads to Kasane and Maun. Earlier we had arranged with our friends, Richard and Anita, to get together later that day at Nxai Pan, a 2100 sq km game park on the way to Maun.

Arriving before them we would set up camp about 5 kilometres from the entrance gate. Their directions were to look for a small rock on top of a large rock which we would leave on the left hand side of the dirt road and then drive at right angles to it through fairly sparse bush for a about a kilometre where they would find us. But the best laid plans of mice and men…

On our way to the pan we stopped off at about 11am in Gweta, a small village on the outskirts of the Makgadikgadi salt pans, the largest in the world. We gravitated to the pub at Gweta Lodge, in those days owned by Margie and Keith Poppleton. Ex British and Rhodesian SAS he was a raconteur deluxe. Within minutes he had us captivated with his bush experiences. And the drinks flowed... and flowed…

During a moment when he was not behind the counter, Margie told us about the time he single-handedly routed 15 patrons who had become belligerent and started throwing punches at him.

It was suddenly dark. Where had the day gone? We should have long since set up our camp at Nxai Pan – a couple of hours away. There was no way we could contact our friends. How awful we'd made it for them.

Next morning, at the campsite near the gate, we caught up with them. Very incisively, Richard reminded us that not only had we stood them up but also that they had spent ages looking for the non-existent rocks. Ouch!

Footnote: Not long after our detour via Gweta, we heard the sad news that Keith Poppleton had been accidently shot by his gun-bearer on a lion hunt in the area. Too far to be carried to his vehicle, he bled to death.

A man of ordinary talent will always be ordinary, whether he travels or not; but a man of superior talent will go to pieces if he remains forever in the same place – **Wolfgang Amadeus Mozart**

Askari's Dilemma

Tim Bax

Darkness had fallen. A cacophony of sounds heralded the excitement of yet another of Africa's nocturnal awakenings. There was an urgent knocking on the screen door. Inside, shrieks of laughter and the tinkling of cocktail glasses dulled even the relentless shrill of the cicada beetles. Mother and father were enjoying sundowners with friends inside a screened boma which served as our family's living quarters. The knocking went unheard.

'*Memsahib.....Memsahib!*' whispered the African askari* opening the screen door just enough to poke his head through. As a night guard, it would have been impolite for him to have intruded any further into the sanctuary of his master's home. He was an old man with white hair and a face deeply etched by years of toil in the African bush; quite how many years he was incapable of remembering. He looked deeply concerned.

'*What is it?*' asked mother, momentarily distracted from her guests. She was standing close to the door and was worried by the grave look on the old man's face.

'*Watoto na maliza. Simba iko karibu sana!*' rasped the askari, his voice raised in alarm. He was sweating profusely in the sweltering, heavy night air, his luminous eyeballs contrasting starkly with the moist sheen of his black skin. He wore an oversized khaki tunic and a matching pair of oversized shorts which ballooned over his spindly legs like the sails of an Arab dhow. In his sinewy hand he clutched a knobkerrie*. It was a far cry from the Lee Enfield he had carried while proudly serving with the King's African Rifles.

'*What's worrying the poor man?*' asked father, suddenly aware of the askari's presence.

'*He says the children are crying,*' replied mother, hastening to the door. '*He says there's a lion nearby.*'

314

As if to punctuate her remark, the unmistakable deep throated grunt of a black maned lion reverberated menacingly through the still, black night. The surrounding bush fell immediately into a deep and uneasy silence. A startled hush enveloped the boma. Even the cicada beetles ceased their chorus, as if silenced by some mystical stroke of a conductor's baton.

Tonight as with every night, the askari had been guarding the open-sided sleeping boma which I shared with my two sisters. It was nestled under the canopy of a large acacia tree a few hundred feet from the living quarters where mother and father were now entertaining. Except for a waist high screen of thatch that surrounded the boma, burgeoning white mosquito nets suspended from a makeshift roof of palm fronds provided the only protection between us and the surrounding bush.

'Well, tell him to chase the damn thing off,' offered father helping himself to another whisky. *'We can't have it upsetting the children.'*

Mother quickly reached for one of the smoking kerosene lanterns that were providing the only light and stepped outside. The dutiful askari followed close behind. *'I'll be back as soon as I've settled the kids,"* she said, clutching her cocktail and moving quickly into the stillness of the dark, moonless night.

The party resumed. So did the persistent call of the cicadas. It was another routine night in the decadence of Colonial East Africa.

*askari – Maasai warriors employed as guards
* knobkerrie – wooden branch carved into club with knob on one end

To witness that calm rhythm of life revives our worn souls and recaptures a feeling of belonging to the natural world. No one can return from the Serengeti unchanged, for tawny lions will forever prowl our memory and great herds throng our imagination. **George Schaller**

The Merry Crab

Greer Noble

It's interesting how a place, sometimes a name can inspire one. In this case it was both. The place was Praslin, an island in the Seychelles, and the name, Merry Crab, was a charming and quaint little pub at the end of a jetty, patronised by visiting yachts. We were one of those visiting yachts. It left an indelible impression, so strong, that I knew somewhere, some place, someday, we had to create our own little Merry Crab… and we did.

One glorious evening the moon pegged the spot for us… we stood looking over tops of silver tinted palms and giant strelitzia, following its magical beam out over a calm sea… the same sea, only very much further south, on Africa's East coast.

We built it from scratch with our own design and had ten years of creative bliss as well as meeting people from all over the world and from all walks of life. They stayed for a night, a week or several weeks and we had many happy returns.

Volumes could be written from our guest book alone which even included accommodating sailors with parrots to all the pilots and engineers from the filming of Blood Diamond, annual air show pilots, golfers, holiday makers, surfers and fishermen, to wedding parties, honeymooners, anniversary celebrations and birthdays. We had topless bathers and the more adventuress birthday-suit swimmers braving the white-crested waves in the moonlight. Compliments flew and our staff excelled.

But with anything in life there were also the mishaps like one particular guest, a friend and local who, after a particularly lively party and one too many, wisely decided to walk home, it being fairly close. Along the way he felt a little light-headed and sat for a while on the curb. One of the two security company vehicles stopped to see how he was, or so he thought. How wrong he was. He was fleeced and, with his wallet taken from his trouser pocket, they drove off. His empty wallet was later found by the police in the bushes. Needless to say we were all shocked more so than he.

But within the bounds of the Merry Crab, great fun and pranks were the order of the day, even the odd April fool prank where we were once ear-marked as the coast's first nudist colony. The number of hopefuls who turned up after seeing and believing the tongue-in-cheek article in the local rag was most amusing. Maybe it was the name, The Merry Crab, which attracted them!

The Merry Crab is now owned and run by a very special couple who have added their own magical touch, expanding and modernising the old place. Most of the original crew continue to hold the fort, quite gallantly I'm told and it's also heart-warming to know that its popularity continues to grow.

'The Crab' as the new owners fondly refer to it, has to be one of the most loved coastal hideouts on the Indian Ocean!

Feeling crabby? Best place to decrab – The Merry Crab (Lodge) in Munster, KwaZulu-Natal, South Coast, South Africa… or its sister 'Crab', Merry Crab (Beach Resort), in Watamu, Kenya's North Coast! – **GN**

The Downfall of an Aristo-Cat

Diana M. Hawkins

In the late 60s I was a member of Air Rhodesia's ground staff at Salisbury International Airport in Rhodesia. Offloaded that day, from a BOAC flight out of London, was a live-animal container bound for Blantyre, Malawi. Two co-workers, Nick and Paul, were on duty in the cargo hangar adjacent to the terminal. Later they described to me what happened.

Attached to the exterior of the container were the usual shipping labels and a list of instructions for feeding and watering the animal it housed. The insurance papers suggested it was a mighty fancy cat because they showed its value to be several thousand British pounds, a huge amount of money in those days. Nick and Paul were incredulous.

The cat had been in transit for twelve hours or more, so in accordance with the instructions, Paul opened the door of the crate to replenish the food and water bowls. The cat, meanwhile, evidently having endured enough of being rudely jostled around and cooped up in the container, saw its chance to escape, squeezed through the narrow opening and was gone in a flash.

The last thing Paul saw was a blur of grey fur shooting out the front hangar doors onto the airport apron. He sprinted after it but it

had disappeared. Paul raced back to get Nick and some freight handlers to help him find it. He was already imagining some of the dire consequences of this fiasco – facing the cat's irate Malawian owners, the filing of law suits, his boss's angry admonitions leading to a letter of dismissal and finally standing in an unemployment line. They had little time to find and capture the cat, since the Blantyre flight was due to take off in less than an hour.

Their search was fruitless. While a dozen employees scoured the area, tractors and trailers loaded with pallets of cargo were sitting idle on the tarmac, waiting to be loaded onto the aircraft. At 15 minutes to take-off Paul had a brainwave.

Close to the cargo hanger were the airport kitchens, frequented by resident stray cats in the hopes of finding food scraps. Paul and Nick raced over and found several rather mangy-looking cats picking through a garbage pile. Nick grabbed the first grey cat he saw.

He and Paul failed to examine the cat too closely until it was safely ensconced in the carrier. That's when they noticed it bore little resemblance to the sleek, handsome, healthy-looking, aristo-cat that had earlier got away. This cat's fur was bald in places, it was missing the tip to its left ear and it looked severely undernourished. There was no time, however, to debate this dilemma so cat and carrier were hurriedly loaded into the pressurized hold of the Air Malawi Viscount, while its four propellers began to rotate, one at a time, and its powerful, prop-jet engines roared into life.

Paul and Nick confessed to me that they had shipped the wrong cat to Blantyre. I commiserated with them for months as they waited on tenterhooks for the anticipated complaints to filter down from the Malawian cat's owners. Incredibly none ever did.

To this day we still wonder how the cats fared -- the aristo-cat which may have become feral or the feral, elevated to a life of pedigreed luxury.

Women and cats will do as they please, and men and dogs should relax and get used to the idea. **Robert A. Heinlein**

A Busload of Guests

Greer Noble

The saying, '*You don't know what hospitality is until you've had Rhodesian hospitality*,' applied especially to Rhodesian farmers. There are still a few of them scattered around the world but these farmers are a dying breed. The spirit of comradery was so great it enveloped everyone around them and, contrary to what some will have you believe, included their staff who were extremely well cared for with schools, sports-fields, clinics, churches and transport.

No stranger went untouched, even a busload of Americans on their way to Kariba who, spellbound no doubt by my brother Noel's repertoire of jokes, never made it out of the Karoi Hotel pub in time to reach their destination before nightfall, Kariba being at least another two hour drive away. Too dangerous to travel after dark, they too were invited home for dinner and to spend the night. My sister-in-law, Bess, used to unexpected guests dropping in, inevitably encouraged by Noel, knew when she saw a huge tour bus, following in the billowing dust of his pick-up, that they were in for one hell of a party.

An Unlikely Mascot

Greer Noble

I wonder how many people have been chased by a leopard... and lived to tell the tale?!

Many years ago, in Livingstone, in what was then known as Northern Rhodesia, I lived with my mother and older sister, Valerie. My father farmed tobacco on a virgin farm in the wilds, many miles away and only accessible in those days by rail.

We shared a three part bungalow, Valerie in one section, my mother and I in the middle and two young girls, Lynn and Veronica also in their late teens like my sister, on the other side of us. Typical of those times these dwellings were designed with gauzed-in verandas to keep flies and mosquitoes out but allow air to flow in for coolness, the days being unbelievably hot and air-conditioning a thing of the future. Access therefore was fairly relaxed as there was no point in locking gauzed doors.

One night all hell broke loose when a heavy-breathing intruder entered my sister's bedroom while she was kneeling, saying her prayers. She screamed, leaped out of the sash window above her bed, thought the intruder had thrown something at her when the picture above her window fell on her head and then ran around to the front still screaming as she feared whatever or whoever it was, was chasing after her. Lynn and Veronica dashed out with their hockey sticks and my mother and I joined them.

My sister had screamed so loudly that the young British South Africa Policemen, as they were then called (even though they all hailed from Britain), whose mess was about 60 metres behind us, also came to the rescue.

Of course everyone knew everyone as Livingstone in those days was a relatively small town. Suddenly our driveway was full of cars and while running around between them to get to my sister, I suddenly noticed a leopard.

Instinctively, I ran faster which was about the worst thing I could have done – it naturally gave chase. Very soon, having scratched my ankle, it was all but on top of me. I too started to scream.

Miraculously the attack I was expecting didn't come. What a relief. Unbeknown to me it was the new police mascot.

The policeman holding the long leash realised what was going on when the leash tightened in his grasp and put two and two together when he heard my screams. Relatively tame, it had probably thought that I wanted to play.

We never did find out who or what the intruder was, always the question as to whether it was two or four legged.

Those who wish to pet and baby wild animals love them. But those who respect their natures and wish to let them live normal lives, love them more
Edwin Way Teale

Great Uncle Harry

Carol Lyes

My great-uncle Harry Bowmaker married a lady called Annie who was a kind, loving woman. They moved to Lusaka, then a frontier town in Northern Rhodesia, now Zambia. Harry became the local blacksmith and undertaker. I don't know if these two jobs were usually linked but Harry did them both. He was not a very happy man as he did not really enjoy his work so he used to drink rather a lot.

He had a pet chimpanzee called Dodo and Dodo frequently accompanied Harry on his drinking binges and would take a sip from each glass of brandy that Harry consumed. When the pair of them fell off their barstools someone would send for Annie to come and collect them.

When Annie felt that Harry was drinking too much she would put him on the blacklist at all the local bars and hotels which meant that the barmen were not permitted to serve him. But after spending a little time giving lessons to Dodo, Harry circumvented the ban. He would simply hand the money to Dodo who would bang on the bar counter to get the barman's attention then push the money across the counter. The barman knew what he wanted so poured a tot of brandy and handed it over. Dodo took his sip and passed the rest to Harry – job done!

Needless to say Harry's drinking got him into many scrapes. Once he was due to do a burial and had the coffin in the back of the hearse when he felt the need for a drink so parked his hearse outside the pub and went in for a quick one. When he came out he drove the hearse to the cemetery, went to the back to remove the coffin only to find it was not there!! Horrors - who would steal a coffin with a corpse inside it? No one surely. So Harry decided he had better retrace his steps to the pub which was the last place he knew the coffin was in the hearse.

As he turned into the main street there it was, in the middle of the road, standing upright on one end. On thinking it over he reasoned that he must have been careless in latching the tailgate, not securing it properly. Being barely sober when he drove off after leaving the bar, he was not aware that the coffin had slid gently out the back landing on its end. Harry hastily replaced it in the hearse and returned to the cemetery where the burial took place as planned.

Another funeral in which Harry was entangled was that of the then colony's governor. Which one will remain unsaid as he might still have family who could sue me. Being the only undertaker in the area when the Governor died, Harry was called in to measure up the body and provide a suitable coffin. He duly arrived at Government House, shown into the Governor's bedroom by a lackey and left alone to get on with his duties. Harry took the measurements he needed then decided that the Governor didn't need that very large bed all to himself, so Harry eased him over, lay down beside him and had a few sips from his hip flask. Unfortunately Harry fell asleep. The lackey returned to find Harry dead to the world next to the dead Governor.

Needless to say this did not go down well with the representatives of HMG. However, they still needed the coffin which Harry delivered a few days later. With the body in place and the lid screwed down, the coffin had to be taken down stairs to the foyer of

Government House where it would lie in state for a day or two. Harry had only one assistant and the two of them could not carry the coffin so they manhandled it to the top of the stairs, lined it up, and pushed hard. It slid down the stairs, bounced a little, then landed in the exact position they had been told to place it. At this point Harry was tersely informed that his services would no longer be required and that the burial would be conducted without his help.

The day of the funeral dawned and Harry found himself a nice vantage point from which he could watch the burial without being noticed. After the ceremony and the departure of the dignitaries Harry made his way to the graveside. There he gleefully informed the officials that they had buried the Governor the wrong way around, placing the foot end of the coffin where the head end should have been. Humble pie had to be eaten and Harry was asked to please dig up the coffin and rebury it properly. Which he did.

When Harry died in the early sixties his funeral was attended by hundreds of people – not bad for a man of little education, wealth or social standing. Buried in Lusaka cemetery next to my grandfather, his legend lives on.

People say maybe we have a soul and chimpanzees don't. I feel that it's quite possible that if we have souls, chimpanzees have souls as well –
Jane Goodall

Lethal Passenger

Mike Ballantine

It had been a long day. I had just driven my small, pensionable pickup truck about 700 kilometres from our beach cottage on the east coast of Natal to Johannesburg. With a dilapidated bench seat, it was not the most comfortable ride but it was more economical, albeit even slower than our series 2 Land Rover.

I can't remember what was on my mind – possibly a nice cold beer – when I had a most curiously pleasurable sensation. I was wearing flip flops at the time and I felt the toes of my left foot being softly caressed.

Looking down was my worst nightmare, its coffin head being a 'dead' giveaway. It was a green mamba, a highly venomous snake capable of causing death with a single bite.

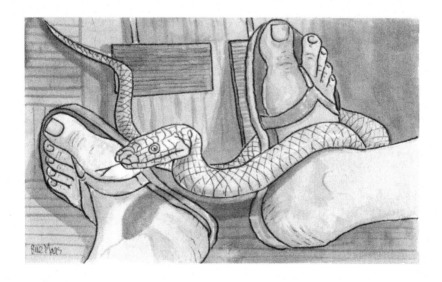

Instinctively, I immediately lifted both legs, steered towards the shoulder of the road, rolled to a stop, applied the handbrake and jumped out.

The snake had disappeared. But even in the small space of the pickup's cab there were many places for it to have holed up. What to do! There was a filling station about 100 metres away so I gingerly climbed back in and made my way there. I bought an aerosol can of insect repellent then asked one of the attendants there to warn me if he spotted the snake while I prodded possible lairs. I don't think he believed me and joked with nearby colleagues until about 10cms of mamba momentarily appeared through a gap in a door panel. Then the reptile *and* the attendant vanished.

I continued to search the nooks and crannies, aided by short squirts of the repellent but disturbed nothing but dust. Gingerly, I drove to the nearby home of my son Scott where I would be staying for a few days and pondered over my predicament and the mamba's future. The next day being Monday, I had several meetings to attend and as I couldn't expect Scott to lend me his car I decided that drastic action was called for and emptied the entire contents of the repellent into every corner of the cab, under and behind the seat and dashboard, into the air-vents, over the threadbare carpets and roof fabric - made sure the windows were tightly closed and shut the doors. I theorised that the snake would find its way out in the same way it had got in.

Next morning, despite it being mid-summer, I wore thick corduroy trousers, heavy jacket, boots and gloves and apprehensively approached the pick-up. I opened the door to find the mamba hanging from a cord under the dashboard, dead. About a metre long, it had obviously 'hitched a ride' from our coastal abode, around which the bush teemed with wildlife.

No passion so effectually robs the mind of all its powers of acting and reasoning as fear. **Edmund Burke**

The Gay Nineties

Greer Noble

Everyone's idea of freedom is different. Growing up, freedom for us was being able to go away, whether for a weekend or weeks on end and to leave home without having to lock a single door. In fact I don't think we even had keys and the only time we ever closed a window was during one of those torrential, tropical downpours. We weren't the exception either. Everyone we knew did the same, even farmers. There was one such gentleman farmer who'd drop in periodically, a bit of a recluse in many ways. Distinguished by his mop of white hair, he wore spectacles with the thickest lenses I'd ever seen which magnified his old, watery blue eyes, making them appear like shifting pools in a mirage.

One fine spring day high up in the Vumba mountains, we decided to call on him for a change. The closest thing to Little House on the Prairie, his farmhouse, a cheerful stone cottage, was set on green pastures of rolling meadows, it's backdrop a wooded area of trees that had been there forever. The little homestead suddenly caught by the rays of the late afternoon sun made it even more surreal. It was the closest step to heaven I'd ever taken.

As was customary in those days to pop in unannounced, we did just that. Looking into his study-cum-lounge through the half open stable door we were surprised to see a tastefully decorated room of surprising proportion, furnished with priceless antiques. Persian rugs were scattered about the wooden floor and those under the inlaid leather desk were strewn with screwed up sheets of paper that had missed the overflowing waste-paper basket, the only indication that anyone even lived there.

'Hellooooooooo, anyone home?' Nothing.

We entered, repeating the call, but still nothing. Peering out another stable door, expecting to see him pottering out back, all we found were signs that our bachelor friend had either had quite a party the night before and had passed out upstairs or was particularly fond of beer and had a very lazy butler or no house servant at all as there was a pile of empties so high it was impossible to open the door!

Knowing him we opted for the latter. Yet, we decided, he must have someone to look after the few healthy looking Jersey cows that grazed the meadow in front of his cottage. Maybe it was knock-off time.

'*You must invite him,*' my mother had made up her mind. The Gay Nineties, an annual show held in the small town of Umtali, was just around the corner.

'*He won't come, you know what a loner he is,*' my father reasoned.

'*I'll catch him the next time you have one of your interminable meetings.*'

'*You're forgetting he's a misogynist.*'

But my mother being the charming and forceful woman she was would not be put off. She bowled most men over as a rule and was used to getting her own way. Maybe this was just a harder nut to crack – besides she could not resist a challenge.

Some days later the opportunity presented itself and, true to form, she got him to agree.

Most people could not believe it... to see my mother there, sharing her sheet music with this old bachelor of note, singing away together.

The entire hall was decorated with the pomp and splendour of a vintage saloon complete with chandeliers. Crisp white linen draped tables resplendent with silver serve; candles and lead crystal were graced by beautifully attired women in glittery, short, flimsy, low-cut-fringed dresses, straight out of the Great Gatsby.

Matching beaded head-bands, long, swinging strings of pearls and elegant Tiffany cigarette holders completed their ensemble. Their respective partners, in keeping with the 1890s theme also looked the part, some sporting braces, neck-ties and Panama hats while others favoured light linen suits and two-tone brogues. It was as if you'd stepped back in time: even an antiquated honky-tonk rolling out nostalgic tunes; a loan leopard strolling through the streets, spotted by a late arrival, a reminder that you were in Africa.

The elevated stage, draped in shimmering street velvet, positively pulsated with anticipation when suddenly the curtains parted and the fun began. Everything from the local rugby team, transformed into hairy can-can girls – which almost brought the house down – the raucous cat-calls, boos and wolf whistles crescendoed to fever pitch especially when the *real* can-can girls followed. Many other acts drawn from local talent included solos and duets sung by pretty girls with sweet voices while the audience were encouraged to join in the chorus; lively Charleston and hot-blooded Spanish dancers from the local dance studio, comedians, magicians and acrobats imported from the big city – even clever clowning dogs. It was a roaring success, the best naughty nineties ever! Even our old misogynistic loner friend came out of his shell – no small feat on my mother's part in twisting his famous arm for he was none other than Sir Edgar Whitehead, the ex-Prime Minister of the then Rhodesia.

It is hard, if not impossible, to snub a beautiful woman – they remain beautiful and the snub recoils – **Winston Churchill**

Hunters' Wager

Ken Tilbury

In the 19th century South Africa's Eastern Cape had an abundance of game and so, with the shortage of fresh beef or mutton for the early settlers, some of them turned to hunting for meat on a professional basis.

In 1827 one William Thackwray boasted in a tavern in Port Elizabeth that he was such a skillful elephant hunter he could creep up to a bull elephant and, without being detected, could chalk his name on its hindquarters. A couple of fellow hunters challenged him and a wager made.

The three hunters duly set off to see if Thackwray could indeed accomplish this feat. Somewhere in the vicinity of where Addo Elephant Park is today, they found a herd of elephants. Spotting a large bull on the outskirts of the herd, Thackwray began his approach, leaving the other two to watch from a hilltop a short distance away.

Carefully circling to approach the bull from downwind so as not be detected by its acute sense of smell, Thackwray slowly and cautiously closed in on his unsuspecting target.

Sue Mais

Eventually, much to the astonishment of the two spectators, Thackwray appeared to be almost underneath the huge bull. Through their telescopes they saw him reach into his pocket, take out a stick of chalk, reach up and write his name on the bull's hide. He had just finished his task and was turning to make his escape when the elephant, sensing his presence, promptly sat down on Thackwray. After a few moments the bull got up and wandered off without even a backward glance. Thackwray did not move. The two witnesses quickly went to his aid but it was hopeless. He had been crushed to death. It was much too far to take his body back to Port Elizabeth, so finding a suitable spot on a hill overlooking the surrounding bush, they buried him there.

The greatest enemy of knowledge is not ignorance, it is the illusion of knowledge. **Stephen Hawking**

A Window of Opportunity

Greer Noble

S ome years back my fastidious, 'never-a-hair-out-of-place', immaculately dressed brother-in-law, trying to impress his VIP American business associates, introduced them to the African bush, a nature reserve not far from Johannesburg. The morning went well until they stopped for a troupe of baboons in the road.

Used to cars and game-viewers, one very healthy young male promptly jumped up and sat on the driver's wing mirror. A little too close for comfort, my brother-in-law quickly wound up his window (automated ones being rare in those days), but in a flash, as if to get his own back, the mischievous youngster peed through the little pivotal vent window onto my brother-in-law's lap.

Seeing the look of utter horror on his face as the primate's steamy fetid urine seeped into his immaculate Savile Row suit, unable to contain myself, I burst out laughing.

I'm not sure if he ever clinched the business deal he was negotiating but one thing is for certain, it was something his guests would never forget!

Footnote – *Primates, mischievous by nature, have a keen and uncanny intuition to seek out the most vulnerable or the most indisposed!* – **GN**

The Devil's Nest

Greer Noble

Have you ever come to a fork road... did I say '*road*'?... more like a barely used track (with a stretch of the imagination) in the dense bush and not know which one to take?

'*I say take the one on the right,*' offered yours truly.

'*No straight,*' insisted my husband Mike and our young son in unison. Outvoted again!

Well the straight track turned out to be an elephant path... leading from pool to pool to pool... yet every now and again, the hint of actual tyre treads reassured us. It was flat wild forest terrain. After a couple of hours we reached a section where the track opened out. It was at this point that we spotted an army jeep in the distance, loaded with wood. Just as suddenly it slipped quietly into the forest and disappeared. It felt surreal... an illusion... a mirage! But on passing the exact spot we craned our necks and strained our eyes. We made out what looked like an army camp, draped in military netting discreetly tucked away in a heavily wooded area. What was an army base doing in the middle of a National Park? And so quiet. It would certainly never be spotted from the air. In fact it was so well concealed that had we not seen the jeep we would have driven right past and been none the wiser!

Puzzled, we pushed on... and on... and on... until half a day later... disaster! We hit a dead end! But not to be defeated we proceeded to bundu-bash through the now sparse undergrowth, thinking... hoping we'd pick up the trail again... only... more disaster. We found ourselves in the thick of a terrible, terrible trap! Thorns, a type of spiny-branched shrub that covered every inch of ground, thorns so tough, so lethal they went clean through our tyres. In all our travels in all the different countries we'd explored in Africa, never had we come across such hostile terrain! By the time we got out of that devil's nest we'd used both our spares... but at least we got out.

Retracing our tracks we resigned ourselves to the fact that we'd made a foolish mistake and would have to go all the way back... a full day's drive. When we reached the forest area again it was almost nightfall so we parked right where we were, in the track, confident that no one else would be coming that way.

That night was eerie. The sounds were somehow unfamiliar. Then at some unearthly hour I woke to what sounded like a thunderous stampede. What could that be? Buffalo? My heart raced. Then just as suddenly, deathly quiet again, too quiet. None of the usual night sounds. But what concerned me more than any wild animal was the army camp, even though it was now more than half a day's drive away. Whoever they were they'd seen us pass yet made no attempt to stop us. They must have known the road (which wasn't even a track) went nowhere. They were obviously trying to be pretty covert. Why the military mesh when the heavy cover of that dense jungle alone provided all the camouflage they needed? A bit of overkill, I thought. No one could possibly see them from the air and they were so well hidden we nearly drove past not knowing they were there. Needless to say for the rest of the night I did not sleep. An awful unease had crept over me. Something I never normally feel in the bush. I couldn't wait for daylight so we could get away from there.

First light and that wonderful first coffee of the day usually lifted our spirits but what awaited us could not have been worse. *All four tires were now flat...* and without a single spare as we'd already used the two spares the day before to get ourselves out of that mess. That nest of fiendish devil thorns had slowly but surely made their mischief.

'*Well there's nothing else we can do but fix all these punctures,*' Mike sighed.

To get a tire off a heavy Land Rover rim using tire levers is quite strenuous work – to get six off is daunting.

'*Where's the puncture kit?*' asked a now slightly irritated voice as the day had turned insufferably hot far too quickly, exciting the tiny mopane bees to enthusiastically kamikaze into any orifice... especially the eyes.

'*It's where it usually is, I haven't touched it,*' I came back defensively.

'No, it's not...'

'Wiseman borrowed it to fix his bike,' cut in our little son. Wiseman was our gardener... well over a thousand kilometres away.

'Dear God!' I exclaimed. Mike rolled his eyes shaking his head and gave a huge heave of despair. *'The blighter forgot to put it back,'* I fumed a little more colourfully than that to myself in utter disbelief. Could anything else possibly go wrong?!

Normally Mike would have packed our safari gear which, when not in use, was kept on a separate shelf in the garage of our home on the coast. But on this trip Wiseman packed the equipment (sans the repair kit which he had left on another shelf) as I had to pick up Mike en route, seven hours away, due to business commitments.

The next thing I knew Mike was draining the radiator. *'What are you doing?'*

'I'm going back to Savuti to get help and I want to make sure you've got enough water to last you because I don't know how long I'll be gone... you are going to have to ration yourselves...'

'No ways!' I was adamant. I couldn't take another night like that and certainly not on my own with our young son for what could be days on end, Savuti being at least a full day's drive away. *'With those soldiers knowing we're somewhere along this track... knowing there's no way out... even suspecting there's a woman amongst us? Who knows who they are or how long they've been there. I refuse! And what about you... what if you got lost? And with all the lion and hyena around... you're mad. Without a weapon, how far do you think you'd get? No, we have to think of another way.'*

We seemed to be in the flight path of commercial airliners... one had gone over during the night and one in the early morning. If we used the worst of the spare tyres and burnt it, would an airliner see us and report our co-ordinates? As we sat pondering I got very excited

when a small plane flew over, much lower of course than the huge commercial aircraft. *'I bet that's Lloyd Wilmot,'* I said as I waved my arms in the air. He ran Lloyds Camp a little further along what was then a dry river bed from the main Savuti camp. Fat chance of Lloyd seeing us in that heavily wooded forest I told myself.

Another brain-wave... we could cut up all our foam mattresses and stuff them into the tyres. I wasn't convinced. Suddenly Mike exclaimed, *'Got it!'* and held up a small tube of super glue he'd unearthed in a cubby-hole full of debris. Then he asked our son to climb up onto the roof of the Land Rover and get the rubber bands we'd cut from old tubes and fitted around our jerry cans to stop them rattling. We set to work cutting patches from the bits that weren't perished and lightly filed one side for better adhesion, doing the same to the punctured areas of each tube – and, very sparingly, used the super glue as the adhesive.

I expect it took four or five hours to repair all the leaks, another couple to get the tyres back on and then... the big test. Would the patches hold? At least we could inflate the tyres using our electric pump that operated off the vehicle's battery. We set it up but only to again be dispirited. It would not inflate the tyre because of a partially perished hose. But shortening it did the trick and Mike managed to pump up all the tyres, even the spares. Amazingly they held, so without further ado, the radiator was refilled and we were off once again, hardly daring to breathe. Our hope of traversing Chobe National Park's Mababe Depression was not to be.

Late that night we limped back into Savuti instead, having kept to the beaten track, extremely pleased to see a few other fellow campers around.

The most remarkable thing was that those tyres eventually carried us all the way home, some 1,400 kilometres (870 miles) thanks to super glue! No, we don't have shares... wish we did... can't even remember the make!

Life isn't about waiting for the storm to pass; it's about learning to dance in the rain. **Vivian Greene**

The Monster of Thokatsebe

Lloyd Wilmot

In the early 1950s and until Independence in 1966 some Bayei hunters would hunt buffalo and other animals with their muzzle-loaders and Martini-Henry rifles not far from Maun in Botswana. They would make bundles of sundried meat, load their dugouts till there was little freeboard and come to sell the meat in Maun. They often passed by Crocodile Camp, my father's base camp for crocodile-hunting operations. The meat usually smelt quite high because of the lack of salt.

In time we began to hear rumours about the monster of Thokatsebe Apparently a large crocodile had taken to attacking the meat-laden dugouts as they passed the *lexanas* (deep pools) of Thokatsebe some distance upstream. It must have learnt this trick from an initial attack which had yielded a lot of meat.

Now, after repeated attacks over a period of months the Bayei people begged my father to come and shoot it. Their eye-witness accounts of a large croc ambushing a loaded dugout and toppling its load of meat became more frequent. As the concessionaire for croc-hunting my father was asked by the authorities to investigate. Accompanied by a visiting friend from Francistown, Ronnie Pook, they set off for Thokatsebe at sunset. My father steered the boat and Ronnie, who had some hunting experience, was briefed on how to deal with the croc if they saw it.

An hour later they reached Thokatsebe and my father slowed the boat as Ronnie shone the spotlight about looking for the tell-tale red eyes. They passed the first pools then as they reached a belt of reeds the monster suddenly appeared in the beam. It was huge and Ronnie, a bit shocked, fired a hurried shot at its gnarled head. The 30.06 soft-nosed bullet blew off one of the heavy ear 'lobes' on the head. It was not an outright brain shot and the croc dived severely wounded. Despite repeatedly searching the dark depths and looking for any sign of bubbles or disturbed vegetable detritus in the water, they could find nothing. They pushed on higher upstream and returned half an hour later but again found nothing. Eventually they gave up and returned to Crocodile Camp.

For the following two days a scratch crew were sent to comb the area in case the croc had drowned from concussion and floated to the surface but it was never seen again. There were no further attacks in the ensuing months so it was assumed the croc had either left the area or eventually succumbed to its wounds in some quiet backwater.

An appeaser is one who feeds a crocodile —- hoping it will eat him last.
Winston Churchill

Satan and the Travelling Priest

Greer Noble

I f ever there was a snake to fear it's the black mamba. It's aggressive, has been known to chase people and is deadly.

A lot is to be said for living in the wilds and bathing under the stars, our toilet being the best. A roofless, doorless, snail-shell shape reed enclosure. Atop a mound, a wooden seat warm from the sun (what could be more inspiring), a rope across the entrance if occupied.

Only black mambas didn't know this because when occupied by a travelling priest, the serpent entered. The priest thought it Satan himself as the poor man explained later. Knees up, he watched in terror as the snake, feeling trapped, slithered around the enclosure. Several rapid Hail Mary's later Satan obliged, found the gap and left!

Safari to Tsavo

Humza Mwita

At 6am on a bright sunny Monday we began our three-day safari from Watamu on Kenya's north coast to Saltlick in Tsavo West National Park and then to Tsavo East.

Taking the Mombasa road we branched off an hour later at Mavueni in the Kilifi district and took the Muram road, a shortcut to Saltlick. We crisscrossed boys and girls in bright yellow and blue uniforms on their way to school, passed Mazeras, the last town before the Mombasa-Nairobi intersection and headed for Voi to refuel. Luckily the highway was not as busy as usual; only a few trailers, trucks and buses either heading to Mombasa or in the opposite direction to Nairobi. After Voi we abandoned the main route and took the Tanzania road which gave us another forty minutes of tarmac. We then branched off again intersecting the Muram road and arrived at Elephant Gate around noon.

After game viewing for twenty minutes we started spotting different birds, among them a large wake of African Vultures circling nearby. I became curious and asked the driver to head over in that direction. Low and behold there was a young elephant about four years old which, until closer inspection, looked dead. Due to the intense heat and lack of water it had obviously become dehydrated to the point of collapsing and losing consciousness. I phoned the head warden who promised to send his rangers to the site. Meanwhile I asked the driver and the three tourists to help resuscitate the animal by giving it the water we were carrying in the vehicle.

Making sure there were no dangerous animals in sight, one tourist, a Mr. Alex, said he would help me to try and revive the animal while the others kept watch for any approaching predators. Thank goodness the area was an open field. I lifted the elephant's trunk to access its mouth and when Mr. Alex, a courageous fellow, held its upper lip I poured water down its throat. Low and behold, after several gulps, the elephant started to respond to our help and opened its eyes.

'Another bottle please,' I shouted to the driver. He brought two. In seconds another bottle was empty. As I started with a third, the rangers arrived.

'Hi guys, how is it going?' They greeted us and praised us for our efforts and courage and said that if we had not found the elephant and given it water it would have died.

They then coaxed the elephant into their truck and took it to the camp's rehabilitation enclosure for release back into the wilds after it had regained its strength.

We continued on our journey to the Saltlick Game Lodge. After checking in we had lunch and relaxed until our evening drive. We spotted many animals including buffalo, giraffe and dik dik, as well as Maasai and Somali ostriches.

Early the next morning alongside the river we came across large herds of zebra, buffalo, various antelope and flocks of water birds, then returned to the lodge to check out and head for Tsavo East and Voi Wildlife Lodge for the night. There, thirty minutes into an evening game drive, we found ourselves on top of a hill giving us a magnificent bird's eye view of the park. On our way down again, low and behold, we saw a leopard coming out of a culvert.

Groaning, it came straight to our vehicle and attempted to climb in. I immediately told the tourists to shut all windows. The animal was behaving very strangely and seemed angry. After realizing that it could not climb into the car it attacked the left rear tire, still groaning and growling. The next thing we heard the hissing sound of the tire being deflated. The leopard had punctured the tire with its claws! Then worse still, it suddenly collapsed and died. I'd never seen anything like this before.

I contacted the warden for assistance. Within a short while other vehicles started streaming in. Then came the five rangers armed with AK47s in a Land Cruiser. We were now safe to change the tire. Meanwhile tourists in the other vehicles were busy taking photographs of the dead leopard. After they were done the rangers loaded the animal into their truck.

While still there, someone shouted '*Snake in the culvert!*' We looked towards the direction of the culvert and saw a big black snake come out and crawl into the grass. A ranger told us that the leopard must have been bitten by the snake, undoubtedly poisonous as its paws were oozing blood. It had suffered a painful death right before our eyes.

On our way early the next morning we stopped to watch a pride of lion feeding on a buffalo kill at a waterhole. Further on we came across elephant, waterbuck and an amazing myriad of birds.

We arrived back in Watamu bursting with news of one of the most eventful three day safaris ever.

The darkest thing about Africa has always been our ignorance of it
George Kimble

Poachers by Firelight

Greer Noble

Poaching in Africa, down through the ages, has been as natural to the hunter-gatherer as supermarkets are to us. On our ranch in Rhodesia, as it was then, our game scouts collected enough poachers snares to fill a ten ton truck... thanks to tsetse fences put up by the government, a futile and costly exercise to ostensibly prevent the migration of game and thus stop the spread of the killer fly. It was soon established that the so-called tsetse fly was in fact the common horse or hippo fly. What it did do was supply enough wire for poachers to make snares for years to come. Worse still, it snared a number of species of wildlife that tried to penetrate or jump the 2 metre high, 70 kilometre long fence.

This became a huge challenge. Hare, antelope and once even a young leopard was snared, a long and painful enough death if hyena or jackal, attracted by their desperate calls as fear turned to panic, didn't eat them alive first. Our scouts were charged by rhino, chased by bees, even a black mamba... lucky to escape with their lives. One day, following a dry river bed, two little spotted cats started playing between their legs. Their surprise soon turned to alarm as they realized these were two little *lion* cubs. Discarding their bikes they ran all the way back to camp..... not a day went by when there wasn't something, only they never caught a poacher.

Then one evening, sitting around the dying embers of our camp fire on the bank of the Mkwasine, a dry (seasonal) river bed, my mother spotted one. *'There, Eric.'* She pointed whispering as sound carries across a river bed at night when everything is quiet and the air crisp. *'Poachers! There, on the other side.'*

'Where?' my father and I said in unison, straining to see... only the penny dropped when my father winked at me. We carried on the charade for some time, pretending we couldn't see them, or rather their bicycle lights... for they were merely the glow of harmless little fireflies! Of course my mother never lived that down and fireflies forever more have been known in our family as poachers.

Eating Crumble Pie

Sue Maas

ot long after we had opened Tiger Bay, a resort high above the banks of the Ume river which flows into Zimbabwe's Lake Kariba, it was my turn to decide on the menu. We served a four course dinner, simple and homely but substantial.

I had the evening off and was able to relax and enjoy the meal with the guests instead of rushing around in the kitchen. The soup was delicious, followed by fresh, succulent Kariba bream and then the main course accompanied by vegetables. I noted that there was one vegetable short of what I had requested but as everyone was having a good time, I decided to leave the reprimands until later.

Dessert followed and it was then that I noticed that some of the guests had a rather strange look on their faces, some even looked positively ill but they were obviously too polite to make a comment. My plate arrived with the accompanying jugs of cream and custard and much to my horror and acute embarrassment, the pudding turned out to be the one vegetable I had missed with the main course. The dessert I had chosen had been baked apple crumble.

Meanwhile the chef had prepared the vegetable in the way I had taught him with a cheese sauce (I seem to recall it being cabbage) topped with a sprinkling of breadcrumbs. When baked it looked just like the apple crumble and our newly trained waiters were not too discerning when it came to serving the strange concoctions we ate. Fortunately our guests were extremely gracious and the evening ended with *real* apple crumble, fresh cream and custard.

Anyone who has never made a mistake has never tried anything new.
Albert Einstein

Fish Fingers

Greer Noble

Thomas Cavendish-Bolton, ex Royal Navy submarine commander, or just Tommy to his friends, was a complex man. He lost his two shipping companies when India gained independence... and his wife who died around about the same time. But he missed his wife the most and would reminisce for hours on end about their life in India. How very grand it must have all been.

He'd lived in Mahé for many years, on the opposite side of the island from Port Victoria, the capital of the Seychelles archipelago, in the secluded residential area of Visto do Mar. I learnt so much from Tommy (when circumstances found us guests in his home) about the islands, the sea and life in general. He showed me a magical emerald light that flashed up over the horizon of the sea at sunset, one of nature's rare phenomena which, he explained, sailors believed would bring them good luck. It took him days, using his instruments to calculate, within a split second, when this would occur. It did only last a split second too. Jules Verne described it as *'...a most wonderful green, a green which no artist could ever obtain on his palette, a green which neither the varied tints of vegetation nor the shades of the most limpid sea could ever produce the like! If there be green in paradise, it cannot but be of this shade, which most surely is the true green of hope! The incomparable tint of liquid jade.'*

One of my favourites was Tommy's story of a notorious governor of the Seychelles who, when a British ship entered the port he'd have the British flag hoisted and likewise, when a French ship showed up, up would go the French flag! He led a wonderful existence on a double pay roll and managed to fool both colonial powers for some 20 years before being discovered.

But what was really amusing was when Tommy was summoned to go to the Amirantes, a group of coral island and atolls about 30 miles southwest of Mahé – by reputation the best fishing grounds in the entire archipelago. I have to mention here that there were two things Tommy hated as much as the Nazis (they shot him full of shrapnel in the back during the war), and that was boats and fishing. He was strictly a submarine man, '*absolutely love them*'. But as there were only two people in the entire 115 island country, with celestial navigation (a prerequisite for chartered deep-sea fishing vessels operating in the Amirantes), he didn't have much choice – and was being paid for his services after all. On this particular occasion, unusually, he came back beaming. It transpired, on the third and last day, while on the bridge having a pee overboard, he accidentally peed on a German.

'*Accidentally Tommy?*' I teased, '*What did the guy do?*'

'*Oh he brushed it aside, closed his eyes and breathed in euphorically in anticipation of more of the same... thinking it spray from the sea.*' Tommy couldn't hide his grin.

'*And I expect you obliged?!*' I didn't expect a reply... and nor did get one but the smug look on Tommy's face said it all.

Then one day Kiwi, a mutual (half German) friend with a marlin outrigger invited us on a fishing trip. Tommy wasn't having any until he heard there would be a couple of damsels on board, of similar vintage to himself.

We set off on a glorious day and for a calmer sea you could not have wished. Kiwi insisted Tommy had a rod out, '*If only to impress the girls,*' he whispered with a wink. '*Come on Tommy,*' he urged, still under his breath, '*you have to look the part.*' Under the circumstances Tommy didn't need much coercing.

Soon elevenses were upon us and out came the G&Ts, ice clinking and Tommy charming the ladies. It doesn't get more perfect than this.

Tommy, deep in conversation stopped mid-sentence. Kiwi grabbed Tommy's rod from its fixed rod-holder and yelled to the skipper to cut engines, indicating to Tommy to take his rod, the reel whirring as the line went with the pull of an imminent catch.

Handing his glass to one of his new found admirers, Tommy reluctantly took it up and started reeling in. It was, of course, all show to impress the ladies because he'd sooner be dead than touch a rod. The engines idled gently creating a slight pull while Tommy reeled in vigorously.

'Quite a fundi there, Tommy,' Kiwi encouraged. *'Keep it taut, that's my man, keep it taut.'*

He did a splendid job, eventually landing his fish. When it did finally come out of the water it did so quite unexpectedly and, with a dull plop, landed on the deck.

First there was utter astonishment… and then peals of laughter. Tommy had caught a box of frozen fish fingers! Compliments of Kiwi of course. But even funnier than his catch, was to see the expression on his face. The girls' eyes were streaming they were laughing so much.

The joke was on Tommy which he didn't much like but merely gave a shrug and a grunt with a comment under his breath, *'I'll get you for this,'* and as nonchalantly as he could, carried on drinking.

Poor Tommy was never allowed to live that down and forever referred to as Fish Fingers!

'If happiness is the goal – and it should be, then adventures should be top priority.' **Richard Branson**

If You Walk Among Lions...

Adele Barton

Walking among lions is always thrilling, maybe a little more thrilling for some. My friend Mads had decided to go on a safari that offered an Encounter with Lions as part of their programme. She went with a friend of hers, Lawrence.

Shortly after breakfast they took off, accompanied by two guides. They walked for a while, then they saw one young lioness off to their right, quite a distance away. They carried on walking, single file, whilst keeping a watchful eye on the big cat. Mads was first in line, followed by Lawrence and then the guides.

Mads stopped at the top of a kopjie, a small hill, and looked around. Suddenly the lioness came charging and ran quickly passed both guides and Lawrence, heading straight for Mads! In true lion style she pounced... on Mads back, digging great big claws into her arms and grabbed her by her neck! Even though Mads couldn't see the lion coming, she knew instantly what was happening. She braced her knees and stood firm. Luckily she was short and sturdy. Somehow she instinctively knew that if she went down she would be killed.

Lawrence and the two guides acted quickly. They shouted and ran at the lioness, hitting her with their walking sticks. Luckily the lioness took fright and let Mads go, running off into the surrounding bush. The group limped back to camp with a bloodied Mads. The wounds were deep. Either side of her spine there were two deep puncture marks, easily big enough for my thumbs to fit. They managed to slow the bleeding down. Mads insisted on having a cup of tea before being taken to the hospital. The wounds were left open so that they could drain and she was given a strong course of antibiotics.

She was very lucky to survive being attacked. The doctors said that if she had not stood her ground, the lioness would probably have snapped her neck. The guides confirmed this afterwards, saying that if the lioness had meant business she would have been killed. The lioness was only eighteen months old and, according to them, was playing with her.

You know you are truly alive when you're living among lions.
Karen Blixen

None So Blind...

Greer Noble

The day had been long, the going rough and normally tempers would be frayed but the man behind the wheel took it in his stride as always. Despite the intense heat... made worse by mosquitoes as nightfall fell upon them, Richard's beautiful calm nature had a way of soothing everyone around him.

Driving in the bush after dark you had two choices; either leave your windows open for air and suffer the mosquitoes or close the windows and die of heat. And no, no air-conditioning... just something else to go wrong. That's Africa... but we still love it – difficult to explain to someone who hasn't been bitten! Richard and Anita were no exception.

'Why are you going so slowly? Anita had hoped to get to their designated rendezvous with the rest of the party before nightfall. *'I could get out and walk quicker,'* she challenged.

Richard smiled his big beautiful charming smile. *'Do you want to tease the lions?'*

Anita was not amused. *'Surely you can go faster.'*

'Well it would help if I could see.'

'Here, give me your glasses.' Even in the dark Anita could see they were coated in dust. *'When did you last clean them?'* She buffed them with soft tissues then handed them back.

'It isn't the glasses,' Richard complained, having put them on again. *'I still can't see properly.'*

Anita had to agree. Something was wrong. *'Stop and let me check the headlights. Maybe we got some mud on them.'*

'From where?' Richard came to a stop. It hadn't been raining and nor had they been through any rivers. *'Could be a build-up of dust,'* he called after her.

Anita checked the headlights and hopped back in again.

'*That's much better!*' Richard couldn't believe the difference. '*What did you do?*'

She had difficulty in trying to wipe the grin off her face. '*These!*' With the flair of a magician she produced their two canvass water bags and held them up for Richard to see. '*You hung them over the headlights my darling.*'

Well that's more or less the way Anita told it to us when we met up with them later. Sorry Richard, but you're never going to live this one down!

The ideals which have lighted my way and time after time have given me new courage to face life cheerfully, have been Kindness, Beauty and Truth. The trite subjects of human efforts, possessions, outward success and luxury have always seemed to me contemptible. **Albert Einstein**

Ferocious Opponent

Rachel Lang

When David Livingstone first laid eyes on the Chobe river, he cried. It is recorded in one of the many journals he kept that he was deeply moved by the extraordinary beauty of the river. The Chobe is indeed a sight to behold – a yawning blue expanse of water, broken by reedy green islands and sun-tanning hippos. It's a playground for elephants and a place where fish-eagles sound the voice of Africa, wild and uninhibited.

Infused in the very same idyllic African scene, I sit comfortably in my camping chair, gathering inspiration for the story I am trying to write. But, alas, my thoughts are up and away, levitating with little pied kingfishers and stotting with the red-brown lechwe on the far bank... then drawn by the whale-like breeching of two romantic hippos popping up in front of me. Ah Africa... never a dull moment.

Suddenly, out of the corner of my eye, I catch something moving, something coming straight towards me. Instinctively I grab my catty (catapult) – baboons and monkeys have a habit of picking on females. It may sound silly but ask anyone who has spent a lot of time in the bush and they will verify this somewhat shameful fact. But I was going to show this one... I may be a girl but I could be tough.

Then I froze. It was not a monkey. As it slunk past I held my breath... grey, black and white with a bushy tail... a honey badger! A honey badger on a mission. And where exactly was this mission leading him? Our rubbish bag. Although hidden between crates under a table, it was all too easily accessible for the badger.

In my mind I run through everything I know about honey badgers, which, despite having done a field-guiding course, is embarrassingly little. Now before you judge my seemingly violent reactions, you must understand that I was the only one in camp. It was my job to be brave camp defender. Besides, how could I just sit and watch this cheeky intruder strewing raw eggs and dirty paper plates everywhere?

I slowly creep clo0er, sneakily filling my pocket with stones and make my way on tiptoe towards the closest tent. Between khaki flaps I take aim. '*Bam!*' The sound makes me jump. I hit the Land Rover! My Dad will be pleased with that. Again I fire… but the animal hardly flinches. I try again. Highly frustrated, I decide to leave my place of safety and pick up a big log from the fire-pit and charge at the badger, almost scaring myself. It stops rummaging and looks up, still for a moment, and I think I see a hint of menace in the creatures eyes … then '*hhhhhsssss!!!*' A ferocious beast is coming for me with claws extended like knives. I have never seen such claws!

Needless to say, I run for the tent and for my very life. Even as I write this it's hard not to shiver. I sit in the tent for another half-hour, until the honey badger trots off, mighty pleased with himself. He disappears into the bush… is he on his way to raid another unsuspecting camper? Whoever they are, I hope they will not be as foolish as I was!

I later learnt that the very powerfully built honey badger has razor-sharp claws and teeth, jaws adapted especially for crushing, that its main defence when provoked is to attack and, no matter the size of its opponent, to go for its groin… and it should be viewed from the safety of a vehicle!

Fear is only as deep as the mind allows – **Japanese Proverb**

Celebratory Hold-up

Greer Noble

The Nagaatsa road to Savuti is not the regular route. We called it 'the back door' into Savuti camp from Kazungula, Botswana's busy border posts with Zimbabwe and Zambia. I'm not sure if anything has changed but some years back the road was pretty bad and little used which made it just that much more interesting and the reason we liked going that way. It's a place where we had two terrifying run-ins with elephant... the one you'll find in this book (*A Night of Sheer Terror*), the other was when an old tuskless cow charged us for no apparent reason in a particularly close call.

I recall spending several enchanting days camped at a serene water hole, our very own little 'nudist colony'! There's nothing like having sundowners in your altogether, watching elephant, lion and a variety of other species come to drink. I've never felt such freedom... try it sometime... and no, they didn't object, after all they do it all the time!

When we eventually tore ourselves away from our little Eden to continue our journey westward, we took a bet as we always did along that road, as to whether another vehicle would come from the opposite direction. On the several occasions we'd taken that route, not once did we see another vehicle or human. The road ran along a ridge for much of the way, the sand build-up forming a substantial centre-mound, making it narrow and, in some stretches, impossible to pass. Some distance along... it happened! We came face to face with two oncoming vehicles, a Land Rover like ours and another indescribable contraption vaguely resembling a jeep and a remote-control car. There was absolutely nothing we could do but stop, get out and meet our head-ons.

'*Merry Christmas!*' we said shaking hands, big smiles all round. They were a couple, about our vintage, and three teenage boys; their fifteen year old with a friend, and their twelve year old who had built the other vehicle from scrap with the help of his architect father!

Our son was intrigued with the contraption and delighted to have other human company for a change.

As it was already noon it seemed the logical thing to pool our food and drink and celebrate Christmas... which is exactly what we did.

What a party we had! Even the meerkats came out to see what all the commotion was about. We exchanged bush stories until the stars came out. One meets the best people in the world in the wilds. We laughed too much and must have drank too much too because for the life of me I cannot recall how our vehicles did eventually pass!

Footnote
Talking of meerkats, in Serondela, Chobe National Park's main campsite where it was common place for any of the big five to stroll through the camp at any time, along with resident warthogs and baboons, the meerkats added to the fun. These little creatures would join us at breakfast, begging for titbits – but it was the entire aura of the place that was unparalleled–**GN**

The Fothergill Pirates

Rob Fynn

Relaxing one evening over dinner on our front lawn at Fothergill, our three girls tucked up in bed, a blood-curdling scream from seven year old Karina or Neen as she was fondly known, suddenly rent the night air.

'Snake, Daddy, Snaaaake!'

I leapt to the door and switched on our generator-driven lights to find a huge python curled around her bed, clearly seeking out her Jack Russell that always slept with her, fortunately inside the mosquito net. Our new guide, whose herpetologist experience was far superior to mine, was called to assist. We gathered Mr Python into a pillowcase to be dropped off on the next morning's game drive. After assuring the girls how nice and friendly pythons were – although they love eating Jack Rusells – I settled everybody back into bed, a little worried that Neen would be troubled by the experience of waking to find a snake's head just next to hers.

All that was alleviated the next morning when excited, Neen related the story to our guests over breakfast, as was her daily habit. Her morning news bulletin, given to each table as she circled the dining room, was one all looked forward to.

'Hello. My name's Karina. My mum and dad own this camp. And, do you know what happened...?!' started most days for newly arrived guests.

This day she recounted how beautiful the big snake looked that had been on her bed last night, what lovely markings it had on its head, and that she'd be drawing it in (home) school that morning. Cath and Rach, her two sisters, listened intently, all having had a good look at Mr Python too, and agreed. What this all did for our guests' confidence in their own sleeping security, I wasn't sure. No ways could we block up all the openings into their chalets.

We decided to build a school and employ a teacher. One of our guides, who was a trained teacher, took on the duty. Richard's teaching and disciplinary measures were delightfully unconventional, filled with humour and motivational fun. I was driving out early one morning on a game drive, our first sighting was the teacher running down the track being chased and pelted with elephant dung by the pupils. I found out later that he'd set up booby traps of flour bags that fell on their heads when they opened the classroom door that morning, his hiding behind the bushes given away by his sniggering.

School started at 0600 and was normally all over by 1000, with a little homework session in the cool of the late afternoon. In between, the children explored. This could mean training frogs, racing beetles, teaching chickens acrobatics, fishing, canoeing, game drives with Dad, or helping Mum. It was a wonderfully free existence.

Neen was the leader of the gang, with Cath a competitive understudy, little Rach following in the rear, agreeing with everything her sisters suggested, trusting them implicitly. They were an inseparable team, known as The Fothergill Pirates by my family in town.

Island dress, spotlessly clean at the beginning of the day and looking like chimney sweeps within hours, consisted of pants and a 'T' shirt, the latter discarded as the day warmed up. A common sight was three off-white bottoms walking down the path, the Lodge's logo of a paw mark clearly displayed, often with a fourth brown bottom, a warthog's, tail high, our latest family addition, all in formation. Always set on another mission, studying a new insect or reptile. They lived in their own world, where school never stopped.

Neen had adopted an orphan monkey found on a game drive, probably having lost its mother to a predator and somehow escaped. It never let her go, clinging onto her neck every waking moment. Neen was protectively jealous of her charge. Cath and Rach would sneak in a cuddle with sleeping Monkey in its box cot when Neen wasn't looking, quickly to be admonished by surrogate mother once discovered.

Days off would be sailing the old Fish, their grandad's boat, to National Park camps up the Ume River.

Meanwhile, back on the base... *'Hello... yes , this is Fothergill Island reception...yes, I'm sure we could...sorry, excuse me a moment...Karina, take the monkey off that postcard stand ...because I say so!... Hello, <u>s</u>orry about that, as I was saying... Ooh nooo...'* Sound of crashing postcard stand... *'Look, I'm so sorry, could I phone you back?'*

It's really beautiful. It feels like God visits everywhere else but lives in Africa. – **Will Smith** (American actor and producer)

Tom Jones

Greer Noble

O h dear, to leave my mother holding the fort... Not to be disrespectful, she was highly intelligent, talented, and the most charming Latin-looking beauty to ever grace that part of the world. Only my older brother summed it up perfectly:

'When the Lord was handing out tact, Mum must have been at the back of the queue!'

I guess you can't have everything. And no better example was when again one day, my mother was left holding the fort. She was making one of her famous salads with fruit fresh from our gardens. Flipper, the newly appointed porter (so named because of his enormous feet), came running down to the cottage and excitedly announced, *'Madam, there are some humans in reception!'*

'Well that makes a change,' my mother smiled at Flipper, trying her best not to laugh. With that she reluctantly left what she was doing and hurried to reception to find three safari type vehicles full of... 'humans'!

Three of them were already waiting in reception.

'Good afternoon,' my mother greeted. It was something to lunch. *'How can I help you?'* she asked in her charming way, her smile hiding her irritation at the inconvenience!

'We'd like some accommodation,' the one fellow began, *'there are sixteen...'*

Before the poor man could finish his sentence my mother cut in... *'Well I'm afraid we're fully booked.'*

We were by no means full... or even half full. With 120 beds if ten rooms were occupied it would have been a lot. In fact it was rather a quiet time for us, pretty obvious I would have thought by the relatively few cars parked there... and the reason none of us were there. We'd taken the opportunity to go out on the lake *because* it was so quiet.

Only my mother would far rather tell everyone we were full (as we were to find out later), as she was in charge of the kitchen, gardens and bedrooms and didn't have a clue as to what went on in reception, nor did she want to know. Once she horribly overbooked incoming guests. She'd erased some confirmed bookings, trying to juggle everyone around to fit in new telephonic bookings and had then forgotten to re-enter the confirmed ones... but that's another story! Let it suffice to say that on that occasion it was so embarrassing we all vanished, including Madeleine, our receptionist, and left my poor father to face the music. Incredulously it turned out well in the end when he had the games room transformed into a dormitory, his Irish gift of the gab coming into play, but my mother vowed never to interfere with reception or incoming guests ever again!

'*Is there no way...*' the visitor implored. '*Do you know who we are...*' he tried a different angle, ' *I'm Tom Jones' manager and he will be arriving.....*'

Again my mother intervened, '*It makes no difference who you might be. We simply don't have any rooms available. I'm sure the Cutty Sark or Lake View can help you.*' (Carribea Bay had yet to be built). '*Here's a map.*' She handed him one of those tourist maps demarcating all the hot spots of where to stay, what to see and do etc.

I'd love to have been there to see the poor man's face. We later heard from the custom and immigration guys, regulars at our hotel pub, that *the* Tom Jones and his entourage had crossed the border into Zambia that very day. Totally deflated they must have headed straight for the border post after leaving us.

My mother casually mentioned that she'd turned away Tom Jones, '*Whoever he is,*' during sundowners that evening.

'*Tom Jones? THE Tom Jones?!*'... we all uttered in unison, incredulously.

I know the mileage Botswana's Chobe Lodge enjoyed after Elizabeth Taylor and Richard Burton spent their second honeymoon there. Why, to this day you can book the 'Burton' suite! Imagine the coverage we might have had, had we accommodated Tom Jones and his entourage - what fun it might have been! And he was eventually knighted! Imagine, 'The Sir Thomas John Woodward suite!'

It was years later that Clint Eastwood transformed the hotel to film part of his 'White Hunter Black Heart' then we later sold it during the bush war and other owners down the line bulldozed the entire hotel into the lake for reasons known only to themselves which is a terrible shame... but what memories!

In the social jungle of human existence, there is no feeling of being alive without a sense of identity **Erik Erikson**

When the Lion Roars

by Addie Kraan

Sue Maas

I used to spend a lot of time in Zimbabwe's Wankie (now Whange) National Park in the late 70s. My VW camper had a PA system which I used to attract lion. That's not the only thing it attracted... all the safaris operators would follow me whenever they saw my camper. On one occasion while looking for lion we came across a load of tourists pushing a Land Cruiser through some sand. In a devilish mood, I slowly came up behind them and when about 50 metres from them I turned on the PA system and made a perfect lion call. You have never seen people disperse so quickly in your life, diving into and under the cruiser. They must have thought their last days had come!

Ultimate Arbiter
Would you believe that an influential Zimbabwean council which employs internationally renowned consultants, relies on its witchdoctor to approve the siting of a tourist camp within its jurisdiction?! – **MB**

Lion Attack at Kaz

Rob Fynn

Still suffering from the shock of being a dad, after seeing my firstborn arrive into the world, I received more heady news. An unforgettable night had also been had back in Kazangula*, our camp on the shores of Lake Kariba's Matusadona National Park. I had taken on a young trainee couple, Calvin and Sue, to hold the fort in my many absences.

It was a particularly dark night, a storm crashed waves on the shore. Moaning trees bent in the wind... an early to bed and snuggle up evening.

Well into the night, a crying and wailing was heard in the direction of the staff tents. Guests thought there was revelry in the air. Some may have stirred uneasily. Calvin and Sue were in an exhausted sleep as all staff was every night. As were Oz and Buhnu who slept by the kitchen.

In the staff tented compound, a lion had clawed its way into where our head bedroom hand, Joseph, was also deeply asleep. He awoke to a lion dragging him by the head out of his camp bed. His brave wife seized a large cooking pot and used it to try and bash the brains out of the king of the jungle, screaming for reinforcements.

Horrified at hearing the lion amidst Joseph and his wife's screams for help, the remaining dozen or so staff members crowded into one tent, also wailing loudly. There was no way they were going out there, certain a whole pride was waiting to devour them. Finally Tyson could stand it no longer. He broke from the tent and, in a frenzied dash through the dark wind-lashed bush to the camp seventy metres away, repeatedly shouted '*SHUMBAAAAAAAAAA...!*' *

Calvin, Oz and Buhnu were quickly wide-awake. Tyson garbled the story. Assessing the situation, they drove round in the Land Rover unarmed as we all still were. Approaching through the trees under urgent directions from Tyson, the lion was picked up in the headlights standing outside Joseph's tent.

The remainder of the staff fled round to the back of the Land Rover hurling themselves in through the rear door.

Buhnu edged his way to behind Joseph's tent, screened from the lion in the dark. Oz stood by, armed with a knobkerrie.* Everybody watched, holding their breath.

Calvin was poised with his foot on the accelerator, ready to charge if the lion moved.

Painfully slowly, Buhnu crept into Joseph's tent, picked up the scalped man in one arm and mauled wife in the other and crawled back to the vehicle carrying them both, all eyes on them and the panting lion standing only metres away.

All fifteen on board, Calvin reversed out and drove back to camp. A casualty station was set up in the kitchen, its mopane* boma the only solid structure in the camp offering a modicum of security. Oz and Calvin woke all the guests and escorted them to the haven, whereupon a dentist and his wife, returning guests, volunteered to stitch up the sorry two, ably assisted by Sue.

Calvin tried to get out in the boat to neighbouring Spurwing Island to use their radio phone, and returned. Too rough.

In the early hours, Buhnu, crouching over the fire, boiling the umpteenth kettle for tea and coffee, suddenly noticed a movement at the kitchen doorway which was simply an opening in the wall of poles. There was the lion, surveying the scene, unnoticed by the activity centred on the stitching operation.

Without saying a word, Bhunu pulled a burning log from the fire and hurled it at the lion. A roar, a cloud of dust, and the fallen king leaped back and disappeared into the dark. Shock and exclamations. Feverish efforts barricaded the doorway with kitchen cupboards and tables. In an uneasy calm the vigil resumed in the emergency room at a renewed level of readiness.

First light found an exhausted but united band of camp guests and staff with two well-stitched and recovering victims. Our only communication with the outside world sprang to life. The Lake Navigation radio. '*Good Morning Lake, this is Kariba*'. Calvin passed an S.O.S.

An Air Force helicopter based at the airport responded and was whirling over the lake in minutes. Our two stalwarts were picked up and whisked to hospital in Harare, with the RhAF's compliments.

Ensuring my new family and just-arrived mauled staff were as fine as they could be, I made haste back to the Lake. Finding a fatigued but exhilarated camp, not a single guest had chosen to leave despite the lion having ransacked four tents. Beds were broken, coir mats torn and mattresses eaten.

National Parks research ranger, Russell Taylor, and his assistant arrived in their Land Rover and took charge of the situation. They shot an impala as bait to lure the lion back with the plan to shoot it, and warned us all to remain in camp.

Later in the evening light, on the spit of land that adjoined our camp to the main land they spotted the lion on the bait. They jumped from their vehicle and opened up on the hapless beast, momentarily forgetting that our camp lay directly behind and in their line of fire.

In camp, settled down for the evening, bullets suddenly zapped through tents and pinged off metal poles. Everybody hit the deck.

Mission accomplished, two proud Parks men stood with a dead lion at their feet. On dissection, it turned out to be an emaciated lioness with severe kidney disorders. Bits of tent, mats, mattresses, and boots from the previous evening's spree were found in its stomach, but no human limbs!

*Kazangula camp in Matusadona National Park, Rhodesia (now Zimbabwe), was so named as its original owner's safari business was based in Kazangula, Botswana, on the Zambezi River where Botswana, Namibia, Zambia and Zimbabwe borders meet.
*shumba –   lion
*knobkerrie –   carved club with a large knob at one end
*mopane boma – enclosure of mopane tree poles
*mopane trees – habitat of fat edible worms, a Batonga tribe delicacy
*RhAF –   Rhodesian Air Force

A lion sleeps in the heart of every brave man – **Turkish Proverb**

Mal de Mer Island Style

Greer Noble

After visiting friends in the neighbouring island of Praslin we took the local ferry back to Mahé... and home. Packed to capacity there was only standing space along the gunnel, midway between the bow and the stern for the half-hour trip. The boat, due to frequent cloudbursts, had a canopy as well as side flaps that could be dropped if necessary. Creoles are particularly prone to mal de mer (sea sickness) and the handing out of plastic buckets in advance by the crew, I thought, didn't exactly help matters.

Standing next to us was a burly, balding, middle-aged German with his buldu, the name given to certain creole ladies who, for a buck, do *everything*! We cast off and as the swells grew, so did the puking. About halfway across, one very old creole woman vomited overboard from the bow. Being downwind, the German and his buldu got the full blast of it and us, to a lesser extent. Thanks to a couple of bottles of the local palm brew we were already several sheets to the wind so saw the funny side of it. He made a dash for the heads and she stood picking bits out of her thick mop of tight curls the rest of the way – a romantic Seychelles sunset ruined!

The Count and the Runaway Bride

Greer Noble

Leo *du* Baudissin*, formally Leo Count *von* Baudissin (no one quite knew why he changed from the German prefix *von* to the French prefix *du*) claimed, nonetheless, that he was of German aristocracy, and proud of it. A gentleman at large, a confirmed bachelor (or so everyone thought), he was, among other things, said to be a remittance man. There were all sorts of rumours surrounding this eccentric character – that he was indeed a German count who had fled Europe under a dark cloud, that he would string his black staff up by the ankles and, suspended from a branch, have them whipped by his boss-boy* (all gentleman farmers in the then Rhodesia had a boss-boy), and left hanging for many hours as an example to his other labourers.

We'd been guests in his home once and I knew people who'd partied there. A very close and mutual friend, Jacque*, confirmed all of the above and also told me that it was Leo's favourite party trick to become morbid and try to hang himself in the bathroom... even to the extreme of stringing himself up by a hangman's noose. But the count is best remembered for his insatiable appetite for the fairer sex.

In the early days there was no TV in that part of Africa. Computers, cellular phones and Facebook were unheard of. Your rather cumbersome telephone was mounted on the wall and by manually winding a side-handle clockwise, using a combination of rings; several turns for a long ring, a brief wind for a medium ring and a half wind for a short ring... or a series thereof, enabled one to get through to anyone in the area or the telephone exchange. Everyone had and knew their own particular ring combination enabling them to make and receive calls.

The problem with this system was that it left it wide open for anyone to listen in on everyone else's conversations... and a lot of bored farmers' wives did. Or even if one had to make a pressing business call for example, you *had* to pick up the phone and listen in to see if the line was clear and sometimes even appeal to the other party to end their call to free the line. As a consequence gossip was rife! A telephonic African Peyton Place!

So it wasn't surprising that Leo's infidelities with married farmers' wives were legendary. But after having *'serviced'*, as he so delicately put it, all those willing and able, he grew bored with that, be it a rather dangerous pastime, and spent more and more time focusing on his pen-pals of whom he had many; a form of modern day Facebook if you like.

There was one in particular called Bianca*. For some time Leo had been corresponding with her. *'A cute little 18 year old blonde honey,'* he confided in Jacque, sucking deeply on the cigarette dangling from his lips, whipping out her photograph as if he were a magician. Even though it was in black and white, she was the epitome of every man's dream; big soft dark eyes and a voluptuous Marilyn Monroe type figure. They'd exchanged photographs.

Their long distance romance blossomed and when Bianca eventually agreed to Leo flying her out from Brussels to join him for a trial run on his tobacco estate in darkest Africa, barely able to contain himself, he told Jacque. The weeks that preceded her arrival had everyone running around trimming lawns, scrubbing walls, sweeping pathways... there was not to be a twig out of place or a speck of dust anywhere. Even curtains were replaced and new linen purchased.

On the Friday in question his blue Jaguar, be it a little dated, was brought out of mothballs, vacuumed and polished to a fine sheen. Clad in his best linen suit, silk cravat and a pink carnation in his lapel, Leo set forth on the three hour journey to what was then the Salisbury International Airport.

Arriving in ample time he stood where he had a perfect view and where he too could be easily spotted. The plane had landed. His heart palpitated. What if she'd missed the flight? He nervously lit his third cigarette, checked his hair once more with a stroke of his hand and waited. Lady Luck was on his side – Bianca was first off the plane.

His heart skipped another beat as he walked towards her in the boiling sun. It had been her idea that he wear a pink carnation in his lapel so that she was sure to recognise him. As the gap closed between them she smiled. It was the most disarming smile Leo had ever seen. He went weak in the knees; he was in love before even touching her.

'*Bonjour!*' she greeted, a kiss on each cheek. '*You... Monsieur Baudissin?*'

She wore a red halter-neck sun dress with just enough cleavage to send his temperature up a few more notches. Her skin reminded him of a porcelain doll. How fresh, how lovely, Leo thought excitedly, catching his composure and her exotic scent at the same time.

'*Charmed...*' he began, taking her hand. He didn't recognise his own voice.

'*Pardon, Monsieur Baudissin*', she interrupted, trying to look past him and on tip toe, all the better to see over his shoulder. Her English broken, she hesitatingly persisted, '*Your son... he is not with you?*'

The truth shall out. Leo had sent her a picture of himself when he was in his twenties. He had just topped seventy!

Late that night there was loud knocking on Danie van Vuuren's* front door. Martha, his wife, woke him. At that time of night it could only mean trouble. Danie reluctantly climbed out of bed, stepped into his rugby shorts, uniform garb among Rhodesian farmers, grabbed his gun and half staggered to the front door. The banging had become more frantic, more incessant.

'*OK, OK, mina boya***', he called out. Then more to himself, '*If it's that boss-boy again I'll kill him.*'

After the weekly wages were paid there was always fighting on a Friday night. The local brew was extremely potent and consumed too rapidly the consequences were always the same. The last time he was woken up, the boss-boy had brought along a very drunk Philemon with an axe wedged in his skull. He'd rushed him off to the hospital in Sinoia, a village some forty minutes away by car. Remarkably the axe victim was back at work on Monday, stitches and all.

He switched on his flashlight, turned the lock and, gun at the ready, threw open the door. Danie's mouth dropped open. He wasn't quite sure if he was dreaming or not. Before him, clutching herself stood the most beautiful naked woman he'd ever seen in his life.

Incensed, Leo consoled himself with God knows how much liquor over the next couple of days then took to the air in his plane which was housed in its own hangar alongside his private airfield behind his tobacco barns. Behaving as if his single engine Cessna was a Tiger Moth he performed hair-raising stunts over several farms in the area, terrorising farmers and their labourers.

Upon eventually and miraculously landing he had a welcoming committee; the head of the local aeronautical club accompanied by the police. He was charged with recklessness and flying under the influence, appeared in court and lost his licence. This was not his first time – he'd had several prior warnings.

The van Vuurens opened their home to Bianca and showed her the hospitality Rhodesian farmers were renowned for. The poor girl had escaped a terrifying ordeal at the hands of their eccentric neighbour who'd obviously tried to bed her against her will. Only she would never talk about it. Running blindly through the tobacco fields she'd come upon this farmstead, its security lights being the only sign of life for miles around on that dark night.

Without money or clothes, returning to Belgium was not an option. The van Vuurens settled her in nearby Karoi, a small farming town where they found her a live-in job at the local hotel. Young policemen, farmers' sons and local salesmen were like moths to a bright light. She fell in love with a local tradesman, a good-looking, salt-of-the-earth Rhodesian who was completely devoted to his *little flower* and, of similar age, they were soon married.

Meanwhile back on the estate a demented Leo descended on his hangar armed with a bottle of Scotch and an axe and proceeded to hack his plane to pieces in between gulps of that fire-water.

Soon afterwards he sold his farm, bought a cabin cruiser and moved to Lake Kariba, about an hour and a half's drive from his farm.

That's where we really got to know him.

*Leo du Baudissin – pseudonym
*boss-boy – foreman
*Jacque – pseudonym
*Bianca – pseudonym
*mina boya – I'm coming
*Danie van Vuuren – pseudonym

'Those who are easily shocked should be shocked more often.'
Mae West

Croc-Bait

Saskia von Sperber

A few years back when I was working in the Northern Tuli Game Reserve in Botswana, my friend Malora and I were having sundowners in the almost fully dried up Limpopo river bed. With us we had my dog and my boss's two dogs that were having a good run and nose around the few pools left from the last flood.

Sitting cross-legged in the sand we were enjoying a beautiful sunset and watched some baboons and kudus crossing the riverbed some distance away when we heard a peculiar noise behind us – both of us turned around and to our great surprise saw a crocodile running towards us through the sand! Maybe only about six foot long this was still a rather alarming sight and both of us jumped up thinking the croc might have mistaken us for a monkey – or baboon – supper! The crocodile seemed to even accelerate its run and with one look at each other, Malora and I burst out laughing and, shrieking, flip-flops and beer cans flying ran for the steep riverbank.

The dogs came running; no doubt alarmed by our shrieks, and when they saw the croc hard on our heels, attacked it with what can only be described as a doggy-rugby-tackle!

377

Dogs and croc rolled around growling, barking, hissing and snarling for some seconds before the croc, thank goodness, admitted defeat and dove into one of the remaining pools in the almost dry riverbed!

Apart from a few scratches the dogs were thankfully unharmed and I doubt they'd had time to inflict any injuries on the poor croc. So Malora and I, still shaking with laughter, gave the very brave and supremely chuffed dogs a much-deserved biltong snack!

On several similar occasions I saw what I thought was the same croc. It again tried to attack and menace me while fishing... and earned me the nick-name of Croc-Bait.

.

The phrase, *'I nearly died laughing,'* springs to mind – **GN**

Hollywood and Lord Dalhousie

Greer Noble

Ollywood happened when, inspired by a wildlife rescue undertaking known as Operation Noah, my father decided to turn a derelict area of several hundred acres into a game sanctuary. It was on either side of a stream that ran through the small border town of Umtali (now Mutari), in Rhodesia (now Zimbabwe).

It concerned him greatly that so many animals would be in such dire need of being rescued during the imminent rising waters of the Zambezi. Spanning the width of that famous river, the big hydroelectric power station built by Italy's Impresit, was all but complete. It was to dam the world's largest man-made lake at that time. The sheer magnitude of it was breath-taking; 400 kilometres from Victoria Falls, it would flood the entire Gwebe Valley and the Zambezi upstream for 300 kilometres.

Despite torrential rains and other setbacks, rumoured by the indigenous Batonga tribe to be the wrath of Nyaminyami the River God, the dam wall was ready and in 1958 the river started to back up into the valley. Aside from the rescue of countless animals, birds and snakes, thousands of Batonga people from both sides of the Zambezi, had to be relocated. The wildlife side, Operation Noah, was led by Rupert Fothergill, a game ranger whom my father knew from Umtali

379

when Rupert had his engineering business there.

With a team of only eleven, including Rupert himself, a breed of men both white and black you'd be hard-pressed to find anywhere, their primary goal was to rescue as many animals as possible from drowning. It was the grit and sheer determination of these men who risked their lives every day, unafraid of what they had to do.

Starvation Island probably proved to be the worst. Crowded within the thick bush, eleven starving lion and four elephant were chased into the water, and all thankfully swam to the mainland beneath the Bumi plateau. To this day elephant can be seen swimming to and from the island. It was the eleven rhino and some two hundred buffalo, among numerous other species, that needed to be subdued to be moved. Finally with no more tranquilizers left it was inevitable some perished, hence the name of the island, but thanks to Rupert and his team, at least two hundred of these animals were rescued.

The ever rising waters were polluted with dead fish floating everywhere, presumably bloated from gorging on the hordes of insects. Partially submerged trees dripped snakes, gibbering monkeys and clawing leopards. Floating islands drifted by, thick with scorpions, spiders and other insects. Elevated ground became islands congested with petrified wildlife as the water continued to rise. Larger animals were nudged and coaxed towards shore or, if flailing, roped to the boats or raft to keep them afloat.

My father arrived in Kariba early one evening in the 60s with his ten ton truck and own small crew. He was met by a very exhausted but exuberant Rupert. The next morning they set to work and within no time, assisted by Rupert and his team, the first animals were loaded for their eight hour journey to Umtali and their new home in the sanctuary. It would be the closest they'd ever get to paradise as it was an expansive area offering ample water, food for every taste... *and* no predators! Home to vagabonds and a hide-out for criminals, it had not been difficult to persuade the local council to declare it a wildlife sanctuary and, in so doing, supply the fencing.

This was the first of several trips to Kariba. While not always possible, pairs of everything were sought, from hornbills to warthog; from impala to pangolin. As big as the sanctuary was, it wasn't big enough for dangerous animals or predators nor was the terrain suitable for giraffe. A series of weirs at planned intervals along the flowing stream formed large ponds for drinking or, in the case of wild birds, paddling. A few pedestrian bridges across the stream, the better to view the game, proved an added attraction. Little did my father know by just how much!

Farmers dumped their peapods and other vegetable scraps daily. Hay was delivered on a regular basis and an enticing thatched kiosk, strategically positioned near the main pedestrian bridge, offered refreshments and curios to the public. Profit went towards the maintenance of the sanctuary. Everything was voluntary and, all in all, a wonderful success and an asset to the town, attracting families, school children, the elderly and tourists.

Only there was one problem – Hollywood. A very large ground hornbill, so named for his long eyelashes, seductive eyes and the way he strutted around. He fancied himself a VIP and clearly ruled the roost. Also a comedian of note, he soon made firm friends with Lord Dalhousie, a feisty little warthog, named after the then Governor General of Rhodesia. The show began when Hollywood would pick up a frog in his beak and Dalhousie would give chase. The next thing Dalhousie would have the frog in his mouth with Hollywood in hot pursuit. This little game would go on endlessly to peals of laughter from any onlookers. Life is a stage and the bush is no different!

But this delinquent bird took it a step further. Deciding the game sanctuary wasn't big enough, he managed to escape. Panic reigned as search parties went out in all directions. It was the owner of the local hotel who found Hollywood – in his pub! He was being treated like a celebrity by the regulars, even a tot or two of beer, until his captors arrived. In disgrace he was brought back to his home in the sanctuary, much to the delight of his friend, Lord Dalhousie. But Hollywood escaped again and again, each time found in the same pub. This wayward bird was incorrigible, his hooligan ways not to be dampened; he became a regular.

Large ground hornbills on critically endangered list – loss of habitat; female lays just 1 to 2 eggs once every nine years – **Africa Geographic**

Living on the Edge!

Greer Noble

B eing interrupted persistently while on the phone is irritating at
best, so one reacts.

'*What is it?*' I turned to my nine year old... and froze. '*My
son is holding a green mamba... I'll have to call you back,*' I said to
whoever it was on the other end, barely recognising my own voice,
my eyes riveted to the unbelievable scene before me.

He had it by the neck! Had I known at the time just *how* lethal it
was – only 30 minutes to get an anti-serum – I don't think I would
have been quite as calm.

'*Throw it into the garden... AT ONCE!*'

Hearing my severe tone he quickly flung it into the undergrowth.
Thankfully it slithered off and, melding with the greenery, was gone
in a flash.

Could this be pay-back time?!

Not a Place for Ladies

Michael Noble Ballantine

During a long safaris with my parents in Zimbabwe I came across a truly enormous abandoned anthill near our camp in the bushes at Tashinga, Matusadona National Park on the shores of Lake Kariba. All of eight years old, I carved a castle out of it with a machete despite it being a favourite habitat of highly poisonous snakes and scorpions.

At times like this some of us tend to feel risks are less up to mathematics, and luck more up to something up there which appreciates enthusiasm for the blessings of creation. And so you go for gold in your innocence. As a tiny tot I relished sitting in crocodile infested water searching for muscles, jumping into a crocodile pit, facing off with an elephant, playing hide and go seek with a rhinoceros...

The oddness of Africa is found in the reputation of the animals who live there: the four legged in their humanity, and in the two legged often in the lack thereof. One of my oldest acquaintances, being something of a Hitler clone, would make casual outbursts about wanting to nuke all and sundry out of dismay at the often wretched psychological states. I found it a shameful topic, though could identify why he was in dismay in this landscape described of as '..*not a place for ladies.*'

As a fourth generation Euro-African I found virtue in the shamanic path like so many of my aboriginal counterparts. From that archetypal search of experience I found myself to be in an intelligent bosom. So when you see an African smoking his calabash pipe outside his hut, know there is a higher purpose at hand.

The rebel in us manifests in different ways; it may be perverse, defiant, even destructive or adrenalin-driven risk-taking often superseding sanity. Woe betide it should become addictive although it is said the most rebellious of all become the best entrepreneurs. **GN**

Pavarotti and Friends

Greer Noble

The door of our small bush lodge stood slightly ajar when suddenly a bossy banded mongoose burst in, hotly pursued by two equally forward warthogs. I stood, my mouth agape! The extremely lively mongoose proceeded to investigate; the vegetable rack, the bedroom, then back into the living area and promptly sat on my foot. Characteristically gregarious (foraging in packs of up to 50), I knew they had a symbiotic relationship with warthogs (a 'grooming service' – piggy gets relief, mongooses feast on juicy tick snacks), but this was definitely out of character. Thinking it must be someone's pet, I cautiously bent down to stroke it. I was wrong. With lightning speed, razor sharp teeth slashed my flesh. That really had me worried; horrors… rabies… what if it was rabid?!

Clutching my bleeding hand, knowing how unpredictable and aggressive warthogs can be too, I feared a reprisal were I to attempt to shoo them out. I felt trapped. Never had I been in a situation like this before. But luck was on my side. Thankfully my husband arrived back and, in seeing my dilemma, shooed the trio out. Nonplussed, they immediately made themselves right at home, languishing on our veranda. Too adorable for words, they earned the title of 'Pavarotti and friends.' There was nowhere to be tested or treated for rabies but as I didn't start barking after a few days we decided I didn't have it after all!

Miss Finland

Mike Ballantine

The quickest route from Kariba to Victoria Falls is via Zambia and will take about eight hours. Just make sure your papers are in order for the cops along this road are particularly vigilant. Alternatively you could drive onto the MV Sealion ferry which runs a relaxing twenty two hour trip from Andora harbour to Mlibizi. From there it's only 3 hours by road to The Smoke that Thunders/Victoria Falls, Zimbabwe. On board you will undoubtedly consume large quantities of your favourite tipple, make new friends, share stories, party and doze in deck chairs. We've enjoyed this voyage several times.

Or you could be just plain dumb and drive overland through Zimbabwe. Well we did – and were delighted with what we discovered. If you were to drive directly to Victoria Falls without leaving the road you would need to allow at least two days for the 1250km trip as the roads are badly potholed, sometimes nigh impassable and tortuous. So it was in the nineties that along the way we stopped to smell the roses – for three months.

On the Binga road from Karoi we turned off after about three hours onto the particularly challenging two hour track to Tashinga, a lake-front National Park campsite in Matusadona. The camping fees for the three of us including our battle-scarred Land Rover and Zodiac-packed trailer were less than one US dollar a day. But you did need to be self-sufficient. There were no hotels, shops or buildings other than the rangers' office, ablutions and a resident ecologist's home all hidden in the bushes – but for the traveller, not even a tent or awning.

It was dicey to order fuel or liquor from the captain of the mini-ferry which called every fortnight. Often he arrived with only fuel and once an eagerly awaited bottle of brandy, whisky being scarce, somehow turned up as a miniature. However, nothing could detract from the site's glorious position on the lake's edge. More often than not we had the place to ourselves – until the Christmas-New Year period when it was pretty full.

That's when she appeared – on New Year's Eve. We christened her

'Miss Finland', among ourselves, for no other reason than that she was Finnish.

My son and I were returning to our camp after a shower when I spotted my wife in the company of a young, skinny, blond 'man' consuming one of my precious beers. My annoyance was only slightly mollified by the fact that 'he' turned out to be Miss Finland.

She had arrived on the mini ferry from Kariba expecting, she said, to find accommodation and food. Being New Year's Eve my wife took pity on her and suggested that she could sleep that night in our supply tent where we stored fuel for our Zodiac, foodstuffs, chairs, a table and sundry clutter from our vehicle. She was made comfortable with the help of some pillows, sunbed mattress and a groundsheet. Our beds were in modified roof-top tents, one being our son's.

Long since having been invited, we spent New Year's Eve with ecologist Mike Murphree who was based at Matusadona, and his visiting extended family. In her early twenties, we arranged for Miss Finland to spend the evening with a newly-arrived overland group of similar age, whose tour guide I knew.

She joined us some time after midnight, strolling back towards our camp when a balding, middle-aged man persuaded us to join another party about a hundred metres away. The night was dark and we briefly lost sight of him and Miss Finland. When she caught up with us she was flustered. '*He pulled me aside and flashed,*' she tittered. He was old enough to be her father.

He had melted into a group of about twenty people who we joined. Perhaps it was the wine but my wife, seeing the funny side of what had happened, related the incident to the woman sitting next to her. When asked who the man was she pointed him out. The woman immediately stood up and, knocking her chair over in the process, stormed off. The villain, it transpired, was her husband – and somewhat incorrigible it seemed, for later in our supply tent to savour a hot toddy before turning in, the flap opened and there he was grinning mawkishly. In less than polite terms I told him to '*get lost*'.

'*What are* **we** *going to do today?*' Miss Finland pointedly inquired when we had all surfaced later that morning. Expecting her to make arrangements to return to Kariba we were taken off guard by her brashness and rather meekly surrendered the day... and the next... and the next... to her desires.

It was exhausting, entertaining Her Highness in a manner she thought became her. Fishing on demand from our Zodiac, helping herself at will to our precious rationed supplies and beers. She'd embedded herself with us in our every waking moment. We didn't like it. But when, with some show, on the fourth day, she presented my wife with a small can of potatoes for our hospitality I cracked. It would have been far better had she offered nothing.

'*We're going for a long walk. When we return she must not be here,*' I cruelly appointed my wife to get rid of Miss Finland while my son and I set off.

We never saw her again but heard that after spending a night or two in the staff compound, much to their discomfort, she was spotted amidst a group of male tourists staying at the Bumi Hotel, on a plateau high above the lake, on the far side of the Ume River mouth.

An 85 Knot Blow Job

Charles Mackie

Having spent a good part of my life in Rhodesia's Department of National Parks and Wildlife Management from 1970 until 1984, I remain active in the same field to this day – 2014. I served in the management branch and held various posts from a junior ranger to warden in charge of several of the country's national parks. Now the duties of rangers and wardens were to fly aircraft – if there was an aptitude and interest. The department had its own fleet of aircraft and several members of the department owned their own aircraft and were paid to use them.

At one time when I was warden at Chizarira, I had the use of a department Piper Super Cub where it was used to serve a number of stations including Chete and Chirisa safari areas, the Sengwa Wildlife Research Area, Matusadona and Mana Pools National Park. This was the heyday of wildlife management where there were animal movement studies and projects, population reduction operations in many of these and other areas in which aircraft were the primary instrument for surveillance, radio telemetry relocations and various ground to air operations and indeed many other uses.

The aircraft types we used were small, high performance, mostly tail wheeled, upper winged machines. I would often leave my station as the sun was rising after downing a double egg-nog and stuffing some sandwiches into the pockets of my overalls, on flying sorties which would sometimes last most of the day. The Piper Super Cub I was flying on the day had its configuration in respect of pilot access through a 'gull wing' double flap opening door on one side. Since the type is slow flying, the doors can be opened in flight and are often opened in such a way so as to be able to throw things out the 'window-cum-door', to people, animals as the case may have been.

On a hot October day I had spent the whole of my time doing aerial relocations of radio-collared elephant at some distant place. I had deposited my rear seat colleague and I had filled my aircraft with Afgas, 100/130 octane fuel, pumped from a 200 litre drum. At some point I had sat on the top of the drum. Now when fuel is pumped through a drum pump there is usually a pool of the contents which oozes from the pump and sits in a shallow pool on the top of the drum. The natural consequence of sitting on the drum was that my cotton flying overalls became saturated up to the waist with the volatile fluid.

As I took to the cabin, and being in somewhat of a hurry to make home by nightfall, I became uncomfortable around the inside of my legs, the cleavage of my buttocks and especially the groin, and other closely associated anatomy! This was particularly so, because in the temperatures of the areas in which we lived and at that time of the year, one sweats profusely. Ambient temperatures easily reach 40 degrees centigrade and in-cabin temperatures may be 10 degrees higher. Added to which the seat of a Super Cub is hardly enough to support a modest posterior and some chafing takes place in the contact zones. The cabin of a Super Cub is a stuffy, noisy and cramped space with a 150 horsepower of engine sitting just beyond ones knees.

Needless to say the sensation soon became sensational. I managed a normal take off (I think) but not long into the flight the sensation turned to pain, followed by agony! Faced with having to take some action, I climbed into the back of the aircraft to retrieve my water bottle. This produced a dramatic effect on the aircraft's flight performance by pitching it upwards and momentarily out of control but this was nothing compared to the effect that it was having on my sensitive anatomy. I proceeded to empty the contents around the appropriate places but the anointment alas, had no effect - all it did was ratchet the undesired effect a few notches upwards.

Opening the front main zips of my overalls, the bottom one as far upwards as to allow maximum air circulation produced little or no soothing effect. In fact, like the water, it simply exacerbated the situation to an even greater degree!

Damned if I was going to turn back and explain this to my colleagues and risk an unnecessary night away from home, I began to look for a place to land in the bush where perhaps, I could somehow relieve myself. This is quite feasible in such an aircraft and there were several bush patches that we used in our active and normal service, available to me. But there was no time for such a venture – it was like the excruciation demanded another, more immediate solution.

There was one remaining, which was to open the doors and drop my overalls to below the waist, I sat precariously on the window ledge flying sideways, my posterior to the slip stream, extended as far as safely possible. The agony began to ease but since I was all but nude and still requiring a complete solution, I then shed what remained of my cladding, which was piled around the control column and my ankles. Then, with my right leg splayed and securing myself with a foot on the wing-strut outside the cabin, I gave myself a full-on, naturally aspirated 85 knot blow job!

This gave greater effect and in due course I landed at my destination, somewhat disheveled and diminutive! Fortunately, being late in the evening, there were no spectators to witness my arrival.

Lovers of air travel find it exhilarating to hang poised between the illusions of immortality and the fact of death – **Alexander Chase**

The Problem with Ned

Gavin Cooper

The problem with Ned was just that... Ned! Up at four every morning of his life, here's 'ein Britisher' married to a rather plump, nagging 'fraulein' from the Black Forest. So, anything to leave the house or get off the farm, just to let one's hair down and find some humour somewhere. By day on the lands, a great life, but what a 'bug up the ass' after vacating the privacy of a bath, as Helga turned up the heckle volume. So one's friends take on an extra special hue and every sojourn off the farm becomes a little piece of heaven!

Like the time not long ago. Ned, already frustrated by Bavarian banalities, was engaging with a less than erudite ethnic bush mechanic in the workshops. Pent up, Ned tried to assist his less than qualified assistant in matching the rear half of a large Ford tractor with the front half, following a gear-box overhaul. Somewhere in the process the mechanic got Ned's fingers pinched in the bell-housing. A fit of pique saw Ned attempt to fill in any gaps in the man's knowledge with a well-aimed fist to the man's overly plump kisser Ned caught him with a round house, sense-instilling blow, crunching a knuckle on a front tooth in the process.

In a day his fist was swollen, inflamed and changing colour. A trip to the quack confirmed all bar-room advice... *'If you're gonna hit some bloody sod don't go for the gob... you'll get gangrene!'* So, the Doc took out Ned's finger, the one next to the pinkie with all the supporting bone structure for a couple of inches behind it. To put things in perspective, Ned was now really pissed off! So was Helga who took it out on Ned when they got home, for being so *'Got in Himmel, stupid!'* To fend off a physical assault Ned locked himself in the upstairs bathroom, from where he plotted an escape somewhat beyond his enfeebled condition. Unable to hang onto much with his right hand, he left the safety of the en-suite boudoir, head first through the window, onto the forty five degree corrugated iron roof covering the downstairs veranda with an air of Victorian grandeur, head first into the rockery below. A resounding crack as shoulder met stone added a broken collarbone to Ned's woes and another good crapping on from Helga.

Another trip to the Doc in the old diesel Mercedes, the sound of the engine drowned out by Helga's fluent Hitler-type blend of oratory and admonishment in the name of discipline and good order. This combination of injuries put paid to any ideas of participating in the coming weekend's pigeon shoot at Walter's farm in the next valley over yonder.   Ned could demonstrate much prowess with a double-barrelled twelve bore. Perhaps he imagined Helga in the sights now and again? Who knows! Broken hand, broken collar bone may be... but, nevertheless, no broken ego!

Come Saturday Ned was keen for a social and left home for a bit of pot-stirring with his neighbourhood pals and got himself over to Walter's where there was a very serious pigeon shoot under way in the corn crop.   Pigeons were gorging themselves and flying hither and thither in vast numbers. Ned found Walter's van parked in the shade and well supplied with after event eats and treats. Oodles of beer, snacks and the traditional South African biltong, and he settled close to it in a folding chair plucked from the back of his truck. Walter was big of heart and always played the role of mein host with a fair degree of generous and hospitable flair. The van was loaded with cooler boxes holding enough beer for more than a fair set of sundowners, bags of thirst-building biltong (salted dried meat) from his farm butchery and inch thick cuts of rump steak for the BBQ, hot off the fire meat with that best condiment ever, coarse salt.

Unable to shoot, Ned sat deep in his chair, and eased into a can of the best whilst slicing slivers of fine dry kudu biltong. Shots were being fired left, right and centre and the odd shower of spent bird shot occasionally rattled through the foliage of the tree under which he was sitting. It wasn't long before a gun dog came belting past his spot, haring in pursuit of a downed bird.

Retriever found bird and was on his way back to his deadeye-dick* somewhere in the corn field when Ned's mischief got the better of him. He gave the dog a wolf-whistle and beckoned it over. Retriever swapped a dead pigeon for a mouth-watering bit of biltong. Has to be so much more rewarding than plain old doggy choc!

A twinkle sparked in Ned's eye and he started to feel great as his mind turned over. He could feel the mirth mounting as he began conjuring some real he-man shit! In one mouthful he had corrupted this highly trained pooch and a couple of grand went gurgling down the plug-hole.

Much cussing started to emanate from deep within the corn as the master of the hound read his dog the riot act for being worse than useless and a *'stupid f****n' mutt.'* Meanwhile this intelligent loveable man's best friend simply traded more birds for more biltong.

As the sun lost its heat to the evening, all the guns came in from the field and gathered round where the fires had been lit by some unseen Man Friday. And there was Ned with no less than eight dozen birds piled high next to his chair and one adoring spaniel at his feet. Not one shot fired and more birds than anyone else! As they say in the classics, the wind blew and the shit flew... one couldn't see a thing for a minute or two. Ned could have been nursing two broken collar bones had somebody not restrained the spaniel's distraught owner and put some distance between the two.

Totally nonplussed, Ned was nowhere near finished yet; he was just coming into his own as life and soul of the party. Helga was out of sight and out of mind. This was time for fun and bonding with pals

As the beer kicked in on everybody's spirits, Ned was heard to mumble something very deliberately, slowly, but loudly... *'You know chaps, the problem with SSG is that it is totally ineffectual after forty metres!'*

Up went the cry *'Ned you're talking a crock mate, bullshit! You don't have to have been shot at to know that SSG can down a donkey at sixty.'*

'Well, let me show you buggers then', was Ned's rejoinder. And of course there were those who rose to the bait. So Ned handed a 'doctored' round to a guy next to him, having earlier taken the SSG pellets out of an SSG labelled round and replaced them with number seven bird shot.

'I'll go up the path forty metres and bend over... you fire that round at my behind!', says our hero with a nudge and a wink - and no small measure of confidence.

Well Mr Incredulous with the gun, knew slightly better didn't he? He must have thought, *'Blimey I can kill him with that!'* Number fours after all are used to knock over everything from bush pig to baboon. So he decided to scale things down just a touch to an in-between round of number fours he still had in the pocket. Brought them just in case he saw a goose float by during the afternoon shoot!

So Ned paced up his forty, dropped his pants and assumed the position, giving the order to fire. Like a man, he took a load of number fours in the behind.

He was last seen hurtling off into the corn screaming like a banshee and calling somebody *'You bloody bastard!'* Luckily he's still all man and has a full set of baubles. They say God looks after drunks and little children... good thing Ned is still such a 'lovely baby'.

* deadeye-dick - *Slang* An expert marksman or homosexual!

I'm all in favour of keeping dangerous weapons out of the hands of fools. Let's start with typewriters – **Frank Lloyd Wright**

Margaruque Peri-Peris

Greer Noble

If you have you ever owned a chicken or more particularly a Bantam, you will know that they're cocky, spunky and quite the most delightful little birds you could ever wish to meet. They're also comical and very pretty. In fact the cockerels are darn right handsome, and do they know it! Strutting about, showing off their spurs, they're feisty, haughty and courageous. And woe betide any other cockerel who so much as glances at *his* hen harem. A very special breed indeed!

I loved my Bantams and would spend hours with them. Dazzled by my buttons they'd peck each one in turn and then squint at all my freckles, similarly pecking at them too. Let's say we had a rather special relationship, an unusual understanding. So when I heard they were coming on holiday with us, I couldn't believe it. Needless to say I was overjoyed.

The journey was long and arduous. We'd left my home town in Rhodesia and crossed into Moçambique as soon as the border post opened which was around six in the morning, although, ostensibly, it was always 'open', be it unofficially – the gate posts, decayed and eaten by white ants had long since fallen over! It was hot and humid and the closer we got to the coast the hotter and more humid it became. But my little feathered friends in their neat reed cage had the best place of all... on top of the Land Rover where a perpetual breeze kept them cool.

The roads were strip roads in parts, otherwise gravel, rough and bumpy at best, and along the way we often came across buffalo and other wild animals except when we went through the sugar cane plantations. I loved it when we reached the coconut groves because then I knew we were close to the coast. The whole aura changed. It was as if the very air, heavy and humid, was charged with excitement. Only first we had to cross a river and, depending on the tide, sometimes had to camp the night and take the ferry at first light. More often than not it wasn't the tide that prevented us from crossing but the thick sand for we invariably got stuck several times.

Whenever we stopped I would talk to my feathered friends and give them water and grain. And we'd have fresh eggs on the island. I wondered if they would enjoy the boat ride across from the mainland because that's the one thing I didn't enjoy. I always got seasick.

Another two nights and we at last arrived on 'our' island. Margaruque or Snake Island as it was also known was very small and uninhabited. Why it was called Snake Island I'll never know because it was totally devoid of snakes or predators of any kind. There was also a beautiful reef attached to the island and the beaches and swimming were superb.

After the long journey the reed cage housing my feathered friends was set beneath some ivory palms for shade. That evening I bid them good night and made sure they were happy and wanted for nothing. Then disaster struck. I overheard my parents and couldn't believe my ears.

'I think we should have chicken tomorrow? Tell Emanuel to prepare some for dinner.'

It was my father talking to my mother. Emanuel was the Portuguese-Moçambican cook we'd brought with us from the mainland.

'I'd say five or six should be enough. We can't count on fish the first day and what's left over we can use for sandwiches to add to our packed brunch for the boat the following day.' Then as an afterthought he added, *'After Greer has gone snorkelling.'*

Yes, my father knew I'd never allow such a thing. MY little friends! How could he! Close to tears, I felt betrayed.

'Emanuel does a nice peri-peri apparently... and potato chips... and salad while it's still fresh,' added my mother almost to herself.

I felt traumatised. I lay awake for what seemed like hours as they chatted softly into the night, sitting around the dying embers of the camp fire. Eventually they all dispersed and went to their designated tents. I made quite sure everything was dead quiet before I stole out into the night. With the sun long gone it was surprisingly fresh with a salty breeze coming in off the sea. There was just enough moonlight to see and I made my way straight to the ivory palms, quietly opened the door of the reed cage and secured it to make sure it would stay that way.

'*Don't worry,*' I assured them, '*you'll be safe now. Charlie, at first light,*' I instructed secretly, '*you must take all your wives for a long, long walk and,*' I whispered, '*DON'T COME BACK.*' Charlie was the oldest cockerel. I think he sensed my concern as he made that special strange warning sound they give if a hawk flew overhead. '*Yes, that's right... be scared,*' I warned. With tears in my eyes I stroked their silky feathers each in turn and bid them farewell. It was sad to be losing my dear little friends. I knew them all by name and I was the only one who could tell them apart. A little less heavy hearted I made my way back to my stretcher. I at least felt relieved that they wouldn't be on the menu the next day.

I was up early, again relieved that I hadn't heard Charlie crowing. He had a huge pair of lungs, my mother would remark, for such a small bird. Now to face the music... I did not have to wait long for Emanuel to report the terrible tragedy.

'*Senhora,*' he addressed my mother solemnly. His head hung low and he couldn't look anyone in the eye, least of all my father. '*The peli-pelis... she is all gone.*' He looked guilty, dejected, not sure of the rebuff he'd get... as if the whole catastrophe had been entirely his fault.

I sat gazing out into the Indian Ocean.

'*Greer?*' my father addressed me slowly, his tone quietly accusing. '*You wouldn't happen to know anything about the chickens' mysterious disappearance, would you?*'

There was never a reprimand or an admonishment. He understood completely and when I didn't answer he simply said, '*Never mind Emanuel, I'm sure we will catch enough fish for supper.*'

Today, over half a century later, there's a village and an airfield on the island and even the little hotel that once sprung up has now been replaced with a few luxury villas belonging, it is rumoured, to some mafia type tycoon who it is alleged, was able to build them for himself and his friends by greasing the palm of some high ranking government officials.

No longer allowed on the island except for day trips to the shoreline reef, we sailed across in an old dhow and spent a wonderful day on the beach, snorkelling off that unique reef with my daughter and grandsons... and guess what I spotted... without a word of exaggeration I recognised that particular breed of Bantam... Charlie's ancestors... an absolute replica of him and his little harem of speckled hens, scratching around under a clump of ivory palms! Was it a coincident that I was to return to that very island nearly six decades on?

It is my view that the vegetarian manner of living, by its purely physical effect on the human temperament, would be the most beneficial influence to mankind – **Albert Einstein**

Musical Taps

Mike Ballantine

Our small bush lodge had two bathrooms, side by side. Being an old thatched building the plumbing was a little antiquated but functioned well nonetheless. One particular morning our adult son entered the one to take a shower only to quickly shut the door again. It was occupied... by a spitting cobra!

The snake fundis were summoned and shut themselves in the bathroom with their equipment and wearing goggles. They knocked around in there for what seemed like hours but eventually came out empty handed. We were advised to seal the gap under the door, lock it and use the other bathroom.

Later that day our son went into the other bathroom and again hastily closed the door. This time he found the cobra draped over the hand shower and bath taps. Mystified as to how it got there we again called the fundis. This time they bagged it. We could only assume that it had used the sewerage pipe connected to both toilets to come and go, in and out of the toilet bowls.

Earlier that week Greer nearly sat on one curled up on her favourite cane chair in our open thatched boma area. Fortunately our gardener spotted it and warned her in the nick of time, her attention being focused on feeding her 'big babies' – kudu visitors – wondering why they seemed so skittish. Could it have been the same snake?

Africa is not for sissies... but definitely the place to be if you're an adrenalin junkie – **GN**

Attack at Third Bridge

Greer Noble

A young woman dived off the deep side of Moremi Game Reserve's notorious Third Bridge as many often did. It's a deep narrow channel lined by reeds and the crystal clear water is as tempting as honey is to a badger, especially in that intense heat. They were a young group of friends having a good time.

Suddenly the young woman screamed then went under, thrashing about as she did so. She was clearly in trouble. Luckily her partner, a well-built rugby player type, dived in to help her and, to his horror, saw she was being attacked by a croc.

He was able to whip her out of the water straight away... only the metre long croc would not let go!

Leaving her on the bridge with the others, screaming in agony, he dashed back, some 50 metres to their camp to get something with which to prize open its jaws. The best thing he could find to hand was a large spanner. She was lucky it didn't start 'spinning' which crocs do to tear off chunks of flesh.

The one and only time I've ever been bitten was by a dog, a dachshund/sausage-dog at that, and also on my bottom. It jumped up and bit me as I was running past its owner's house. I can remember the pain to this day. It was agonizing. But to be bitten on the derriere by a croc, even if it is a relatively small one, must be excruciating... especially when it won't let go!

The young lady had to be casevaced from Maun to South Africa for remedial surgery.

To think we quite happily sat in our collapsible camp chairs on so many occasions in the water on the shallow side of the bridge, be it with a wary eye mind you, sipping chilled beers!

The power of the crocodile is in the water – **African Proverb**

Terror on the Zambezi

James Lepper

I am the most disorganised person on the planet. I married Kim, the second most disorganised person on the planet and chaos has slowly been taking over the world ever since. She said that the honeymoon had to be Africa.

Our tour started in South Africa. We took in some of the well-known tourist spots including Notten's bush camp, a brilliant place to stay when in the Kruger National Park.

We then flew on to Livingstone in Zambia where the real excitement started. We had decided that we would like to do three things in Zambia; to game view from an elephant, an awesome experience where you get really close to other animals, to see the Victoria Falls which Kim admitted was as every bit as good from the Zambian side as she remembered it from the Zimbabwe side in her youth and thirdly to canoe down the Zambezi. The plan was to drive about 40 miles upstream, spend an afternoon paddling on the river then to overnight on an island in mid-stream and carry on down the Zambezi the following day.

Initially we each canoed with a ranger in our inflatables, towing a third canoe. I was with Dominic and Kim was with Cliff. Dominic was very knowledgeable about the river and Cliff, a wiry little man of surprising strength, manoeuvred Kim's canoe with ease. When we reached the island we found that everything had been thought of including a shower, a long drop loo and pup tents. Food supplies were ferried over to us from a hotel opposite the island then cooked on an open fire. Dawn came - and so did the smell of breakfast. With Dominic's encouragement, Kim and I clambered into one of the canoes and, with our rangers in the other two, soon reached the rapids. At first they were really mild, then really exhilarating as we arrowed through the turbulent white waters. Great stuff! After about 45 minutes we were through and on the widening reach of the river. We moved towards the shore away from some hippos, past a huge crocodile basking on the bank, some waterbuck at the river's edge and an eagle wheeling in the azure sky.

We saw more hippos near another island and were keeping a wary eye on them when our canoe juddered. I thought for a moment that we had hit a submerged object until I found myself falling backwards out of the rear section of the canoe which had instantly deflated. When I surfaced our canoe, with Kim hanging on, was already some distance away and low in the water. Dominic was about 30 yards away while Cliff was already nearing Kim.

I struck out like a fish then paused for a millisecond after about 15 yards as I remembered the instructions. Swim away from the canoe if attacked by a hippo; hold onto the canoe if it's a croc to prevent it dragging you under. Then I thought, '*I don't know what attacked us*' followed by '*don't be a bloody idiot get into the nearest canoe now,*' when Dominic's hand reached out for me.

Cliff, in the meantime, had come alongside Kim. She too was baptised in the mighty Zambezi when she lost her balance trying to step into Cliff's canoe. Having had time to really think about how dangerous her predicament also was, Kim immediately grabbed his outstretched arm, hauled herself upwards and slithered over him.

We recovered the punctured inflatable and examined it once back at the hotel. It had a spread of teeth marks in it that Dominic reckoned was the bite of a 17 foot long Crocodile.

Back in England and the parents' house in Essex a couple of days later we started to relate our tale of crocodiles and canoes. When the brandy was produced I realised that for the first time we genuinely had a story to dine out on!

Nyaminyami Nabbed

Greer Noble

To the Tonga tribe, Nyaminyami, believed to be half fish, half snake, is their Mudzimu, their ancestral spirit. The Tongas lived along the Zambezi long before it was dammed to form Lake Kariba; Nyaminyami, it is said, lived in Kariwa Gorge (Kariwa meaning little trap while Kariba is the European corruption of Kariwa) where the dam wall is now situated. They believed Nyaminyami protected them, allowing them to cut meat off his belly during times of famine. They pledged their allegiance to him by performing ceremonial dances and rituals.

To honour Nyaminyami a beautiful stone carving placed high above the dam wall placated somewhat, the chiefs, elders and ngangas (witch doctors), but one day it was stolen… ripped from the plinth in which it was embedded. Speculation was rife as to who the thief was and word soon spread that something so bad, in fact unprintable, would befall the culprit unless he or she returned it immediately. A reward was also offered to anyone who could identify the culprit. The worst of it was trying to keep it from the Tonga people – bush telegraph having a way of communicating great distances. How to return it without being caught must have been of serious concern to the thief too. Nyaminyami was obviously very angry – Kariba had one of the worst electric storms in many years during which the Nyaminyami carving was thankfully returned.

405

A Featherless Bird

Colin Lowe

Some years ago I was phoned by a farming friend of mine who asked me to take a group of schoolchildren on a one day canoe trip down the Zambezi River. I ran a tourist company in Livingstone that specialised in canoeing this majestic river so the request was not unusual. My friend, Marty, although not a teacher, often helped out with these bush trips that the school arranged for its pupils. Marty was quite specific about the object of the trip; to enlighten the pupils of the value of wildlife and its habitat to humans and how we needed to protect and preserve all our fauna and flora, from the tiniest insect to the largest elephant, and from a blade of grass to the mighty baobab, for the benefit of future generations. This request was also not unusual as I often took biologists, researchers and environmentalists down the river so that they could feel the pulse of this part of Africa.

'Colin, you need to talk about the devastating effects of commercial poaching, the balance between crocodiles and the fish in the river and to identify all the common trees and birds as we paddle down. Some of the kids are really keen birders.'

'OK, so quite a serious learning expedition then. How many pupils are we talking about?'

'There should be about twelve of us, boys and girls, including me.

I'll come on the canoe trip to give you a hand.'

'OK, and what age would they be?'

'Probably between ten and fourteen.'

That day dawned bright and beautiful as only it can on a crisp May morning in Zambia – the rains had just ended, the bush was still green and the sky was that deep, deep blue that heralded another stunning day on the river. Marty arrived with the children, all bright eyed and eager to get going in their canoes. First, though, I had to

406

give them a safety talk and a chat about what we might see on the banks of the river. I emphasised that the quieter we kept, the more we would see. After settling who would partner who in the two man kayaks, we set off with the current gently pulling us along at a comfortable pace, I in the lead and the rest stretched out behind me like ducklings following a mother duck.

Every now and then as we saw something of interest they would crowd around me in their kayaks and we'd talk about what we'd just seen, be it a croc sunning itself on the bank, a family of hippo grunting amongst the waterberry trees or the identification of some wading birds in the shallows. The children were enthusiastic environmentalists, great company and seemed to be really enjoying themselves.

As we progressed down the river we encountered more islands and I constantly scanned ahead with my binoculars, always looking to where we would be in ten minutes, to give us time to take evasive action in case there were elephant or hippo in our particular channel. One of my favourite islands, Chundu, was just coming into view. When the river level was down, as it was then, the island had a large sandbar extending out and upstream. These dazzling white sands were always inviting for a twenty minute refreshment stop, although this time there was something different about the sandbank.

At first I could not identify what it was but gradually, as we drifted closer, I realised it was a small two-man tent. This was quite unusual as camping was prohibited on this island and I wondered who it could be. I continued to search with my binoculars and suddenly spotted one of the occupants – she was lying on her stomach, stark-naked on the sand, soaking up the warmth of the sun, about twenty metres from her tent. I turned to the children and indicated to them to be quiet and to even stop paddling. We drifted towards the sandbank in absolute silence – anyone who has ever been in a canoe will know how completely noiseless a canoe can be. The children were totally engrossed in watching this woman. Those who had binoculars silently passed them over to their friends, although from twenty metres out they were hardly necessary. The woman shifted position and lay on her back but I could tell she was feeling uncomfortable – perhaps she could sense she was being watched but didn't know from where.

We all gently beached on the sand with a slight crunching sound less than a few metres away from her. She lifted her head, unable to identify the noise. Then firstly in astonishment then horror she looked into thirteen pairs of eyes gaping at her. For a few seconds she lay frozen on the sand, unable to comprehend what she was seeing. Suddenly, with what can only be described as a strangled shriek and still naked as the day she was born, she covered the distance to her tent in a few seconds, disappeared into it like a rabbit into a burrow and zipped it up firmly behind her.

With that the children collapsed into giggles which gradually turned into eye-watering hysterical laughter as only children can enjoy. Through my own tears of laughter I indicated to the group that we'd move on to another island and we left the woman to contemplate her embarrassment. I later found out that she was Austrian and with her partner had started their canoe trip some sixty kilometres up in Botswana, hadn't seen anyone else on the river as they paddled down, and believed that they had the Zambezi to themselves.

Marty paddled up next to me. *'Well Colin, this is an expedition that these kids will never forget. I'd call that bird watching with a difference!'*

'God made Africa first, while he still had imagination and courage.'
Alexandra Fuller

Hip Litunga of the Lozi

Greer Noble

E very April the Barotse Litunga, king of the Lozi people in western Zambia, leaves Lealui, his dry-season residence west of Mongu, with his entire court. Driven by the encroaching Zambezi flood waters, he rides in an elaborate royal oar-propelled barque, the replica of a huge black elephant on top, with mechanically flapping ears. His wife's barque has a huge cattle egret with similarly flapping wings. This is followed by a flotilla of mokoros (dug-outs), to his high-water palace in Limulunga. Known as the Ku-omboka festival, this ceremony is said to date back hundreds of years, the only one of its kind in the world to actually celebrate floods in this manner.

An old friend of ours who ran the local rag downstream in Kasane in neighbouring Botswana, made the trip to Mongu some years ago. It was ostensibly to interview the king about the upcoming festival but mainly to get him to reveal something of his clandestine existence. Ushered into a large reception hut she waited, be it a little nervously, not quite knowing what to expect. The next thing a rather hip young man in shirt and jeans burst into the room, swaggered across towards her wearing Ray-Ban sunglasses and a huge grin and introduced himself in Oxford English as the Litunga, then said, *'Not quite what you expected, am I?'*

409

Too Close for Comfort

Greer Noble

F latdogs, for the uninformed, was the name given to crocodiles by the Rhodesian Armed Forces. They had a language of their own - words and expressions, many of which have lived on to this day. I presume that is how the camp in Zambia's South Luangwa Valley got its name.

For those of you who've never been to Flatdogs you might be interested to know that it is so wild that, as a guest of this gem of a camp, you're escorted from the rustic open African-Bohemian style restaurant to your bungalow or tent at night by an armed guard.

It was our first night there and tucked safely into our little pup tent (our first trip ever without our usual rooftop tent), on the banks of this semi-dry river, screened from blood-lusty female anopheles mosquitos, we settled down, listening to those wonderful night sounds of the African bush. It was a hot, muggy night with not the hint of a breeze but there's something about the wilds and the earthy scents that is so calming... we soon drifted off.

In my dreams I could hear this sniff, sniff followed by a weird churning, squelching sound. Then a nudge, nudge again followed by a snuff, snuff... no wait a minute, I'm not dreaming! I opened my eyes... wide, not daring to move. Between my head and the noise was a thin piece of canvas. Then it suddenly dawned on me, remembering seeing the pools in the dry river bed – of course, hippo-pools! A HIPPO! *OMG*, a piece of lousy canvas between me and a hungry hippo, one of, if not *the* most dangerous animals in Africa. There he/she'd been chomping away RIGHT AT MY HEAD... NUDGING ME in an attempt to get a better grip on the hippo 'salad' growing *under* our tent. A terrible dread enveloped me... while my husband slept like a hibernating bear as only men can (in case you're wondering I also have older brothers!) Now one could argue as to who had the right of way here... but dammit, this was OUR tent, therefore OUR territory! There was only one thing to do.

'*PUSH OFF*!' I shouted as loudly as I could. Well OK, a little more colourfully than that.

'*What have I done now?*' my wounded husband uttered, turning over.

I held my breath, wondering if I'd been too hasty with my outburst and what reaction it might promote. I hadn't thought of that. So far there was complete silence from outside. Then with landslide relief I could hear the oversized piggy plod off, seemingly as offended as my husband – it must have been a male!

Now I wouldn't suggest that anyone try this... you might just come across an antagonistic female and you could very well find yourself sandwiched in-between your tent or her tusk-like teeth – not a pretty thought.

Footnote
I wish campsites within/bordering other national parks would take a leaf out of Flatdogs' book – armed escorts are so much more thrilling than the diamond mesh fences many of these camps and parks use. They're not only unsightly and costly but deprive locals of much needed employment and bushwhackers like us of so much more fun! Half the charm and charisma of Flatdogs is that it does NOT have this unsightly prison-of-war barracks type appearance and restriction! – **GN**

The FUD

Rory Young

Canoeing safaris are potentially extremely dangerous. The only thing that makes them safe is the guide knowing what he is doing and the clients following his instructions to the T.

Hippos have to be avoided carefully whilst choosing the right route round them. There are a whole bunch of things that will upset them, like going through the deep channel when they are in the shallows or getting between them and the low bank or exit-chutes. Surprising them is also a really bad idea. Getting these things wrong will get your canoe bitten in half if you are lucky and get you bitten in half if you're not..

There are crocodiles up to fourteen foot long and lots of them. Just trailing your hand in the water can mean losing it or losing your life.

Then of course there are all the land animals, including Cape buffaloes, lions, elephants, leopards, hyenas, mambas and so on.

We were mid-way through the first day and these people had signalled to me that they needed to stop. When we had pulled into the bank two of the middle aged housewife-type ladies had requested to go to '*the bathroom*'.

I had been continuously signalling them all morning to get behind me because they kept wandering across the river. Clearly they did not understand the extreme danger, despite the hour long safety talk.

I pulled my rifle out of its jacket and climbed out of the canoe onto the river bank. I told everyone not to move and then walked the immediate vicinity, checking for 'scaries'.

Once I was sure it was all safe I explained that they must go behind THAT termite mound and NOWHERE ELSE! I explained it was dangerous, there were all sorts of things that could kill them and so on. I could see it going in one ear and out the other. I was starting to get irritated.

I offered them 'Doug' the spade, a toilet roll and a box of matches. The idea was to burn the paper carefully before burying the ashes and whatever else had been created. They declined. Okay, not a safety issue, just gross for a woman I thought. Still I was there to keep them alive, not to admire their personal hygiene.

As I hopped back into my canoe, they toddled off in the opposite direction to the agreed upon termite mound. Now I was pissed off. There was a tiny bush very nearby the way they were heading. Couldn't be that, it was too close. They must be heading for the distant bushes that hadn't been checked.

Now I had had enough. Now I knew I really had to do something about it before someone got killed. I jumped out of the canoe and started towards them just as they reached the small bush. They stopped in front of it.

Then something happened that caught me totally by surprise... Both standing, they put their left hands on their hips and their right hands in front of them and started peeing. Yes. Standing. Just like blokes. Now I am not a prude at all but this was just bloody weird.

It was too confusing. What happened to the plump American housewives I had been sure they were? I turned back to my canoe and looked at their husbands. Both gazed at me with poker faces.

I sat waiting for them to finish their pee and thought about some of the strange people that I had encountered.

There had been the Greek chap too with a phobia for germs and insects who had covered himself from head to toe in bright purple gentian violet.

There were the Danish naturists. No one had warned me that they were naturists or Danish. I had turned around in the middle of the first day to discover a flotilla of naked people following me down the river with big smiles on their faces. Lunch on the first day had been a trial of eye control.

Before I could reminisce any further about all the odd-balls I seemed to end up with, the ladies came back.

Before I could say anything they both swished their right hands in the river. I was just about to let them have it when one said, 'Oh sorry, we're not supposed to put our hands in the water.' She really did sound like a woman. And then, 'We just needed to wash our fuds.'

'Pardon?' I said, 'What is a fud? Blasted weirdo foreigners. Now they were really confusing the hell out of me.

'Oh here, look,' she said and handed me an oblong shaped cup with a pipe sticking out the bottom of it, 'It's my Female Urinary Device. FUD.' Then, 'May the fud be with you', she said and I fell over laughing.

Needless to say the rest of the trip was a laugh-a-minute with this lot. Definitely one of the most enjoyable canoeing safaris I did. Long live strange, middle-aged Americans!

You have little power over what is not yours – **Zimbabwean Proverb**

A South American in Africa

Greer Noble

I've always hated seeing anything caged and that's why I bought Pedro. At the time he cost thousands (which I could ill afford) but what could I do, he stole my heart. I named him Pedro after King Dom Pedro, the Emperor of Brazil, from where he hailed... after all, only fitting for such a brilliantly feathered turquoise and yellow Macaw. Fully grown, of how many years I do not know, I could see how miserable he was, caged, on exhibition in a shop, poked at and teased by children and strangers all day, then lonely nights and Sundays alone.

The huge ornate cage took pride of place in my warm sunroom with sliding doors, sky-lights, a Jacuzzi, large potted palms, open plan kitchen and long oak table where we'd eat and entertain. All other rooms in the house including bedrooms led onto this expansive living area.

The first thing I did was open his cage door which then stayed open forevermore. Pedro gingerly climbed out and sat on top of it.

As the days and weeks passed he became a different bird. He

415

flapped his wings, preened himself and started talking. He regained his confidence and was soon bossing everyone around including our Lhasa Apso, English Pointer and ginger cat, but most of all his namesake, Peter the cook. Peter was very taken with him. He'd clean Pedro's cage every day which Pedro found most fascinating, watching intently. His favourite was to walk outside in the garden, more of a waddle really, trailing his long tail feathers to where Peter sat on a little stool on the lawn, polishing the silver in the sun. Pedro loved this and would pass the shiny cutlery to Peter, one piece at a time, his eyes dazzled by the glinting silver.

Soon Peter and Pedro became bosom pals and Peter would help me clip his one wing to prevent him flying away. I didn't like doing this, as much as Pedro objected to it being done but it was for his own protection. On one occasion I was a little lax in doing this and disaster struck – Pedro flew away! I was devastated and afraid for his safety. Having been reared in captivity he knew nothing of the dangers of the outside world; the hawks, snakes and heaven knows what else.

I was preparing to make 'Lost Bird' notices when Peter said the gardener had spotted him next door. Being smallholdings, our German neighbours had a dam surrounded by willow trees; home to various species of duck and a variety of water fowl and guinea fowl. Unfortunately the owners were overseas and the property locked up so we couldn't get in but managed to get fairly close trying to coax him down from high up in a willow, armed with mirrors (a typical male, he loved admiring himself!), delicious fruit, seeds, rusks and all forms of the proverbial 'carrot'! But we were totally ignored.

As evening approached I became quite fretful, afraid of what might happen to him when he suddenly decide he'd had enough and simply flew back across our property and to the safety of his cage. Peter and I both felt a bit foolish but most relieved. I'm sure Pedro enjoyed the entertainment; antics of his fellow species and probably had been dying of curiosity for some time.

The pleasure Pedro gave us is among my fondest memories.

I hope you love birds too. It is economical. It saves going to heaven
Emily Dickinson

Heads or Tails?

Mike Ballantine

While Zimbabwe's Kariba Lake is renowned for its tiger fish which give sportsmen an exhilarating fight, as edible fish they're extremely bony. So the camper's choice of fish is bream. Its meat when pan-fried is firm and succulent and a good deal of time is spent trying to hook a few.

After several weeks of trial and error I found that by fishing in the shallow inlets in our Zodiac which had a draft of no more than a dozen centimetres my success rate was much higher than if I tried in open water. On this occasion I beached the dinghy up a creek to fish with more aplomb on terra firma.

In no time my bait was taken. The resistance was too unyielding for it to be a small vundu or a barbel. Perhaps it was an eel that had looped itself around an underwater root. Yes, I reasoned, it was an eel.

The breaking strain of my line was greater than it needed to be so, ever so slowly, I winched in the resisting weight until it suddenly slithered out of the muddy water. It was a crocodile, more than a metre in length!

Greer's immediate reaction was to insist, 'Croc steaks!' Although rather an intimidating prospect, a change from bream was a tantalizing thought. Keeping up the tension I looked for my sheath knife. It was on the bank some four or five paces away.

My mind raced. I had never killed a croc before. Even with the knife in hand, how would I subdue it sufficiently to deal it a mortal blow? Grab the croc behind its head? Then what about its threshing tail? Grab its tail? Then how do I avoid its leering jaws? Mercifully, wisdom prevailed. I released the tension and, in a flash, it somehow managed to eject the hook from its jaws and plunged back into the creek. Hours later I confessed to having engineered its escape.

This adds a whole new meaning to the expression *'tight-lines'* – **GN**

An Eccentric English Gentleman

Greer Noble

' I never knew a morning in Africa when I woke up and was not happy,' Ernest Hemingway once said. I know the feeling so well. It was one such glorious morning at our hotel on the shores of Lake Kariba. Madeleine our receptionist, and I sat chatting in reception when in drove a black vintage Rolls Royce. It was truly a sight to behold... and I'm sure we were too, with our mouths hanging open. Out stepped a tall, very stately old gentleman with a handle-bar moustache.

In those days the hotel was undergoing a huge transformation. The simple white round tin huts called rondavels were being replaced by proper brick and mortar buildings. Being moveable the original huts were practical in the early days when the water of what was then the biggest man-made lake in the world kept rising. But had now outgrown their use as the lake had stabilised.

By the time our distinguished guest had reached the tin longdavel, our soon to be replaced reception, mercifully we had recovered our composure. Greetings over, he asked what accommodation we had.

'We can offer you an en-suite shoreline bedroom with air-conditioning,' Madeleine ventured proudly, as the first of several lakefront rooms had recently been completed.

'Good lord, no,' came the surprising response. 'That's exactly why I booked out of the Cutty Sark... can't stand the infernal things.' By that he was referring to air-conditioners.

This really threw us. 'Well then all we can offer you,' Madeleine stammered somewhat deflated, 'is a tin rondavel with ceiling fan, on top of the hill. It has a nice view of the lake but you will have to use the communal ablutions as it has no en suite facility, only a hand-basin.'

'That would suit me just fine,' he beamed, his moustache rising to the occasion.

'The noise,' I quietly reminded Madeleine.

'Oh yes, sorry sir, I forgot to mention the noise. We are building at the moment and the builders start early to avoid the heat of the day.'

'That will be no problem,' he said without hesitation. 'I'm an early riser.'

'How long will you be staying, Mr..er?' Madeleine wanted to know as she handed him a pen to sign the register.

'I've no idea, my dear. All depends on how I like it here.' He didn't mince his words.

So it was settled, the porter summoned and off he went.

As it turned out he stayed for several weeks. He didn't fish or go game-viewing by boat which was odd. Heaven knows what he did during the day but every evening he met us for sundowners. It transpired that he was an ex Indian army major with a particular penchant for Africa. He shipped his vintage Rolls out every year from the UK and motored all the way up from Cape Town, some three thousand kilometres away. Other than that he was a bit of a closed book and all we learnt was his secret for keeping slim... *'A chocolate or two every evening keeps my constitution going.'* He must have had quite a collection of bedtime chocolates from all the different hotels he stayed at in his travels as he presented Madeleine and me with one each every evening.

One of the many eccentric characters one meets in Africa, running a hotel in the wilds.

When you leave Africa, as the plane lifts, you feel that more than leaving a continent you're leaving a state of mind. Whatever awaits you at the other end of your journey will be of a different order of existence.
Francesca Marciano

Grand Theft Towel

Greer Noble

O n safari in a remote, little used, Moçambique game reserve, we were the only campers left at first light. We packed up quickly, deciding to breakfast on the road, when the party who we thought had continued on their journey, unexpectedly returned. Suddenly a big commotion broke out. *'Where's my towel?'* someone yelled. Thinking nothing of it, but urged on by my friend Lily (not her real name) we happily set off ourselves. I couldn't understand why Lily had uncharacteristically gone quiet and worried that I might have said something untoward. It was only at the end of the long, hot, dusty two day journey, when we reached Monkey Bay on the shores of Lake Malawi that she confessed to having taken their towel. Like us she thought they'd left and it seemed a shame to leave such a good towel for the lurking baboons to run off with. By the time the party returned it was too embarrassing and too late to have us unpack and then admit to these strangers she'd taken it. We all had a jolly good laugh especially when she later exchanged it on the beach for a hippo's canine tooth or fighting tusk – a beautiful specimen, measuring nearly 50 centimetres, suggesting the hippo had probably died of old age. Presented to us in memory of the best holiday she'd ever had, we have the tusk to this day.

Dying in Africa

Colin Lowe

A lthough I shouldn't have been surprised I was still shocked to hear that eighty-three year old Bill Sykes had died that afternoon. He was overweight, had difficulty with his breathing and even walking was an effort for him. I had been helping him write his memoirs about the more than sixty years he'd spent in Africa, mainly on the copper mines in Zambia.

His wife Mabel phoned me from Kadonga Hospital to tell me of the sad news so I went along to offer my condolences. Under the old colonial system this hospital was used only for indigenous patients and had been in a poor state of repair since independence with many doors missing or hanging on one hinge, windows broken or repaired with plastic sheeting and walls which hadn't seen a lick of paint in forty years.

I found Mabel sitting on her own, on the steps outside Ward 5, and comforted her as best I could. Marvin, her son by a previous marriage, had gone off to find Lionel, another one of their many relatives. Mabel was so distraught that I offered to help in any way I could, not knowing at the time where this would take me. Mabel was overwhelmed with grief and couldn't face looking at Bill who was still on the bed where he had died and in full view of both patients and visitors. So I asked a couple of nurses if they could put some screens around him which they did before going off duty.

I introduced myself to Johnson, the male nurse who remained on duty. He told me that he couldn't manage as he was by himself and could I assist him? I assumed he needed help with filling out forms so I waited patiently in the duty room while he tended to other patients. Filling out the form took the best part of an hour as Johnson was constantly interrupted by cell phone calls and patients needing his attention, particularly one Zambian who was clearly on his way out. His death rattle reverberated around Ward 5 and was even louder than the TV blaring out at the other end. After three or four attempts at completing the form, and having established Bill's full name and date and place of birth, we came to the question – Cause of Death. I fully expected Johnson to write this up as he had attended to Bill

423

when he had been admitted earlier that afternoon. Johnson looked quizzically at me.

'So what was the cause of death?'

I took a while to realise that he wanted me to answer this question.

'Johnson, you are the attending nurse and represent the hospital, I am just a visitor and it is me who should be asking you that question.'

'Yes, but you should know, you are the relative.'

'Actually, I'm not the relative, in fact I'm not related to him in any way; I'm a visitor and a friend of the family and I wasn't even here when Mr. Sykes passed away.'

Johnson was not to be put off by this logic and insisted that I answer the question. Now, I am not an avid watcher of medical reality TV programmes, in fact they make me slightly queasy, but I have garnered enough superficial terminology from ER, Holby City and Private Practice to sound impressive and besides, I'm married to a nurse, and over the years I've picked up a few phrases.

'OK, he died from myocardial infarction exacerbated by influenza.'

I have no idea what the first bit meant but I knew how to pronounce it. Johnson raised his eyebrows, clearly impressed by my grasp of medical matters, and he laboriously copied my diagnosis down on all five copies. He stamped the forms, signed them with a flourish and instructed me to take them to the Central Police Station to get another stamping and bring all the copies back to him. He added rather ominously,

'Because I'm alone I'll need you to help me when you get back.'

I didn't like the sound of that but I'd dug a hole which seemed to get deeper as the day progressed.

The Police Station was relatively easy and I returned back to Ward 5 at the old Kadonga Hospital slightly apprehensive at what Johnson might have in store for me.

'Ah, there you are. You must help me bandage the body now.'

My heart dropped. When I'd come to the hospital to offer my condolences this is not what I'd had in mind. '*Johnson, I have no medical training. Shouldn't you get some nurses from another ward to help you?*'

'*No, I'm alone and this white man is heavy, very heavy – you have to help me.*'

His attitude was clear - hey, the dead man's white, you're white and you're his relative, what's your problem? And besides, aren't you the guy that came up with the cause of death?

'*Can you go over to Ward 3 and ask the Sister-in-Charge for some bandages to wrap a body.*'

He waved vaguely in a direction over his shoulder and hurried off on another task. After ten minutes of wandering around I eventually found Ward 3 where half a dozen nurses were lolling around the nurses' station. I briefly considered asking them to help with the bandaging but after their languid response to my search for bandages realised that this was not an option. One of the nurses slowly shlopped her way to a cupboard, seemingly reluctant to lift the soles of her feet. She returned with three small rolls of cotton bandages and gave them to me. I stared at them in dismay. This would barely wrap Bill's head, never mind the rest of his body. I mean, wasn't the procedure to wrap him up like an Egyptian mummy? Clearly not, judging by the giggles coming from the collection of nurses.

'*Tell Johnson that he can keep whatever bandages are left over.*' More giggles.

I returned to Ward 5 and gave the bandages to Johnson.

'*OK, now we must tie his hands and feet and then we must put a sheet around him, but first you must put on these gloves before touching the body.*'

Fortunately Lionel had now arrived at the hospital and was willing, in fact anxious to help. With the gloves on and feeling like an extra on ER I approached the body with some trepidation and gingerly prodded it. Even through my new gloves I could feel that the body was still warm.

'Johnson, are you sure he's dead?'

'Yes, of course he's dead. I can't feel a pulse and you haven't seen him move, have you?'

We all shook our heads solemnly and agreed that Bill hadn't moved.

'OK, hold his hands together while I tie them up. OK, now lift his feet while I tie them together.'

These two operations were done easily and, for Zambia, quite quickly. My confidence increased in that I would be able to manage the next couple of hurdles. I should say at this juncture that Johnson was spot on when he said that Bill was heavy, very heavy. When Bill was alive he could not fit the seat belt in his car around his body and neither could he lift his own weight out of a chair. He easily weighed over 250, maybe as much as 280 pounds.

'OK, now we have to wrap him up in this sheet before tying him up. Try to lift the body while I pull the sheet through.'

There was absolutely no way that we could lift Bill – so we devised a plan that was not easy or quick and took a huge effort from Lionel, Marvin and myself. We pushed Bill up on his left side and then balanced him there while Johnson quickly put down the sheet where he'd been lying. Suddenly I noticed that Bill had started to overbalance which would have meant that he'd land on the floor and that would have been a disaster – we could never have lifted him back onto the bed. I scrambled to the other side of the bed and put my shoulder into the body to stop it falling off. After averting that near disaster we then let him roll back and reversed the procedure for the right side, this time with more care. We could now pull the sheet through but to our dismay found that the sheet couldn't meet on top due to Bill's bulk. Fortunately Johnson found a second sheet and we repeated the procedure - and yet again when Johnson tied the bandages over the sheets and around the body.

Whilst tying the bandages Johnson said to Lionel, *'Haven't I seen you around the hospital before?'*

'Yes,' said Lionel, *'I used to be on the Hospital Board, but now I'm freelancing.'*

In Zambian terms that means unemployed and the conversation continued in this light vein, exploring Lionel's career path, interspersed with the occasional *'Watch out, he's falling'* or *'Quickly, push on his shoulder'*. This whole performance had attracted the attention of everyone in the ward and that included sundry visitors, the two who'd been watching TV and, with the exception of 'death rattle', even a couple of patients who lifted their heads off their pillow for some light entertainment.

By now we were all quite exhausted and a thin sheen of sweat covered my body. Unfortunately, due to the exertions, the latex gloves had broken and all my fingers and thumbs were poking through and I resembled a twenty fingered monster from a horror movie.

Marvin, a slightly built coloured man, kept bursting into tears and proved to be ineffective. I should also add that Johnson was not the neatest body wrapper because, for some reason, Bill's right foot protruded from the sheets, but by this stage this minor detail no longer bothered me.

'Right,' said Johnson cheerfully, *'now you must take the body to the mortuary.'*

What I liked about Johnson was the fact that he included us in all his decisions and despatched Marvin to find a gurney. I was pleased to see that it was lower than the hospital bed but that it had a shiny stainless steel tray which was obviously quite slippery. The two lengths of galvanized piping welded on either side of the tray to stop bodies sliding off sideways I should have taken as a warning.

'Johnson, you'll have to get us some help to get the body off the bed and onto the gurney.'

'OK, no problem,' he called and went outside and summoned two security guards squatting around a fire. He then rounded up the visitors in the ward, most of whom surprisingly volunteered. Bill was partially rolled over and landed with a resounding thud on the gurney, albeit slightly crooked with his bound legs hanging over the edge. I now realised how slippery the surface was when the rest of the body started to follow the legs and only another try-saving dive rescued the situation.

'Eish, this white man was too heavy – he must have been very rich,' was the consensus of opinion from the volunteers.

Johnson had disappeared, apparently to find keys to the mortuary which was situated in a separate building away from the hospital. So Lionel and I were on our own in having to wheel the heavily laden gurney down the cement path to the mortuary. Fairly steep, it was cracked and uplifted from tree roots that grew next to it forming unofficial rumble strips. Positioned at the front of the gurney I turned around to face the direction in which we were going, my hands grasping the handle behind me. It only took a few seconds for the first problem to arise when I felt Bill's feet slam into my back as his body slid on the slippery surface of the tray and the gurney did its best to run me over as it gathered speed.

'Lionel, for goodness sake, hold on to the gurney,' I shouted over my shoulder.

'I can't, I've got my slippery shoes on and in any case I'm holding on to the body – it's trying to slide off.'

I dug my heels in and fortunately found some potholes in the pathway which slowed us down to a trot as we arrived unceremoniously at the mortuary with Bill piled up against my back and my legs splayed out in front of me like a learner skier.

After some judicious shuffling of smaller bodies we found fridge space for Bill and luckily it was at a lower level than the gurney. I pulled the wheeled stretcher out of the fridge as far as it would go and we attempted to slide Bill onto it. No such luck. This once slippery corpse that had done its best to find the ground now refused to move one centimetre on the rough surface of the fridge stretcher.

'Lift the back of the gurney up,' it was suggested.

'We can't, it's too heavy.'

Once again we had to round up some volunteers who hoisted the back of the gurney into the air and we all but got Bill into the fridge. I say 'all but' because when we tried to close the fridge door it wouldn't shut. Bill's head and shoulders were still protruding over the end of the stretcher. There was nothing for it but to shove the body in as best we could.

With a final huge heave we got him in and slammed the door shut. Mission accomplished - but it had taken the best part of four hours since I'd first arrived at the hospital and as I removed my now useless gloves I pondered over the lessons learned from this episode.

Never ever buy condoms made in China and if you're white and of a delicate nature, don't die in Africa if you can possibly help it.

Dying is a very dull, dreary affair. And my advice to you is to have nothing whatever to do with it – **Somerset Maugham**

Mama Nick's

Greer Noble

At this âpres party café we frequented after the ungodly hour of midnight, in the avenues of Salisbury (now Harare, Zimbabwe), Mama Nick would routinely nod off after serving everyone, snuggly wedged in her special, high bucket stool. This inevitably caused a few stifled giggles by the uninitiated.

While we were sipping coffee, seated at the counter on one particular night, something happened that almost caused us to fall off our bar stools. Without any disrespect intended, Mama Nick was, let us say, a rather voluptuous Greek mama with ample bosoms. What really slayed us was the huge shiny cockroach that suddenly nosed its way out from between her cleavage, scuttling off across her shoulder and disappearing down her back.

Granted it most likely dropped from the ceiling as it never happened again, not to my knowledge… but the word soon spread and from then on business really picked up at Mama Nick's with everyone taking bets, waiting with baited breath for an encore.

Old Enemies

Greer Noble

There's no truer idiom than the title of this anecdote when recalling an incident while on safari in Botswana's Savuti area of the Chobe National Park. The Savuti Camp itself is very spread out, in thick, thick sand – the only designated camping area we've ever come across where low range four wheel drive is required IN the camp – and it is not often that one hears other campers. But of course there are always exceptions to the rule. We had just turned in when we heard blood curdling screams, shouts of terror and all sorts of noises, thumps and clangs, as if the whole camp was under attack by some marauding tribe… except there were no villages for many miles around.

A large group of family and friends from South Africa were gathered around their camp fire, sipping after dinner coffee when all hell broke loose. Before their unbelieving eyes, close enough to touch, a lone hyena brazenly tore into their midst, heaving, frothing at the mouth, its eyes crazed. *'Was it rabid?'* was everyone's immediate reaction? Although rare, this is not unknown. Panic-stricken they all leaped up with camp chairs flying in all directions, wildly clambering for whatever cover they could find.

A sudden growl in their midst had them momentarily freeze, as if it were a party game, one of those Freeze Dances where everyone stays as they were when the music stops. On seeing a full maned-lion between them *and* the hyena, renewed terror reigned. It was akin to being trapped in a forest fire on a stormy night.

Screams, menfolk shouting orders, shrieks, people bumping into one another diving for bins, climbing trees and clambering up ladders into rooftop tents - it was pandemonium. Only the lion was not remotely interested them. His sights were firmly fixed on the unfortunate hyena which had done something to really antagonise His Highness.

Unperturbed he rushed at the equally frantic, momentarily confused, hyena which resumed its flight. Not long after, the death knoll sounded. The hyena let out a weird yelp and breathed its last.

A crescendo in the great orchestra of a wild African night, it was over as quickly as it had begun. On hearing the kill we knew something had met its maker so decided it wise to stay in our rooftop tent and find out the full story the next morning. This we did through much laughter and ribbing. It's easy to laugh afterwards at all the different antics and behaviour but, at the time, a terrifying and sobering experience nonetheless.

Footnote
Whenever we're in the Chobe area, my husband, around sunset, goes into hyena-mode and emulates them calling with a series of long, manic whoops punctuated with intermittent 'oooooh-WHUP' yelps and manic giggles, at which stage everyone joins the chorus unable to stop themselves giggling, especially when his harem start closing in on us. Literally coming closer and closer they call back, salivating I'm sure, in anticipation of a friendly fellow clan boasting about a juicy kill! – **GN**

Some Dumb Little Human

Tollan I Wade

After my 'long' military medical where the medic looked into my eyes and made me cough, I secured my backpack onto the rear seat of my Honda and zoomed out of Salisbury on the road northwards to join my buddies in Kariba.

Police speed traps were only common in built up areas in the 70s. The limit was seventy miles-an-hour but after leaving the outskirts of the city I lay on the fuel tank and let the bike do what it did best, travel. The road was flat and had long straights of miles in length and soft rounding curves. Nothing in the world would stop me cruising at a decent speed of ninety, ninety-five. At this speed I felt the closest I had ever been to actually flying a jet.

By the second fuel stop the African night was pulling its curtains together quickly on the diving sun, like it always did in this part of Africa.

The most desolate part of the trip was still to come with miles of tarred road dropping down into the Zambezi river basin and finally ending at the water's edge of Lake Kariba ninety-five miles ahead. Finally darkness arrived and the African bush made an appearance right next to the road. The basin's high trees and increasing growth was a total change from the dry savannah up above. Tropical forests and thick bushes appeared ghostly out of the dark as the road quickly dropped into the escarpment below.

Still keeping the Honda's speed at around eighty, the curves tightened until I was sweeping left and then right down the escarpment like a racer making his way around the Alps on the Monte Carlo Rally. The night was dark but a full moon was about to appear. I had never ridden this road before and found it exciting traveling along it and, with headlight on full beam, I used up the whole road, completing each tight curve on a good and fast racing line. Through some of the tighter curves I had to lift off the throttle a little but still I was doing close on eighty miles an hour when I

433

approached what seemed to be the last tight 180 degree turn at the bottom of the escarpment. A large shock awaited me.

I couldn't believe my goggles! There, right in the middle of the road, was the largest elephant bull I had even seen getting rid of his heavy load of dung right in the center of the bend about seventy yards ahead of me! He must have heard my bike as he was looking directly towards my oncoming headlight. It was too late to change my racing line. The Honda and I were already well into the curve and since the bike was leaning at a sharp angle to the ground, with my outstretched knee nearly touching the surface, it would be catastrophic to apply brakes. There was nothing I could do to stop myself going through the middle of the huge mound of steaming hot elephant dung.

I had about a second and a half to hang on tight. All I could do was to close the throttle, grip the bike and tank hard and try to hide the rest of me behind the now very thin looking handlebars. It became one of those times in life where time itself slowed down to slow motion, I slowly watched the pile of dung get closer and closer. I must have been going well over seventy when I hit, but had straightened the slowing bike up at the last minute as I had just had a moment to notice an open space between the trees on the other side of the road.

'*Jesus...!*' I started praying, but didn't have much time as SPLAT! was the only noise around as the bike and I hit the steaming mess!

It felt like a giant hand had smacked me all over the road. The Honda immediately went into a serious wobble and it was pure luck that I kept it upright by blindly punching the ground with both boots to try and keep it on its tires. Luckily I had worn goggles and with the back of my hand managed a quick wipe of the left eye-piece of my blackened goggles and slowly brought the slipping and sliding bike to a halt between two giant baobab trees, thankful that the elephant itself was nowhere to be seen.

Every part of me as well as parts of the bike was covered in a very smooth and concentrated layer of still-steaming dung. I felt like I had a muddy face-pack on from a spa, except for one thing, the smell! My nose wanted to close down and leave my face forever! I stank! The bike stank! Everything stank! After coming back to my senses, I grabbed some large leaves from the side of the road and cleaned as much of the evil smelling excrement off me and my bike.

The bike fired up and once again I was on the move, with bits and pieces of elephant dung flying off the parts of the bike and me that I couldn't reach.

Finally, I drove into the open camping area in Kariba and rode up to some of the guys who had been waiting up for my arrival next to a small fire. Their clownish remarks and gestures when they spied my mien suddenly became quite obscene when they realised that the new revolting animal smell came from me. There being no showers in this campsite, I had a quick bathe in the warm lake water a hundred yards away. Not wanting to be eaten by a crocodile I had someone stand by me with a lantern.

That wasn't the end of my encounter with elephants that night. The last of us late-nighters got to bed around one in the morning. Some of us slept around the fire in sleeping bags and when I awoke, refreshed from a deep sleep, I noticed a huge foot print right next to my sleeping bag. At least a foot and a half across and it hadn't been there when I went to sleep.

Over cups of coffee we figured that an elephant must have smelled the excrement from my brush with dung and death earlier and come to investigate the odour of a possible foreign male in his area, walked right through the camp, stopped where I was sleeping and smelt me with his trunk. *Some dumb little human smelling like elephant shit!* he must have thought and carried on...

It was amusing to hear from a fellow overlander that in some parts of North Africa *bikers* had been fined for not wearing a seat belt! – **GN**

Alien in the Toilet

Mike Ballantine

Our offices were located in South Africa's semi-rural Natal coast. Early one morning I went into one of the toilets and found mud on the toilet seat, on the floor and on the walls. *'Who could have left it in such a state and what had they been doing to cause the mess?'* I asked myself. *'Of course, it must be Greer'*, I reasoned. She was the gardener, regularly introducing new pot plants into the office. But on showing her the mess she was surprised. n

'What on earth...?!' she exclaimed. With that the girls in the office came running in and gaped at the toilet. Theories abounded... even 'aliens' were considered but none seemed feasible.

Late that afternoon alone in the office, I heard swishing, slapping sounds coming from the toilet. I crept through and there, covered in mud, was the perpetrator. On seeing me, it climbed up and slithered into the toilet bowl – and vanished! It was a leguaan, an amphibious monitor lizard, about 75cm long, which had gained access through the exterior vent pipe that had broken off at ground level. It was having the time of its life diving in and out the toilet bowl, hence all the mud... As you can imagine we were all shocked to think that we might have been using the toilet at a most inopportune time.

A Thief in the Night

Mike Ballantine

Some years ago we yet again found ourselves at Botswana's Savuti camp, a bushwhacker's must, and again made camp on the banks of the then dry river channel. From our slightly elevated position we regularly enjoyed sightings, often close up, of elephant, antelope, warthog, an occasional pride of lion, and birds, big and small, our favourite being the gregarious yellow-billed hornbill. One balmy, starless evening the night quickly closed in on us – and soon the glowing embers of our fire were the only source of light.

Suddenly a torchlight flashed about 150 metres away. It began weaving towards us. Loud voices from behind the light reached us. They sounded agitated. We were mildly annoyed – unlike domesticated, urban camp sites only metres apart because of restricted space, bush sites generally were out of normal hearing range from each other, all the better to enjoy the heady night sounds of the wild.

The light suddenly illuminated us.

'Sorry, sorry,' the torchbearer apologised. *'We're looking for a briefcase, a large one like those used by pilots.'* Then he expanded. *'There's a dozen of us. We were enjoying an ABF* when one of the wives shrieked when she spotted a hyena sneaking off with the case.'*

'I wouldn't look for it now,' I offered. *'It's too dark. You'll be trying to find the proverbial needle. I'm sure you will find it somewhere in the channel come sunup.'*

I spoke fairly confidently, having on past trips found more than a few campers' possessions discarded in the channel including tog bags, shoes and sandals – the discarded spoils of hyena grown quickly bored with the items' lack of taste. But my advice went unheeded – and we learnt why later. For hours we witnessed their frantic search as their torch-beam bobbed to and fro, up and down as they scoured the bush around the camp.

Up at dawn as usual, I rekindled our fire. While waiting for the water to boil for that delicious first cup of coffee, I looked cursorily up and down about fifty metres of channel in front of us - and there it was, the brief-case, large as life, unceremoniously dumped on its side next to a small bush.

There were thank you's, sighs of relief and much nervous laughter when I returned the case. It belonged to a tour guide, contained several bottles of whisky – and... the passports of everyone in his party.

*ABF - absolutely bloody final drink

Footnote:
After being dry for nearly 30 years the Savuti channel quite unexpectedly started flowing again.

*The funniest thing in the wilds at night is to hear hyena giggle – the heavens hold not the only stars – **GN***

Old Lofty

Belinda da Costa

Here I am, no longer two bricks and a tickey* high but still wet behind the ears, as evidenced by my first ever hangover-induced misery. It is in this delicate state, following my eighteenth birthday that I am slouched on the back seat of a car with a skill reserved solely for teenagers. I'm trying desperately to ignore the sweltering heat, the drone of the tyres on tarmac and the erratic growl from the diesel engine. I already miss my once-hometown of Bulawayo* (Zimbawe), somewhere in the distance behind us, but I'm half-heartedly looking forward to the long queues at Beit Bridge Customs and 'Irritation'. Anything to get me out of this tin can on wheels.

Our driver is mean today, probably a product of his own vodka induced misery, and it takes several hours before someone in the car finally convinces him to make a pit stop.

'We've just passed Todd's Motel. Why didn't you ask five minutes ago?' He grumbles pulling over on the side of the road.

With sweet relief, we all pile out of the hot box and scatter like thieves into the bush.

'Men on the right – ladies on the left.'

I find a suitable spot behind some low thorn bushes, clear of long grass and hidden from the road. I glance around quickly to check the coast is clear. The only sign of humanity is my aunt's head bobbing up and down like a meerkat above a nearby shrub as she also scouts.

Deep breath, shorts down, in position, watch for splash-backs (men really don't appreciate how difficult this complex operation is for us girls) and then… relief!

'Lindy!' My aunt's frantic stage whisper stops me in mid flow.

'What?' I mouth back, fear prickling icily in contrast to the heat of the African sun.

'Don't... move.'

'O... kay?!' Yeah right! Eyes first, I follow her frightened stare over my shoulder. Then, open mouthed, my gaze drifts up to the heavens. How the hell did such a big animal get within two arms' length of me without me hearing it? For several long seconds, the giraffe and I gaze curiously at each other. Neither of us moves.

A scramble in the bushes behind me tells me that my aunt has decided on self-preservation and gapped it swiftly back to the car.

Myself? Well I'm torn. I love nature and getting so close to it is a huge privilege. To say I'm in awe would be an understatement as my shorts-around-my-ankles-and-nether-regions-exposed   situation   is temporarily forgotten. But this is Africa. And this is a wild animal with legs and a head that could do me some serious damage if it felt so inclined.

'Hi!' I bleat feebly, rising slowly to my feet, shorts following. Should I be embarrassed if a giraffe can see my less tanned bits? I decide to reserve that question for another time.

Avoiding fast movements, I secure my clothes and shuffle in reverse until my tree is now between us. The animal's long neck is craning to one side to see me better. I thought this tree was bigger? The giraffe then seems to get bored with me and proceeds to rip a few sparse leaves from my tree to graze.

Feeling slightly insulted now by the giraffe's apparent disinterest, bursting my ego-filled bubble that I had perhaps shared a moment with this beast, I straighten my shoulders and my pride and turn to stalk back to the car with one short glimpse over my shoulder.

My friend-for-a-second watches me with abstract boredom. He makes no move to follow as he chews his way through a mouthful of thorns and leaves.

Navigating the shallow storm drain separating me from the road, I grow more certain that the endless motion and drone of the car will be soothing rather than grating and my hangover is miraculously fading to a distant memory.

* tickey – three-penny coin in circulation before decimalisation of currency

*We've found giraffes too be rather placid creatures – they will not harm you if you keep calm and show you're not a threat. We've walked within a few paces of them in the wilds. They're more curious than anything else. In fact they can become quite forward when they get to know you. I used to feed them oranges. But don't be fooled by their gentleness, their kick has been known to kill a lion. **GN***

Deadly Intruder

Greer Noble

Have you ever read a newspaper, propped up in bed, then folded it and tossed it on the floor? Nothing out of the ordinary about that... only this time my hand was dripping wet. Strange, but anything's possible in Africa. My immediate reaction was to look up, expecting to see one of those juicy, fleshy, transparent looking geckos, clinging to the ceiling by its suckered feet, clucking and sweeping its tail back and forth, vying with a rival for a moth or some other mouth-watering delicacy. Nothing. Puzzled, I looked down... and that's when I saw it. I froze.

Coiled and rearing up was my worst nightmare; a fully hooded banded cobra, its beady eyes fixed on me, swaying in strike mode, its tongue flicking. *Dear God, what was I to do!*

Only that morning I had my bedside pedestal removed so that my little daughter's bed could fit in next to our double bed in preparation for unexpected guests. Friends due to arrive the next day would be temporarily accommodated in her bedroom in our two roomed lakeside cottage as our hotel was full to capacity.

Now she lay asleep and, to my horror, her little arm hung over the side of the bed, her hand precariously close to this deadly intruder. I prayed she would not stir. I knew one move of her hand and it would strike. It had already sprayed me with its putrid 'milk' and was clearly agitated, at the ready. It would only take the slightest provocation... the blood drained from me in anticipation of what could happen. I had to act fast.

'*Wake up!*' I shook my other half next to me.

His reaction was instant. On realising our daughter's life was at stake he wasted no time, leaped over me onto her bed, swooped her up in his arms and bounded out of the room with her, so swiftly, that even the cobra was confused. In a tizz, it flared its hood even more grotesquely, swaying furiously, as if prompted by the flute of the devil himself. Thankful that my daughter was safe, I didn't wait to see what would happen next.

By this time the night watchman had arrived and both men armed with broom-sticks went into the now closed room. The 'hood' was nowhere to be found! Then a huge scuffle ensued with beds scraping the stone floor and shouts and thuds... then silence.

The door opened and there was one very dead snake, its hood no more.

A dear old friend staying with us at the hotel, Dr Marr, an ichthyologist seconded by the local fisheries to study Lake Kariba's species, after dissecting it the next morning to see what the big lump was in its body, said that if it hadn't eaten the frog we could have indeed come off second best.

My father may not have approved. '*Leave wild creatures alone and they will leave you alone,*' was his dictum. Hmm... I was beginning to doubt those wise words of benevolence. There's always the exception and this time it was a little too close for comfort.

The Elephant and the Church Mouse

Rory Young

It was golden hour. The warm glow of the African sunset bathed the already gorgeous scenery of Lake Kariba and the Matusadona mountains making its already magical beauty seem almost surreal. We were seated in an open Land Rover quietly observing the old elephant. Serenity. Then he began to extend his gigantic penis. Yes, it's enormous, the largest of any land animal. Up to a metre in length and fifteen centimetres thick. It also has two muscles, so it can be moved, which elephants seemed to do when being observed by men.

I waited quietly for the response from the two couples seated on the back. Responses were usually varied. They ranged from the elderly's, '*good grief!*' to the Australian Bruce's, '*That would come in handy on a picnic!*' Whilst both the men were pretty laid back and chatted normally and asked questions about the wildlife, their wives couldn't have been more different. The first lady just couldn't shut up. She talked incessantly and was giving me a headache. The second lady was the exact opposite. She was petite, demure and did

445

not say one word. I was starting to wonder if she could speak at all.

I noted with a feeling of great relief that the garrulous lady had now gone completely quiet. But then so had everybody else. I waited till the silence was deafening and then decided to break the ice. '*This is a male elephant*', I said, '*You can tell from the shape of the head.*' There was a round of chuckles from behind me and I tackled the subject head on, '*The elephant's penis extends 160cm in total length, including what you don't see and the testes are internal, close to the spine, which is why you don't see them.*'

Then, as I rambled on, I was interrupted by a quiet little voice from the very back. It was the girl who had not yet said a word. '*How do elephants have sex?*' she asked.

A surprising first question. Quite obvious I would have thought. As usual I bit back my first answer, which in this case was '*Not in the missionary position...*' and began to explain how the male's penis has to curve to reach and therefore had the two muscles and so on and so forth.

When I had finished our quiet little angel said '*Oh*'. I waited. Then, '*I always thought their sexual organs were in their feet*', she said.

'*I beg your pardon?*' I said. I hadn't yet realized who the naive party in all of this was and now expecting to have to explain the birds and the bees to a honeymooner.

'*Because when it stands on you you're f****d*' said the little church mouse.

Life is far too important a thing ever to talk seriously about – **Oscar Wilde**

'Don't Kill Charlie!'

Greer Noble

B esides mosquitos, scorpions and spiders, even tsetse fly can be nocturnal... yet they all have their place and they're not all harmful. I was once about to deliberately stand on a huge hairy ginger hunting spider as big as my hand, to squash it, when two men jumped up and shouted in unison, *'Don't kill Charlie!'*

I subsequently got to know and love Charlie. He appeared every night to feast on insects attracted to our Tilly lamp placed next us on the ground where we sat around our camp fire. He'd rush in, grab a beetle then run off into the bush to devour it. The most amazing thing of all was the way it got to know us and actually came to my father when he scratched on the canvas of his chair. It would then take a beetle from his fingers.

If these spiders are crushed they disintegrate into nothing.

Footnote: *Je suis Charlie* slogan was created by French art director Joachim Roncin and adopted by supporters of freedom of speech/freedom of the press after 7 January 2015 shooting at the offices of the French satirical weekly newspaper *Charlie Hebdo*.

The measure of civilized behaviour is compassion – **Paul Theroux**

Fight or Flight

Rory Young

I used to run a wildlife sanctuary and safari operation in the Zambezi Valley on the Zambian side of the river. During the wet season the area was inaccessible by road so very few people came to visit. That's when we spent most of our time doing anti-poaching work. But as two other nearby camps from where anti-poaching patrols had also been active and had been attacked I used to sleep in a different room or tent every night with a loaded rifle next to the bed.

One night I awoke to a sound of voices whispering. I rolled off my mattress and picked up the rifle and torch I had ready and quietly went to the gauze window and peered out. In the moonlight I could make out several figures moving along a path towards the main building. They had one small torch.

I had no doubts. There had been no sound of a vehicle or boat. My own team would not risk being shot by walking around the camp at night without giving verbal warning first. So I steeled myself for a fight. Knowing the paths I was able to quietly sneak up on them. There were four.

A few feet behind them I raised my rifle and switched on the torch, which I held under the barrel, at the same time shouting in the local Goba language for them to surrender.

They froze, several screamed. Two elderly European couples stood in front of me with shock on their faces. They had turned around and were also shining their torch at me.

I cleared my throat and said, '*Sorry, I thought you were poachers.*'

They said nothing and even more strangely the two women were looking everywhere except at me, whilst the chap with the torch was now pointing it behind him. It slowly dawned on me... I was stark naked.

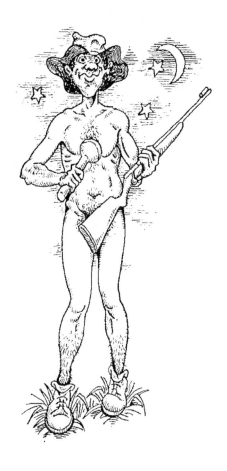

There was nothing for it but to behave perfectly naturally so I said, *'How can I help you folk?'* I casually slung my rifle over my shoulder and put one hand on my hip trying to somehow look normal.

After a long pause one of the men said, *'Our boat hit a sandbar this afternoon and we have been stuck most of the night on the river. Eventually we managed to push it off but we couldn't get it started and paddled downstream till we saw the light at your jetty.'*

I directed them to the dining area, casually excused myself and nonchalantly walked off to get some clothes on. I later fed them and organized rooms for them and the next day got to know them. They were farmers from one of the tobacco growing areas. Everyone was polite enough not to mention my commando outfit of the previous evening and I naively thought that was the end of the story.

A couple of months later I was in Zimbabwe and met a couple who also farmed tobacco. They had never even been to the country where I worked. They asked me what I did and where I was based. I told them.

There was silence and I wondered what I had said wrong. Then the woman said to me, '*Are you the guy who runs around naked in the bush at night hunting poachers?*'

Footnote
Rory Young has devoted his life to saving the African elephant, his anti-poaching methods already having swept through many African countries, inspiring hope for the survival of the species where many others have already given up. To me he's a legend, having risked his life on so many occasions, not only in war-torn countries but also in the face of killer diseases such as Ebola. I do not think he gets the recognition he deserves, nor the funding. I'm hopeful, be it in a small way, word will out by whoever reads this – **GN**

Chameleon Calamity

Greer Noble

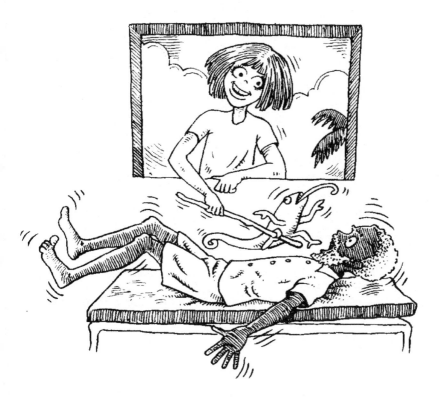

In the old Rhodesia*, ancestral mythology was an integral part of everyday life and our cook, of the Shona tribe, was a mine of information. We'd often sit having lunch together, dunking sadza* into relish*. One that made a lasting impression was the reason chameleons were bad luck – their spirit god had sent a chameleon to tell everyone to bathe in a certain pond. Only the chameleon was so slow in delivering the message that by the time his tribe got there, only enough water remained for the palms of their hands and the soles of their feet.

One day my friends the Baker twins and I found a chameleon in their garden. The three of us proceeded to cook up some devilish mischief. Lynn and Dawn lived with their grandparents on a grand old estate bordering Mozambique. In fact we were neighbours. Their grandmother, being the wife of the local magistrate, did a lot of

451

entertaining which she could not have managed without her chef of 20 years. We planned it for siesta time. Balancing on their shoulders, I was able to access the high window above his bed. As he lay dozing I carefully lowered the chameleon onto his chest from the end of a stick. As the little fellow mounted Cookie's chin, Cookie's one eye shot open. Then all hell broke loose. The chameleon went one way, Cookie the other and we collapsed in a heap of uncontrollable laughter as only 12 year olds can. We were still giggling when we were summoned. Cookie was so upset he wanted to resign but a good stiff brandy and profuse apologies from all three of us sorted that out... or so we thought.

Happily we recovered the chameleon and put him back in the garden. But as it turned out Cookie had the last laugh as he was instructed not to cook for us for the next two days I was with them. We had to fend for ourselves.

*Rhodesia – now Zimbabwe
*sadza –   maize meal cooked into stiff porridge – staple African diet
*relish –   stewed greens of the spinach variety usually with tomato

You are only young once, but you can stay immature indefinitely.
Ogden Nash

Al Crapone

Greer Noble

Stories about long-drops are legendary. A wonderful invention but high maintenance what with wood-rot, a variety of termites and even the likes of bush pig and aardvarks have been known to burrow in and around them. This can undermine the very structure of this endearing form of latrine. Needless to say, if not regularly maintained, they can become high risk, the most common culprit being white ants.

At a popular beach camp in Moçambique, while a group of us were enjoying sundowners, Derek, one of our party, in using a long-drop, failed to make it out in time. Like a sinkhole, it very unexpectedly caved in and, at a most inopportune moment too, caught him completely by surprise. Unable to secure a grip, the force of gravity

453

was completely against him and in he went. Being a well-used latrine it had built up quite a pile of human excrement turned into fine sludge, work of the worm inhabitants. This had now become a noxious tomb as the fumes were putrid beyond belief. Howling in terror, treading the worm liquefied excreta, he gagged between squeals, all the while straining to keep from submerging altogether... as was later related to us in all its finer, gory detail.

Fortuitously, our cook in passing heard the poor man's muffled yelps and, fearing the worst, rushed to inform us.

After an emergency extraction, a rather unpleasant, messy affair with inebriated comments flying around as much as the debris did when hosing him down, a very long swim in the sea ensued. This was followed by copious amounts of hooligan-soup (brandy and coke), which he poured down his gullet while the splinters were removed from unmentionable parts of his anatomy.

In the meantime Dave, our host, having surreptitiously dashed off up the hill to his permanent residence, returned sometime later and presented our unsanitary hero with a hand-made medal on which was inscribed *Al Crapone* – one medal that was *not* worn with pride! And for some odd reason (and nothing to do with the stench that stayed with him for days on end), that name stuck – from then on Derek was known as Al Crapone.

If you're going through hell, keep going. **Winston Churchill**

Diamonds are for... Birds

Keith Wright

When we were in USA, in the Africa section of Disney Animal Kingdom, a parrot, an African Grey, sat on my wife's hand, walked carefully up her arm, got to her shoulder, turned around, walked all the way back to her hand, bent down, pecked the stone right out of her ring and flew away!

Footnote
Keith did admit it wasn't an expensive ring so possibly the stone wasn't that well set.

It Could Only Happen in Maun!

Connor Eddles

This story was told to me by a safari lodge owner I met in a bar in Maun – as the cicadas droned endlessly and the swollen African sun languidly crept towards the horizon, a marvellous tale of misadventure unfolded...

While not its main sport, cricket is still rather widely played in Botswana, to the extent that local towns furiously compete against each other. The night before one such match the visiting team hit upon a brilliant, if somewhat drunken plan to amuse themselves.

The cricket pitch just happened to border a small crocodile farm where young crocodiles were raised for bush meat and more profitably, their hides used for shoes and handbags.

What these men did was utterly extraordinary; not only did they break into the farm, they also made off with about ten juvenile crocs which led them to an obvious conclusion; sword-fighting!

Several bite marks later, one of their numbers drunkenly crawled into his tent shouting abuse, threatening unspeakable things that would befall anyone who dared to disturb him. As an act of revenge, the snappiest of the juvenile crocs was chosen and deftly chucked into the tent which was then zipped up and cable-tied shut with remarkable alacrity.

The screaming which shortly ensued from within soon gave way to a disparate wailing; the victim of the prank had managed to cut a hole to slip through – unfortunately, his plan came awry when his prodigious beer gut became wedged in the hole. This set a rather interesting scene; a small, hairy-legged tent sprinting about with no particular destination, panic stricken shrieks of hysteria emanating from within. His wily teammates quickly pulled him free before sprinting off into the night – leaving behind a croc-infested cricket pitch to be dealt with in the morning.

A boy's story is the best that is ever told – **Charles Dickens**

Now you see it...

Greer Noble

We took great pride in growing our own fruit for our hotel on the shores of Lake Kariba, Zimbabwe's own Riviera. Granadillas, papayas, bananas – and no small thanks to my mother whose green fingers and ardent determination was mostly responsible. It was a full time job continually having to ward off elephant, hippo, warthog, hornbills and a plethora of antelope and insects. Whoever would have thought vegetables needed round the clock security guards!

As we were known for our delectable tropical fruit salads, it came as quite a surprise when one day a lunch guest complained to one of our waiters of being served *'pig fodder'*, demanding to see the manager. As it was a family run hotel there was no manager as such but being my mother's department she was naturally summoned.

'How may I help you?' she offered politely.

'Explain,' began the acne-faced youth, jabbing the air with his finger, *'what THIS is doing in my fruit salad?'* He had spooned out a sizeable chunk of thick glass and dropped it with a clunk onto his side plate.

My mother who had, as always, made the fruit salad with her own hands, peered down, picked up the piece of glass, examined it and not recognising it or knowing what to do with it, tossed it into the rockery amidst thick undergrowth. *'There,'* she said matter of fact, *'It's gone now.'*

The guest looked astonished while everyone else at his table began to snigger. The ungracious youth went red in the face, stood up and stormed out of the dining room. Later his party, who'd popped in for the day from Zambia, had difficulty settling their bill, despite the fact that the price of the fruit salad had been deducted.

The staff knew nothing of the broken glass and while we had our suspicions that he may have put the glass in the fruit salad hoping not to pay for his meal, it remains a mystery to this day.

Shocking Warthogs

Adele Barton

It was a typically hot and humid day in Chiredzi, nestled in the Zimbabwe lowveld. We arrived at the sugar estate early in the morning and had just settled down to a hearty breakfast on the terrace which overlooked the sugar plantations which are protected by an electric game fence that circumnavigates the entire estate.

Off to our right we saw a group of warthogs starting to gather on the other side of the fence. At this time the manager came and sat with us. He told us to keep our eyes on the hogs. It was as if they were rounding up the troops, spurring each other on. They kept looking longingly at the ripening cane.

Suddenly one plucked up the courage, broke free from the crowd and ran, tail standing straight up, through the fence. Once on the other side he appeared a little confused, not sure of himself. Then another broke free and ran through the fence, then another, and another, until all of them were on the side of the cane. All of them looking disorientated!

Then, as abruptly, the whole process started again, back to the other side, where they gathered as if to strategize. Once they had re-grouped they were off, back through the fence again. This carried on for hours and hours and was a most bizarre sight to behold.

'How come they got into the crop but don't eat anything?' we asked the manager. *' Why do they keep running back and forth?'*

He told us that the electric fence was **not** working that day but the warthogs were so conditioned to getting zapped then eating their reward, they weren't going to eat unless they got zapped.

Footnote:
Although I've never witnessed it myself I've heard and also read that it is not uncommon for warthog to kill lion, buffalo and wildebeest by ripping their stomachs open with their lethal tusks 'when running below the abdomen.' Their hard skeletal face plate apparently makes them almost 'impervious to a frontal attack.' Having lived among warthog I'm not surprised they have few predators, other than predators in groups. And while a fully grown warthog has few single land-based enemies it can, of course, be attacked by crocodile. By reputation, the African warthog is one of those 'bad-ass animals of lore' up there with the honey badger. **GN**

Leguaan Lunacy

Greer Noble

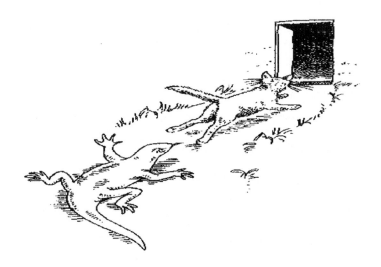

When you have eleven ginger toms, each with their own turf (lions are not the only cats that are territorial), even if spread over 46 acres, life can get pretty interesting. Snookums was my special boy. At 14 lbs (6kilos), he was the biggest, had the strongest markings and the deepest voice. He was also possessive and God help any other cat, even from the same clan, that ventured anywhere near our cottage.

Once, when still a kitten, no sooner had we rescued a baby leguaan (Nile monitor lizard) from our hotel swimming pool than his curiosity got the better of him. He made a beeline for the little reptile which instantly latched onto his lower lip in a vice grip which sent Snookums into what can only be described as a psychotic frenzy. It took two of us to hold him down as he clawed wildly, while a third prized off the wee leguaan as gently as possible with screwdriver and pincers, trying not to hurt the victim or perpetrator.

So when some years later I saw him streaking down the tradesman's entrance and bolting into the hotel kitchen, hotly pursued by a rather large, equally swift and very angry leguaan, I knew he'd been nosing around her egg nest. Lucky for him – while they have no teeth, only bone, that grip has more tenacity than a bull dog.

Savuti Streaker

Greer Noble

Some very strange things happen in the Okavango and especially at Chobe's renowned Savuti camp. Hyenas running off with anything that looks remotely edible – having your car tyres chewed by these normally carnivorous scavengers; hornbills admiring themselves in your rear-view mirrors; hippos honking in the night; lions calling; you may even see the odd snake; hear or see a kill... the list is endless, but none so plentiful as elephant. The elephant stories, like the hyena stories are legendary. They wander right past you or through you, strolling quietly, unhurriedly often at night too, leaving their big round pad spoor in the thick soft sand... and then there's the unexpected... like nude women streaking past your camp!

Talk about a double-take!

'*What's going on?*' my husband wanted to know, consumed with curiosity.

It was early evening and as is customary we were sitting quietly, as one does enjoying a sundowner, when this woman streaks past like a flash of lightning. You begin to question your sanity... '*Is my imagination playing tricks on me?*' ...more particularly as we were oblivious of anyone else in camp!

My husband being the gregarious type couldn't bear the suspense so went to find out for himself.

In certain parts of Africa we have to really wait long and hard for the rains to come. Day after day the sun mercilessly scorches the earth until any pool or other source of water dries up. And during a drought the rains don't come at all. It was one of those times. The animals become desperate. The hippo die as their pools evaporate and the elephant come into the camp and have the intelligence to dig up water pipes and will even knock down ablution blocks to get to the water.

On this occasion the unfortunate woman in question, after a long

462

hot and dusty journey, was enjoying a rose-less shower – all the shower roses having been removed or stolen. In the midst of shampooing her hair the water suddenly dried up. Bewildered, covered in soap-suds she looked up to see an elephant's trunk through the frameless window sucking on the shower pipe as if it were his own personal straw!

Terrified she took flight, running all the way back to the camp where the rest of the party were relaxing.

People in cities cannot imagine what they miss by not experiencing the wilds. No two days or nights are ever the same. The entertainment is unparalleled, varied and endless... you even get streakers with your sundowners!!!

A Letter Out of the Blue

Dear Greer,

Your book, Veiled Madness, apart from being an intriguing read, unlocked many memories of Rhodesia where we lived for four years. We travelled the country, loved Inyanga, Mermaids Pool and particularly Kariba where we stayed at your hotel and also met you and your family - your father was building at the time.

We spent a couple of magical evenings around a fire on the beach with your brother Noel, drinking cane spirits and listening to stories of adventures in the bush. He invited us to a weekend at his tobacco farm and took us shooting guinea fowl for the pot.

An incident that really sticks in my mind was when Marian, my wife, and I got up early one morning and heard a commotion around the kitchen area only to see your mother with a broom, chasing a large elephant out of the compound. It had been putting its trunk through the kitchen door and stealing the breakfast pawpaw.

Once, just after descending the escarpment into Kariba, we came across a big bull elephant in the middle of the road. I backed onto the verge to give me the option to make a run for it but then he trumpeted and a herd crossed the road on both sides of us – my father was so excited he got out of the car to get closer!!! I had to force him back before they took too much interest in us. The bull did give us the once over then thankfully went on his way.

The bush war saw our departure but unable to settle in the UK we returned, this time to South Africa. I started taking overseas contracts in Mauritius, Greece, Iran, Oman, Nigeria, Saudi Arabia, Abu Dhabi, the Caribbean and the USA - but I never found another Rhodesia. We'll never forget the magnificent sunsets over Kariba and God's firework display, as my father called the storms, but also the people. Now we rely on photographs and writers like yourself.

With kind regards,

Ron and Marian Watts

Cecil

I'm just another lion
So why the fuss and bother
Though some say I was chosen
To end this game of horror

What manner, earthly predator
Is the jungle king to fear
Without bolt or bullet
No man would ever cheer

So take my head, my skin, my claws
A trophy for your wall
I roam no more nor watch my pride
Nor see my cubs mature

But from afar I see it all
A broody silence prevails
Savanah plains once teeming life
Now devoid of animal trails

Are we the new age dinosaurs
Lifeless clones of bone
Glass eyes stare across the halls
Will museums become our home

I'm just a lion called Cecil
But with a wish or two
I hope to touch your hearts
The way I used to do

Please stop this senseless killing
Let my cubs explore
Pursue the freedom that was mine
And enjoy forever more

GN

I am not African because I was born in Africa... but because Africa was born in me – **Kwame Nkrumah**

Introducing Contributors

Here we all are, alphabetically by surname, and a little bit about us. *To contact any of us or submit a review please email:* kariwa@ymail.com http://greernoble.com/my-funny-africa---blog.html

Mike Ballantine – Sometime journalist, PR man, estate agent, property developer, bushwhacker and adventurer. Born and brought up in Africa. Lives between Africa and Europe.

Michael Noble Ballantine – Student, researcher, explorer, adventurer, amateur horticulturist, conservationist, human rights sympathiser, animal cruelty activist, vegetarian, nomad.

Russell Barnett – Born in Rhodesia, now lives in Cork, Ireland. An artist, he specialises in pictorial map making; natural history; botanical and fine line work; calligraphy and hand lettering. https://www.facebook.com/russell.w.barnett?fref=ts

Sora Barnett – 14 yrs old, lives in Ballingeary, West Cork, Ireland. Has a dog called Sausage, loves anime and especially likes to draw manga. Loves Africa and is crazy about animals even though bitten by a mongoose in South Africa.

Adele Barton – Writer, animal and wildlife enthusiast. Budding ornithologist. Actress, adventurer, bush-whacker. Born in Kenya. Now lives in Zimbabwe. https://www.facebook.com/adelebarton

Tim Bax – Brought up in Tanganyika, UK & Canada, highly acclaimed author, ex-Rhodesian Army & Selous Scouts lieutenant, now assists in survival courses – read more here: http://www.timothybax.com/

Jeremy Bentley – Mad engineer, goofy socially civilized bachelor, secretly adventurous, dreams of adrenalin filled explorations. Fairly normal bushwhacker, occasionally suffers agoraphobia, vertigo, claustrophobia, arachnophobia. Rhodesian born & bred Now lives in S.Africa. https://www.facebook.com/jeremy.bentley.357?fref=ts

Nick Bornman – In tourism for 30 years. Mobile Go Wild Safaris, Botswana then 'See Africa Tours, Namibia. Owns and runs guesthouse, Oyster Bay Beach Lodge, Oyster Bay, Eastern Cape. http://www.oysterbaybeachlodge.co.za/

Bruce Brislin – Geophysicist, served with RRAF during bush war, artist, published author (Zimbabwe), 6th generation African, lived in Rhodesia, Botswana and now resides in the UK. https://www.facebook.com/bruce.brislin

Ginny Brock – Journalist turned author, metaphysics student. Born in Johannesburg, lived in Seychelles, Rhodesia and with family in USA, Dubai, Singapore. Now lives in Virginia, USA. http://www.ginnybrockwriter.com

Colin (KK) Brown – Born Singapore 1948. Taken to Africa, aged 2. Schooled in England. Escaped back to Africa. National Service Rhodesia during Bush War. Chartered accountant work in Swaziland & South Africa until 2012. Now lives, Hampshire, England. https://www.facebook.com/profile.php?id=100000606013092 &pnref=friends.search

Heather Clark – Born and raised Rhodesian. Worked in safari industry in Botswana. Hosted trips into national parks helped her see funnier side of life. Sometime singer and artist – from Maun.

Gavin Cooper – Independent financial adviser – MBA in rocket science. Lived in Rhodesia/Zimbabwe, South Africa and Botswana, now based in East Africa. https://www.facebook.com/gavin.cooper.965?ref=ts

Bella Costa – Published author - Adventure and romance novelist. Professional ocean freight-forwarder. Rhodesian born and raised, currently residing in the UK https://www.facebook.com/bella.costa.7503

Tinka Christopher – Artist/sculptress extraordinaire, sculptured and painted for famous international personalities and celebrities. Her studio and home is on a beautiful farm in the Eastern Cape, SA.

Connor Eddles – College student, brother-teaser, globe-trotter, born and brought up in Africa and Britain. Now lives in rural England, Hampshire. https://www.facebook.com/connor.eddles

Vered Ehsani – South African born, educated in Canada. Civil engineer, multi-book author, own radio show Africa Creates Talk Show Host – International – Artist First Radio Kenya Network – Nairobi http://veredehsani.blogspot.co.uk/

Rob Fynn – Author; professional game guide; developed and owned Fothergill Island Game Lodge. Rhodesian bred, trained Royal Navy officer, BSc (Cive Eng) Bristol. Lives – Zimbabwe. https://www.facebook.com/pages/Angel-in-a-Thorn-Bush

Marilyn Garvin – Former farmer's wife outskirts of Mutari, now a housewife in Harare. Born and bred Rhodesian/Zimbabwean. https://www.facebook.com/marilyn.garvin.1

Chris Goldswain – Works in IT; BCom (Hons), BSc Environmental Studies. Worked: Gold and diamond mines, banking, education, manufacturing. Lived in Southern Africa – now lives in UK. http://facebook.com/chris.goldswain1

Jane Goodall, PhD, DBE – Founder – Jane Goodall Institute. UN Messenger of Peace. World renowned for pioneering research on wild chimpanzees. Her efforts today inspire every individual to protect the environment we share. www.janegoodall.org

Reiko M Goodwin – Primatological researcher – Conservationist. Born in Toyama-shi, Toyama, Japan. Speaks English, French, Japanese. Lives in New York. https://www.facebook.com/Guenon.Conservationist?ref=ts

Kevin Graham – Born and raised in Africa, extensively travelled, currently in UK, haunted by the memory of a lost paradise. https://www.facebook.com/wildmanfromafrica

469

Angie Gullan – Founder, 1994, Africa's 1st Wild Dolphin Swim Program, Ponto do Ouro Marine Reserve, Mozambique. Supports Marine Mammal Monitoring & Research. www.dolphincenter.org

Gary Hannan – Native of Zimbabwe, soldier (Rhodesian Army then South African Special Forces), commercial diver, talented artist, songwriter - first single released 2012 in the USA. http://garyhannanproductions.com

Diana M Hawkins – Zimbabwe-born former journalist, environmental writer. Published author of adult and children's books. Resides in USA. http://dianamhawkins-books.com

Eve How – Conservationist, adventurer, bushwhacker. Crazy about animals & wilds of Africa. Brought up in Rhodesia, now farms Eastern Cape, South Africa https://www.facebook.com/eve.how.75

Trish Jackson – Published author/several romantic suspense novels. 2nd generation Rhodesian sparked love of adventure and romance influencing her writing. Lives in USA http://www.trishjackson.com

Brian Jackman – Freelance journalist, author, lifelong passion for eco-tourism & wildlife - 3 years under canvas in the bush. Travelled worldwide. Best known as Britain's foremost writer on African wildlife safaris. Fellow of the Royal Geographical Society. Patron of Tusk Trust. Trustee of the George Adamson Wildlife Preservation Trust. http://www.brian-jackman.co.uk/index.html

Joe Khamisi – Former politician, political analyst and author. Born in Kenya. Widely travelled. Divides time between Kenya and USA. http://joekhamisi.wordpress.com/

Addie Kraan – Retired engineer, 48 years photographing wildlife in Zambezi-Binga area, Rhodesia. Master scuba diver, Zimbabwe Bisley shottist, Hospitality, Commercial fishing. Lives in UK. https://www.facebook.com/addiekraan

Tom Lang – Born and brought up in Rhodesia/Zimbabwe. Military background. Great love of the wilds. Now lives in South Africa. https://www.facebook.com/tom.lang.9461/info

Rachel Lang – Privileged to have travelled much of Southern Africa from an early age - plans to pass on her bush knowledge to children. Based in Cape Town. https://www.facebook.com/BushBoundGirl

James Lepper – Royal Agricultural College graduate married a 'crazy' Rhodesian-raised lady who took him to Africa for an adventure. Now safely back living in England. https://www.facebook.com/kim.lepper.3

Kim Lepper – From Rhodesia. First recollection of wildlife - dawn viewings of white lions at Timbavati. Loves observing game in its natural habitat. Now a housewife in rural England. https://www.facebook.com/kim.lepper.3

Colin Lowe – Zambezi River canoe safari specialist for 25 years. Kariba based tracking instructor during bush war. Rancher. Born and bred Rhodesian. Now lives in Livingstone, Zambia.

Carol Lyes – Born & bred Salisbury, Rhodesia; lived in Zambia, Kenya, S.Africa. Only son lives in London. Loves wilds of Africa and all its creatures. https://www.facebook.com/carol.lyes?fref=ts

Sue Maas – Celebrated wildlife artist. Born in Rhodesia/Zimbabwe, lived in Mozambique and Lesotho. Previous partner of Tiger Bay Lodge, Ume River, Lake Kariba. Now lives in South Africa. https://www.facebook.com/suemaasart?ref=hl

Vic MacKenzie – Illustrator/Rhodesian Herald Editorial cartoonist. Book publishing industry. Rhodesian born and bred. Now lives in USA. https://www.facebook.com/victor.mackenzie1

Charles Mackie – Conservationist engaged in field work in the former National Parks and Wildlife of Rhodesia – latterly flying for various international conservation organisations in a number of African countries. Born and lives in Harare, Zimbabwe.

Humza Mwita – Professional safari guide, water sport instructor and Part-time soccer coach. Based in Watamu, a beautiful coastal village and tourist hot spot in Kenya. www.eastafricasafaris.kbo.co.ke

Greer Noble – African fiction and non-fiction author, conservationist and seriously addicted bushwhacker. Runs a little beach bush camp on the East Coast of Africa. http://greernoble.com/index.html

Larry Norton – Zimbabwe born, internationally acclaimed wildlife artist of 20 years, based in Victoria Falls. Worked with galleries in New York and London – Extensive travels/expeditions across Africa including a year with bush pilot Tom Claytor flying through 18 African countries. www.larrynorton.co.za

Gareth Patterson – has dedicated his entire adult life to the greater protection of the African lion. His many books include his autobiography, My Lion's Heart – www.sekaiafrica.com www.mylionsheart.com www.garethpatterson.com

Bob Shacochis – Acclaimed American novelist, short story writer and literary journalist. He teaches creative writing at Florida State University. http://en.wikipedia.org/wiki/Bob_Shacochis

Wilbur Smith – Born 1933 in Central Africa, educated at Michael-House and Rhodes University, became a full-time writer in 1964 after successful publication of *When the Lion Feeds*. Has since written over 30 novels, all meticulously researched on his numerous expeditions worldwide, now translated into 26 languages. http://www.wilbursmithbooks.com/

Ken Tilbury – Commercial farmer, crocodile breeder turned novelist of several books. Lived in Swaziland and Rhodesia where he served in PATU during the bush war for 12 years. He speaks Siswati, Shona and Afrikaans. Retired in UK. www.kentilbury.com

Will Travers OBE – Co-Founder and President of The Born Free Foundation and Born Free USA – Internationally renowned wild life expert who's dedicated his life to stop wild animal suffering and protect threatened species worldwide. www.bornfree.org.uk

Saskia von Sperber – Born in Germany, Saskia following her dream and travelled to Africa. Her "funny stuff" got her elected Runner Up Wildlife Artist of the Year in Botswana. Now based in Germany. **www.africawild-at-art.com**

Tollan I Wade – Born in England, banker father transferred to Southern Rhodesia where he grew up... now a successful indie writer he lives in the USA. http://tiwade.com/

Ron Watts – UK born. Project\Dev\GM Resort\Management. Avid Globetrotter. Favourite country Rhodesia. Worked/lived in S.Africa, Iran, Nigeria, Saudi Arabia, Abu Dhabi, Oman, Caribbean, USA Mad about wild-Life. https://www.facebook.com/ron.watts.391

Lloyd Wilmot – Born in Francistown, legendary conservationist and safari guide of 43+ years (Lloyd's Camp - Savute, 19 years) Botswana culture enthusiast – speaks Setswana fluently. Maun based. http://www.wilmotsafaris.com/

Tamsin Williams – Hampshire. Amateur wildlife photographer, inspired by David Attenborough since childhood, Africa being her favourite destination.

Bart Wolffe – From Zimbabwe – now lives in England where he continues to write. Former creative director, actor and author working with radio, print, film and television in Africa. http://www.lulu.com/spotlight/bartwolffe

Rory Young – Born in Zambia, raised in Zimbabwe and Malawi. Professional game guide – Exceptional wildlife knowledge – Life dedicated to wildlife protection. Works and trains anti-poaching units across Africa. http://youngrory.wordpress.com/

Reviews

More Amazon Reader's ★★★★★ Reviews (some truncated)

In Love With The African Bush And Its Wildlife
The undoubted privilege of having lived in the African bush along with its wildlife and particularly the magic of the Zambezi River is threaded throughout Greer Noble's 'My Funny Africa' like a gold ribbon. The short stories so lovingly collated are true to life, unbelievable though they may appear to some who haven't lived in the African bush.

A Book To Treasure.... A Collector's Item!
The work that has gone into this book, including the artwork… could only emanate from a person deeply passionate about Africa. Such a rare collection of true-life adventures… must surely have genuine historical value… exciting and compelling to readers young and old… would make it challenging for college students; a rare opportunity of analysis of such variety of African-English literature… and enlightening to what life is like on the world's second largest continent.

Great Bushwhacker Tales!
The old East African bushwhacker is a breed apart and Greer Noble's collected tales certainly live up to her title of My Funny Africa… not only a human quality to do silly things, for the animals too are responsible for many surprising and endearing acts, quite out of character with their wild personas… these tales open a doorway to understanding how animals behave in the wild... this adds value to an already enchanting book.

My Africa Too
I sent off immediately for the book and eked it out by only reading a few chapters a night. I went to sleep with Africa on my mind. Some I read with acute attention… to find that was it. Oh no – shock horror. I wanted more. Africa beats in my heart and to this end the book has given me jogs that woke my own memories. It would be unfair to mention my favourites but one thing is for sure, I will be reading the book again… soon.

An absolutely wonderful collection of African anecdotes by some of Africa's very BEST authors. I have three copies, but have removed the one that was previously in the guest loo, because visitors were spending far too long in there. 'My Funny Africa' reminds me a little of the Christmas Stockings that Santa used to leave at the bottom of my bed: so much to see that one scarcely knew where to start! Wonderful.

UK : I have just finished reading 'My Funny Africa' (for the second time), and can only say that it is an absolutely SUPERB selection of African tales, anecdotes and sketches! It would be curmudgeonly even to attempt to pick out favourites, because they are all so different: although possibly Wilbur Smith will have to pull up his socks a bit if he wants to get into the next edition. Seriously, this is a really fabulous selection and would make a wonderful present. Being of Scottish extraction, might I suggest that if you treat your copy very gently you will probably be able to wrap it for someone as a late Christmas gift saving any further outlay. Having read it though, I doubt that you will want to give it away.

UK : It is very seldom that I pick up a book and by the time I have read 30 pages I know that I can expect to be entranced on every page – but 'enjoy' isn't a word adequate enough to describe my feelings in this case. The book to which I refer is Greer Noble's 'My Funny Africa.' Having contributed minimally to its content I was thrilled to receive a complimentary copy through the post a few days back. The title says it all; it is a light-hearted romp through moments in the lives of people who have spent time enjoying the wildlife and magnificent vistas of Africa. 'My Funny Africa' brought a rush of treasured memories flooding to mind – when the world was less politically correct, where people *lived* rather than just existed. The book is packed full of anecdotes by people across the social spectrum, each providing a window into a lifestyle that is almost extinct now. It might be pretentious to say it will be historically important but I firmly believe it will. I cannot do other than recommend it whole-heartedly to people with a soul, a sense of humour and a love of wild-life. Best of all, for those that buy it, they will be contributing to the Born Free Foundation.

I never knew of a morning in Africa when I woke up that I was not happy
Ernest Hemingway

Printed in Great Britain
by Amazon

34639713R00264